Virginia Woolf, Fashion and
Literary Modernity

Virginia Woolf, Fashion and Literary Modernity

R. S. Koppen

Edinburgh University Press

© R. S. Koppen, 2009, 2011

Edinburgh University Press Ltd
22 George Square, Edinburgh

First published in hardback by
Edinburgh University Press in 2009

www.euppublishing.com

Typeset in 10.5/13 Adobe Sabon
by Servis Filmsetting Ltd, Stockport, Cheshire, and
printed and bound in Great Britain by
CPI Antony Rowe, Chippenham and Eastbourne

A CIP record for this book is available from the British Library

ISBN 0 978 0 7486 4284 7 (paperback)

The right of R. S. Koppen
to be identified as author of this work
has been asserted in accordance with
the Copyright, Designs and Patents Act 1988.

Contents

Illustrations

Abbreviations

AROO   *A Room of One's Own*
BTA   *Between the Acts*
CDM   *The Crowded Dance of Modern Life*
CR 1   *The Common Reader*
CR 2   *The Common Reader, Second Series*
CSF   *The Complete Shorter Fiction*
D   *The Diary of Virginia Woolf* (5 vols)
DM   *The Death of the Moth and Other Essays*
E   *The Essays of Virginia Woolf* (6 vols planned; 5 published)
FR   *Freshwater*
JR   *Jacob's Room*
L   *The Letters of Virginia Woolf* (6 vols)
M   *The Moment and Other Essays*
MEL   *Melymbrosia*
MOB   *Moments of Being*
MD   *Mrs Dalloway*
ND   *Night and Day*
O   *Orlando*
PA   *A Passionate Apprentice*
RF   *Roger Fry: A Biography*
TG   *Three Guineas*
TTL   *To the Lighthouse*
TW   *The Waves*
TY   *The Years*
VO   *The Voyage Out*

Acknowledgements

My scholarly debts are acknowledged in the text and notes, but let me mention here my personal gratitude: to all those whose conversation and advice have contributed to the writing of this book. First, colleagues and friends at the International Annual Virginia Woolf Conferences in Portland, Oregon 2005 and Birmingham 2006 for responding to early versions of my arguments. Special thanks to Dr Catherine R. Mintler for proposing and co-organising the panel on Woolf and Fashion for the 2006 conference, to Vara Neverow for her suggestions for Chapter 5, and to Maggie Humm for kindly answering questions about the *Three Guineas* photographs. Thanks are also due to my colleagues and friends in the TAS (Text, Action, Space) research group for their enthusiasm and support for this project over several years. I am especially grateful to Professor Lars Saetre for providing generous opportunities to present and discuss parts of this book at conferences and workshops in Chicago (Department of Germanic Studies, University of Chicago), Paris (Centre de Cooperation Franco-Norvegienne en Sciences Sociales et Humaine), and Bergen (University of Bergen). Thanks to the Andrew E. and G. Norman Wigeland Memorial Endowment and the Department of Germanic Studies, University of Chicago for their generous invitation to 'A Norwegian-American Conversation' in February 2007, and in particular to Eric Santner and David Wellbery for stimulating discussions. For time to complete this project I am grateful to the Faculty of Humanities, University of Bergen, and to my colleagues in the Department of Foreign Languages. For invaluable help with the illustrations I thank staff at the National Portrait Gallery, the Tate Gallery, the Harvard Theatre Collection, Houghton Library, the Society of Authors, and the estates of Nina Hamnett and Vanessa Bell. Lastly, and most of all, I thank Stella and Bengt for their patience and support.

Preface

A range of stimulating books on the theory of modern fashion and the connections between fashion and modernity have become available in recent years, many of them published as part of Berg's 'Dress, Body, Culture' series, confirming that the connections between *mode* and *modernité* far exceed the etymological. The interrelationships between literary modernism and modern theories and practices of fashion have been much less consistently explored, however. Clair Hughes and Mark Anderson have written valuable books on the connections between dress, fashion and fiction (Hughes's *Henry James and the Art of Dress* (2001) and *Dressed in Fiction* (2006), Anderson's *Kafka's Clothes* (1992)). Within Woolf studies a number of recent essays have been devoted to aspects of Woolf's famous 'clothes-consciousness', proposing readings of her work in the contexts of shopping, masquerade, and cross-dressing, as well as exploring the complexities and contradictions of her engagement with a fashionable modernism, commodity culture and the cultural marketplace. These contributions are highly valuable, but remain uncollected and relatively scattered. A comprehensive reading of Woolf's work as cultural analyst and writer of fiction, set in the context of the modern interest in fashion as theory and practice, and in clothes as things, commodities and symbols, is still lacking. My own book is intended to begin to fill this gap. It directs itself to the current interest in the traffic between literary, material and visual cultures, assuming that writing engages with the look and feel of culture in complex ways, and that exploring this engagement reveals more not only about what it means to be modern, but about the projects of literary modernism and the exchanges of some of its leading proponents.

The book places Woolf's writing in the context of sartorial practice from the Victorian period to the 1930s, bringing out its 'look through clothes' and its engagement with theorists of dress and fashion from Thomas Carlyle to Walter Benjamin, Wyndham Lewis and J. C. Flügel.

For Woolf as for contemporary historians, sociologists and psychologists, sartorial fashion serves as a privileged metonym of modernity as well as a focus for various modernist projects of resistance. Like them, but differently, she 'thinks through clothes' in her representations of the present, her explorations of the archives of the past, and her projections for the future. For her, as for them, sartorial items appear as objects of the everyday, phenomenal world that are particularly suited not only to investigations of modern relations between subject and object, but to the experience of a 'modern materialism', imbued with the potential of alternative rationalities and the existence of other worlds.

Chapter 1

Modern Clothes-consciousness

Clothes have a curious presence in modern fiction, a presence which at once asserts and denies its significance, and whose relation to character, much like that between an individual's physiognomy and his or her secret subjectivity, hovers uncertainly between the synecdochic and the allegorical. The purpose of this book is to explore some aspects of that presence, based on the assumption that clothes matter to the construction as well as the reconstruction of a historical moment and its literary representations. The relations of clothes to culture can be thought of as constitutive to the extent that clothes as embodied cultural practice contribute to bringing forth and performing culture, and as reconstitutive to the extent that they, as cultural products and images, take on a historiographical or 'mnemotechnological' function.[1] Such relations and functions are tied to the nature of clothes as objects, things and signs. They also arise from the many performative dimensions of sartorial language, grounded in its double semiotic function as both system and event. As a symbolic system clothes may serve to interpellate and discipline, to signify the place of individual bodies in social, economic, or sexual orders; as event, on the other hand, they offer an opportunity for individual performance, in Butlerian terms, as the idea of variation within a set of discursive possibilities. Beyond the material and the symbolic, clothes matter because they come with a deeply anchored phenomenology and an equally fundamental imaginary, and because they are invested by tradition with the ability to speak otherwise, in or as allegory. Sensations, smells and even sounds of clothing, our own or others' – of being swathed, wrapped, dressed; or sensing, smelling, hearing the proximity of another's clothed being – are probably among our earliest experiences and in some cases constitute our earliest memories. The connections with allegory, with topoi and vocabularies of transcendence, emerge from clothing's palpable yet ghostly character, of screen or veil, of mobile, three-dimensional surface, of translucence and semi-transparency, of envelope and tabula, site of inscriptions and imprints, traces and stains. 'Seeing through clothes'[2] in all these aspects entails bringing out different contours in the terrain of literary modernism by tracing the intersecting lines of aesthetic and everyday practice; the traffics between material and literary culture, high and low, art and trivia.

Most immediately, perhaps, clothes are objects of use that display a look and a style that tie them to a particular aesthetic and historical moment. Their materiality connects them with a process of production and its technology, with the history of everyday life and the practices of the material *habitus*. As commodities, they enter into the exchange-systems of economies and markets as well as the logic and temporality of fashion, thus making them a favoured metonym for modernity, as we shall see, suggesting that the connection between *mode* and *modernité* far exceeds the etymological. Clothes are also imbued with the material-ity of things, however, and things, as theorists of material culture insist, are neither objects nor commodities. If we think of objects as framed within objectivist discourses, things present themselves to us in their phenomenal irreducibility. The thing can never be reduced to a fact, and as such, in the words of one exponent of thing theory, 'names less an object than a particular subject-object relation', or even 'that enigma that can only be encircled and which the object (by its presence) neces-sarily negates' (Brown 2001: 4–5). A material approach to history raises questions about the ideological and ideational effects of the material world; 'what work things perform' (Brown 2001: 6–7). The materiality-effect of clothes, however, is not quite like that of other things, primarily for the reason that it takes place on a boundary, the interface of subjec-tive and objective worlds. Garments, as we normally encounter them, do not exist as separate entities; they are seen on a body, brought into movement and animation by a living corporeality. A garment presents the body to the world as image and as thing, while performing its work on the body as imagined extension of self and as inorganic other. Empty clothes enter into yet another phenomenology, another imaginary regis-ter, which is no less an evocation of the interface even though the body is absent. As Thomas Carlyle noted in *Sartor Resartus*, the capacity of death to turn people into things while bringing inanimate objects to life, works with particular poignancy on garments and shoes, whose creases, folds and stains trace the physical contours of absence. In such cases the garment, more evocatively than other 'material hauntings', seems to gesture towards the topos of the boundary and the figure of chiasmus, interstitial crossings of subject and object, animate and inanimate, life and death (Carlyle 1869; Stallybrass and Jones 2001).

In part, it seems, it is this materiality-effect at the interface that makes clothes particularly suggestive things in modernist art and writing. If, as Bill Brown argues in his introduction to 'Thing Theory', modernity is the condition in which the enigma of the thing has ceased to exist – where the dominance of objective over subjective culture is in effect the dominance of reification, commodification, and alienation – the work of the modernist avant-garde of surrealists and dadaists deliberately refused such ontological distinctions between inanimate objects and human subjects, between people and things (Brown 2001). The purpose of this modernist materialism was to think the materiality of things outside the system of commodities and their fetishisation, and to show that the central preoccupation of modernity ought rather to be the exchange – the patterns of circulation, transference, and displacement – between the 'quasi-subjects' and 'quasi-objects' of which the world is composed (ibid.: 10–12). Incorporating garments into their materialist project, dadaists and surrealists invested clothes and accessories with a mystery that became apparent by means of spatial and/or temporal dislocation. As Ulrich Lehmann argues in his book on modern fashion, clothes, rather than their owners, could be seen to act out the visual and verbal plays devised by dada and early surrealism, during the 1910s and 1920s, in which a number of sartorial items recurred as actors: the hat, the monocle, tie, dress, glove and shoe (Lehmann 2000: 283, 354). Garments, estranged from the bodies on which they were worn, disconnected from their ordinary, 'simple' purpose, were foregrounded as strange and surreal signifiers, keepers of secret myths and fantasies, like the hats photographed by Man Ray for Tristan Tzara's essay 'D'un certain automatisme du goût' (1933), exploring the resemblance between different shapes of women's hat and female genitalia (ibid.: 356). A different type of displacement occurred with the translation of nineteenth-century sartorial items or accessories from their original temporal frame to a modernist one, as with André Breton's surreal evocation of the corset in a 1919 poem; a collage of cut-out advertisements entitled 'Le Corset Mystère', or the Paris dadaists' adoption of the monocle as a favourite prop in a gesture of quotation which altered the object as well as its wearer. Again, Ulrich Lehmann's book provides valuable documentation and analysis, showing how, with the wearer's efforts to keep the monocle in place, the inorganic encroaches on the organic, affecting the body's movements, gestures and facial expression, imbuing it with the quality of the statue or machine.

In Walter Benjamin's historical materialism, clothes are counted among the things that give access to the real of material history. The object liberated from historical continuity and thus invested with a thingness at once surreal and indicative of the circumstances of its

Figure 1   Man Ray, photograph for Tristan Tzara's essay 'On a Certain Automatism of Taste'

production, supply the material of a dialectical historiography of the fragment. The reconstructions of nineteenth-century Paris in *The Arcades Project* (1999) fasten on the boom in the textile industry (producing the arcades and department stores), together with the figure of the ragpicker feeding on its waste products, as the opposite ends of the commodity capitalism which defines modernity. The arcades signify the modern phantasmagoria; the ragpicker its detritus, the latter supplying the model for Benjamin's own method of dialectical ragpicking. Within the Benjaminean dialectic clothes also appear as objects of fashion, however; as modernity's primary commodity, manifestations of capitalism's fundamental logic. Here, clothes take on a double function which indicates that their place in the constitution of modernism is less that of the margin than the foreground: at once a metonym for the condition of modernity and a focus for various modernist projects of resistance.

   That Benjamin is not alone in working with clothes as an image of modernity is confirmed through the writings of a number of nineteenth-century commentators, many of which are cited in *The Arcades Project.*

Repeatedly, in these writings, the fashion industry, the fashion dynamic with its sociologies of gender and class, even individual fashions, are given exemplary status, appearing as paradigms and heuristic devices in investigations of the being and doing of modernity – its sociologies, its economies, and its mentalities. Thus, 'fashion . . . corresponds entirely to the constitutional character of our age', writes the German novelist Karl Gutzov in 1846, a statement which is echoed three decades later by the literary critic Friedrich Vischer's observation that fashion expresses 'what is . . . common to the peoples of the modern civilized nations' (Gutzov 2004: 197; Vischer 2004: 155). In turn, this 'constitutional character' or 'common element' of the modern is generally defined by contemporary commentators in terms of rapid mobility and change; of commodity capitalism; of modes of social regulation that allow for a degree of individual freedom within a framework of 'voluntary cooperation'; and finally as the age of the bourgeoisie, of a movement towards homogeneity and obscurance of marks of class distinction. In his chapter on 'Fashion' in *The Principles of Sociology* (1902), Herbert Spencer makes use of fashion to draw the boundaries between modern and 'primitive' or 'ceremonial' societies ruled by compulsory cooperation and forms of enforced, ceremonial reverence (Spencer 2004: 331). 'Our century has done away with dress code regulations', writes Adolf Loos: 'Everyone now enjoys the right to dress as he pleases, even like the king if he wants. The level of a nation's culture can be measured by how many of its citizens take advantage of this newly acquired freedom' (Loos 2004: 94). This higher level of culture, however, as both Spencer and Loos agree, is inseparable from the existence and operations of a consensus enforced by unembodied opinion. Fashion, writes Spencer, is a form of social regulation analogous to constitutional government. Just as voluntary cooperation has replaced compulsory cooperation in the social as in the political domain, in both fields, too, one has seen

a growth of this indefinite aggregate of wealthy and cultured people, whose *consensus* of habits rules the private life of society at large. And it is observable in the one case as in the other, that this ever-changing compromise between restraint and freedom tends towards increase of freedom. (Spencer 2004: 332)

Spencer's points are developed by the philosopher and sociologist Georg Simmel, whose *Philosophie der Mode* (1905) constitutes the first comprehensive academic study of the philosophy and sociology of fashion in the context of modern urban life. First, in Simmel's analysis, modernity's break with the past brings about an accentuation of the present which at the same time emphasises the element of change. Under these circumstances, fashion – 'which always occupies the dividing line between the past and the future, and consequently conveys a stronger feeling of the present . . . than most other phenomena' – inevitably increases its power and extends its original domain (Simmel 1971: 303). The present moment, moreover, is the historical consequence of a 'civilizing process' that entails a much greater tolerance for the foreignness that fashion represents. The exotic origin of fashion as foreign import, or as otherwise originating outside a social circle, perhaps associated with the stranger, does not pose a threat to the modern man of culture – on the contrary: 'Whatever is exceptional, bizarre, or conspicuous, or whatever departs from the customary norm, exercises a peculiar charm upon [him], entirely independent of its material justification' (ibid.: 300). Modernity's break with the past, then, constitutes fashion not simply as the garment of the present, but as a generative principle which ensures an endless series of presents, or as Walter Benjamin was later to call it, the 'eternal recurrence' of the foreign and the new (Benjamin 2006: 155).

Fashion's position at the boundary of subjective and objective culture is the second factor that invests it with particular explanatory force in Simmel's reading of modern metropolitan life. For Simmel, the history of society turns on a fundamental duality of two opposing principles, the principles of subjective adaptation or imitation, on the one hand, and of differentiation or individuation on the other. While the full demands of these principles can never be met, social institutions – of which fashion is a microcosmic manifestation – serve to reduce their constant antagonism to a form of cooperation. As the imitation of a given example fashion satisfies the demand for social adaptation. At the same time, however, and in no less degree, it satisfies 'the need of differentiation . . . the desire for change and contrast' (Simmel 1971: 296). This latter tendency, as Simmel demonstrates, works along a vertical as well as a horizontal axis. On the one hand, there is the 'constant change of contents' observed above, 'which gives to the fashions of today an individual stamp as opposed to that of yesterday and tomorrow'; on the other hand, fashions differ for different classes, 'the fashions of the upper stratum of society . . . never identical with those of the lower; in fact, they are abandoned by the former as soon as the latter prepares to appropriate them' (ibid.: 296). Thus, the principle of constant renewal is driven also from below, by imitation motivated by desire for social advancement, which in turn drives the upper classes towards confirming their unity and apartness – their distinction – by adopting the ever-new.

The contest between adaptation and differentiation, as Simmel understands it, is rendered particularly acute by the metropolitan condition with its bodily closeness and lack of space. Under such circumstances, fashion serves to protect against the proximity of other bodies, preserving mental independence and apartness by its 'levelling cloak' under which the individual is invited to 'seek refuge' (Simmel 1971: 312). Simultaneously, however, fashion offers that 'measure of conspicuousness and individual prominence' which allows the individual to make him- or herself noticeable, to grasp the attention of the social world (ibid.: 309). In the metropolis the need to 'appear to-the-point, clearcut and individual' follows partly from the 'brevity and rarity of meetings . . . allotted to each individual in the metropolis as compared with social intercourse in a small city' (ibid.: 336–7); partly from the habit of intellectual, objectifying response to impressions which follows from the complexity of metropolitan life and which corresponds to the logic of the money economy. In a mental climate where quality (individual difference) reduces to quantity (exchange value), fashion offers a mode of individuation which is always looked upon as proper, and a mutability which operates at the 'periphery of personality' and so presents no threat to the 'stability of the ego-feeling' (ibid.: 311).

Fashion, as Simmel sees it, then, affirms the metropolitan condition as one of individual freedom – not only by preserving mental independence and apartness, but by making individual bodies into signs of their incomparability and irreplaceability rather than undifferentiated parts of a larger body:

> That we follow the laws of our inner nature – and this is what freedom is – becomes perceptible and convincing to us and to others only when the expressions of this nature distinguish themselves from others; it is our irreplaceability by others which shows that our mode of existence is not imposed upon us from the outside. (Simmel 1971: 335)

Simmel's employment of fashion as heuristic device serves not only to illustrate the modern social formation as a contest of subjective against objective culture, but as a relation between fragment and totality. The development in the fashion industry from tailor to department store illustrates 'the economic-psychological aspect' of metropolitan life – the 'overgrowth of objective culture' and the delimitation and fragmentation of individual perspective (Simmel 1971: 327, 337). 'Since the division of labour destroys custom production', writes Simmel,

> the subjective aura of the product also disappears in relation to the consumer because the commodity is now produced independently of him. It becomes an objective entity which the consumer approaches externally and whose specific existence and quality is autonomous of him. The difference, for instance, between the modern clothing store, geared towards the utmost specialisation,

and the work of the tailor whom one used to invite into one's home sharply emphasises the growing objectivity of the economic cosmos, its supra-individual independence in relation to the consuming subject with whom it was originally closely identified . . . . It is obvious how much this objectifies the whole character of transaction and how subjectivity is destroyed and transformed into cool reserve and anonymous objectivity once so many inter-mediate stages are introduced between the producer and the one who accepts his product that they lose sight of each other. (Simmel, *The Philosophy of Money*, quoted in Lehmann 2000: 135)

Fashion here constitutes the fragment that allows Simmel to theorise the totality: the fragmented abstraction of modern social reality. The change from a structure of individual encounters and transactions to the ano-nymity of the market – the reification and alienation of supra-individual exchange-networks – is connected with the metaphor of *das Gewebe* (fabric), through which Simmel figures the social formation (Lehmann 2000: 129). Society as *Gewebe*, and fashion as fragment, suggest a fabric which extends beyond the individual field of vision and knowledge, and to which individual lives must be understood as opposed, as Simmel puts it, if not in actuality then *in abstracto* (Simmel 1971: 328–9).

From what we have seen so far, fashion emerges as something of a shorthand among contemporary commentators – a metonym and privileged exemplum of life in the metropolis, of commodity capitalism and modern materialism (understood as the particular mode of appear-ance of material objects-as-commodities). Thus, being jostled by the crowd, which Baudelaire and Benjamin think of as a defining modern experience, is to come into contact with dressed bodies, rather than an unmediated corporeality. Likewise, the perceptible manifestation of what Benjamin called the phantasmagoria – the ideological trans-formation of commodities into fetishes and the blurring of boundaries between the organic and the inorganic – seems to occur with particular *Anschaulichkeit* in the case of clothing. And 'no line of consumption', as Thorstein Veblen put it, 'affords more apt illustration' of the principles of the 'pecuniary culture' – 'conspicuous consumption' and 'conspicu-ous waste' – than 'expenditure on dress' (Veblen 2004: 278). Within the modern social organisation where people are placed 'in juxtaposition' rather than actual contact, as transient and in principle unsympathetic mutual observers, one's apparel – 'always in evidence' – 'affords an indi-cation of one's pecuniary standing' (and, by proxy, of the nature of one's character) 'to all observers at the first glance' (ibid.: 278).

Among the defining characteristics of fashion is its particular dynamic or temporality, which, as Gutzov and later Benjamin were to see, 'prepares the way for a conceptual definition of the modern' (Gutzov

2004: 197). The dynamic of fashion is the principle of the avant-garde: to be ahead of the mass, to be unique. Characteristically, this striving, which is also 'always the striving to get out of fashion', takes the form of a return, rather than a simple rejection of the old-worldly. Thus, in Gutzov's words from 1846: 'The modern does not reject the old, but rather either moulds it according to its own taste, or drives it to an extreme where it becomes comical, or refines it in some other manner' (ibid.: 197–8). Such a conceptual definition of the modern as an ongoing proclamation (of modernity) in the form of a return, seems particularly appropriate to describe the relations between nineteenth- and twentieth-century modernities. If the nineteenth-century modern was caught up with fashion and the sartorial object in many ways, this turned out to be no less the case for the modernities which continued to be proclaimed in the early decades of the following century, when fashion provides a perspective on and a shorthand for the past, a field of play, as well as force, in which to stage one's encounters and battles with the outmoded. As we shall see, fashion at this time also becomes a field for the articulation of competing aesthetic and ideological formulations of the modern as being and doing. It is not just that fashion is a metaphor for a conceptual definition of modernity, in other words; equally important for a historiography which looks 'through clothes' is the extent to which fashion and the sartorial, quite often in a dichotomous relation to directions in anti-fashion and body-work, provide the cultural site, the discourse, and the tropology for modernism as an ongoing, contested, and polymorph project.

Virginia Woolf's work as a cultural analyst and writer of fiction, extending from the turn of the twentieth century to the early days of the Second World War, provides a particularly complex and comprehensive perspective on the modern fascination with clothing, grounded in its involvement with the worlds of fashion and anti-fashion, its preoccupation with modern identities and modes of being, and its deployment of a sartorial tropology in evocations of an archival past as well as a modern present. Woolf's personal relations with the world of fashion, as is well known, were fraught with contradictions. Readers of her diaries and memoirs will be familiar with what she alternately referred to as her 'clothes-consciousness' and 'clothes-drudgery'. The visits to dressmakers and department stores recorded in her journals follow the transition from made-to-measure to off-the-rack manufacturing while remaining fraught with tension, not least the tensions of class: the failed encounters of server and served, the hopes and humiliations of fittings at which the intimacies of one's body and one's 'pecuniary strength' appear to be on trial simultaneously. There is the reluctant and haphazard shopper who goes off 'with teeth set' to do 'what of all things [she] loathe[s]', reviews twenty coats at Marshall and Snelgrove's, decides against them all on score of price, then takes the first shown at Peter Robinson, 'at a price quite ruinous', out of sheer boredom (*PA*: 249–50). And there is the 'literary figure' twenty years later, the author of *Mrs Dalloway*, who has appeared in *Vogue*'s 'Hall of Fame' as 'the most brilliant novelist of the younger generation', off dress-buying with its famous editor Dorothy Todd, 'trembl[ing] and shiver[ing] all over at the appalling magnitude of the task I have undertaken' (*Vogue* late May 1924: 49; Reed 2004: 24–5; *D* III 78; Noble 1972: 172).

The everyday figure seemed constitutionally, physically, unable to merge with any crowd, to the extent that, as Leonard Woolf observed, she would make 'nine out of ten people' – whether in Barcelona, Stockholm, London or Lewes High Street – 'stop and stare and nudge one another', even 'go into fits of laughter', at the sight of her (Woolf, L. 1963: Vol. 3, 29). The derision of the crowd, however, as recalled by family and friends, was not caused by her manner of dress, though the stories of the knickers that came off in the street, the hat that looked like an upturned wastepaper basket, and the silk rags pinned up with a brooch, might suggest otherwise (*D* I: 103–4; Noble 1972: 171, 85). Leonard ascribed the public attention to his wife's disquieting aura of 'genius'; her clothes in themselves were usually rather quiet and nondescript. Individual rather than fashionable – out-of-synch with the times – they seemed somehow part of her being, merged in her. Rosamond Lehmann recalls her 'dressed like an aesthetic don': 'There was something about her that made one think of William Morris and the New Age and the Emancipation of Women' (Noble 1972: 62). Others remember her 'look of great distinction' even in the most ordinary everyday clothes, long tweed or corduroy skirts, brown or blue silk jackets to match (ibid.: 56, 86, 157).

Clothing represents more than style and aesthetic statements. Among other things, it is an immediately available way of proclaiming different corporealities, different ways of being a body in the world, and different interpersonal relations, whether of gender or class. When Woolf's 'Georgian cook' performs like a modern subject in 1910, she famously embodies the character of the age as 'a creature of sunshine and fresh air; in and out of the drawing room, now to borrow the Daily Herald, now to ask advice about a hat' (*E* 4: 422). The terms of change are sartorial as well as spatial and intellectual, the hat serving as a visual shorthand for the moment when the constitutional character of the age extends beyond the bourgeoisie to what used to be 'the lower depths' of the Victorian house, as the servant, albeit on a scale more modest than that of her employer, comes to participate at once in the modern illusion of self-fashioning and in the collective affirmation of the look and meaning of the contemporary moment. Depending on the context in which such proclamations and acts of self-fashioning are made, such moments are also fraught with risks and tensions, as Woolf's painful recollections of attempted sartorial insubordination show. Within the sartorial regime represented by her half-brother George, the young Virginia Stephen's rather banal experiments in dress take on the force of conscious threats to cultural practice and to the norms and assumptions it embodies.

Virginia Stephen's home in 1900, Hyde Park Gate, as she herself describes it, 'was a complete model of Victorian society', of which the following is a specimen scenario:

> Society – upper middle class Victorian society – came into being when the lights went up . . . . At seven thirty dress and hair overcame paint and Greek grammar. I would stand in front of George's Chippendale mirror trying to make myself not only tidy, but presentable. On an allowance of fifty pounds it was difficult, even for the skilful, and I had no skill, to be well dressed of an evening. A home dress, made by Jane Bride, could be had for a pound or two; but a party dress, made by Mrs Young, cost fifteen guineas. The home dress therefore might be, as on one night that comes back to mind, made cheaply but eccentrically, of a green fabric, bought at Story's, the furniture shop. It was not velvet; nor plush; something betwixt and between; and for chairs, presumably, not dresses. Down I came one winter's evening about 1900 in my green dress; apprehensive, yet, for a new dress excites even the unskilled, elated . . . [George] at once fixed on me that extraordinarily observant scrutiny with which he always inspected our clothes. He looked me up and down for a moment as if I were a horse brought into the show ring. Then the sullen look came into his eyes; the look which expressed not simply aesthetic disapproval; but something that went deeper. It was the look of moral, of social, disapproval, as if he scented some kind of insurrection, of defiance of his accepted standards. I knew myself condemned from more points of view than I could then analyse . . . He said at last: 'Go and tear it up.' He spoke in a curiously tart, rasping, peevish voice; the voice of the enraged male; the voice which expressed his serious displeasure at this infringement of a code that meant more to him than he could admit. (*MOB*: 147, 150–1)

George 'had over a thousand a year in unearned income. He could supply frock coats, hats, shoes, ties, horses, guns, bicycles, as the occasion required. Thus furnished and equipped society opened its arms wide to him and embraced him' (*MOB*: 152). The code he embodies and enforces is that of reserve and conformity, the defining features of the elegant bourgeois male. At the turn of the century which did away with dress code regulations, to be dressed well is to have 'outgrown ornament' and to stand out 'as little as possible at the centre of culture . . . in the best society' (Loos 2004: 94–5), which in the modern age is to say bourgeois society, with London as its 'true enduring metropolis' (Fuchs 2004: 320). The inconspicuous functionality identified as modern by contemporary commentators followed from what was perceived as the modern masculinisation of culture. As Eduard Fuchs puts it in 1912, 'bourgeois culture is an altogether male culture; its orientation is toward production and creative drive' (ibid.: 319). Reflecting this, male dress is 'the clothing of the working, restlessly active person' rather than of effeminate gallantry (ibid.: 320). If bourgeois man 'abandoned his claim to be considered beautiful' in what J. C. Flügel famously terms 'the Great Male Renunciation' (Flügel 1930: 110), he did not abandon his claim to inconspicuous elegance. As D. L. Purdy writes in *The Rise of Fashion* (2004), the male sartorial style of reserve was designed to facilitate the moral and psychological scrutiny to which respectable society subjected its male members, a scrutiny which zoomed in on facial features, bodily gestures and seemingly anonymous sartorial details, such as lapels and cuffs, as signs of character. The individual who successfully passed this heightened surveillance was integrated into the operations of society as a morally and financially reliable individual, himself empowered to participate in the exercise of power (Purdy 2004: 6–8).

For the bourgeois woman the rule of conformity was no less insistent, although informed by a contrary logic. Where, as Vischer authoritatively proclaims, men's dress is to make itself inconspicuous so that 'the man himself within it may assert his personality', 'for woman the formula runs like this: you should make yourself inconspicuous by not deviating from everyone else in certain principle [*sic*] articles of clothing . . . however conspicuous these principle articles, these basic forms, themselves might be!' (Vischer 2004: 157). Within a strictly coded world of social action feminine sartorial conspicuousness was aligned with the stylisation offered by cosmetics. The Victorian obsession with Nature has finally come to an end, exclaims Max Beerbohm in 1896, ladies are once more 'dipping their fingers in the rouge-pot', the trade of the makers of cosmetics has increased twentyfold the past five years, and 'the use of pigments is becoming general' (Beerbohm 2004: 227–8). Deploring the feminine 'invasion of the tennis-courts and of the golf-links, the seizure of the bicycle and of the typewriter', Beerbohm hails the 'pervasion of rouge' as the end, at least as applied to women, of the naive reading of soul from physiognomic surface. With the revival of cosmetics, 'surface will finally be severed from soul' and the face, for so long 'degraded . . . to a mere vulgar index of character or emotion' will once more enjoy the autonomy and the reserve of the aesthetic object (ibid.: 229–30).

The suspension of physiognomic scrutiny, however, does not entail the suspension of 'the one great permanent law', to the effect that 'clothing addresses an erotic problem – that of the passive, but constant sensual courting of two sexes of one another', and that 'clothing is for both sexes an ally in the competition for reciprocal favor and sympathy' (Fuchs 2004: 323). As the man takes the active role in this relationship, his clothing is erotically more neutral, designed, as we have seen, to offer the most immediate indication of his character and, inseparable from that, what Thorsten Veblen would call his 'pecuniary repute', with the woman appended to him as his 'vicarious' or 'ceremonial consumer' providing a further indication of his pecuniary strength (Veblen 2004: 278). The unattached female, for her part, must trust in the attraction of sartorial display, as confirmed in Karl Kraus's 'Eroticism of Clothes' (1906), which concludes that 'the configuration of eroticism has gone hand in hand with the configuration of clothing' to the extent that, 'in our unconscious experience eroticism and clothing are no longer at all separable from one another' (Kraus 2004: 241–2). On the same note Virginia Stephen's 'Thoughts upon Social Success', recorded in her journal from 1903, address the need for the upper middle-class woman to perform a femininity which seems to be constituted as well as mediated by the optics and embodied feel of clothing:

> You have, for a certain space of time to realise as nearly as can be, an ideal. You must consciously try to carry out in your conduct what is implied by your clothes; they are silken – of the very best make – only to be worn with the greatest care, on occasions such as these. They are meant to please the eyes of others – to make you something more brilliant than you are by day. (*PA*: 168)

'A Garden Dance', also from 1903, depicts a similar choreography, as ladies in light dresses are shown 'flowing out of the windows & falling in cascades of lace and silk down the slope [of the garden]. It was like some French painting' (ibid.: 171). A day at the seaside in contrast describes a respite from the regime of display and surveillance which appears almost surprising in its freedom, even to the contemporary observer:

> people seem to strip themselves of some of the integuments in which they wrap themselves where the criticism of eyes is to be dreaded. We seem to have come to a common agreement here not to look surprised at bare heads & hands; to accept hair flying in the wind, & bathing towels wrapped round the neck, as the simple and natural things. This unconventionality of dress is reflected in the tanned faces & the free stride of the legs . . . ladies . . . shorten their skirts, throw aside their bonnets, & caper as they walk, consciously, almost defiantly as though they asserted a right which your mild glance of inquiry would deny them. (*PA*: 296)

To this picture of bourgeois dress codes it should be added that alternative, if not directly competing, sartorial definitions of the modern were in circulation in respectable society at this time. Fixed by George's observant scrutiny Virginia's green dress sets off alarm bells presumably because it carries associations of the 'artistic', though it may not have been her intention to emulate the look of so-called aesthetic or artistic dress. Recycling the Pre-Raphaelite iconography of the Jane Morris dress (transformed into a marketable commodity by Liberty's in the 1890s) and continuing the rural romance of the Arts and Crafts movement as well as the late Victorian fashion for Orientalism, 'artistic' dress, in the minds of Woolf and others, seems to have been a composite of soft fabrics, subdued colours and organic shapes, with drapery as the main form of ornament. This sartorial ideal dominated a parallel respectable society about which Virginia, characteristically, entertained no illusions, as is evident from her sketch of 'An Artistic Party', The Royal Academy's Annual Reception at Burlington House in 1903:

> This crowd, I say, has a character of its own. Every other person you feel must be distinguished: the men wear a surprising number of decorations . . . . The women, as though to atone for their want of definite orders, dress up in the oddest ways. We found some queer specimens . . . the most usual figure was the typical artist, or artists wife – clinging Liberty silks – outlandish ornaments – a strange dusky type of face . . . . I am always impressed by the splendid superiority of these artist men & women over their Philistine brethren. They are so thoroughly convinced that mankind is divided into two classes, one of which wears amber beads & low evening collars – while the other follows the fashion. Each thanks God that it is not as the other – but the artist is the more intolerant. (*PA*: 176–7)

Adopted as a model for late nineteenth-century women's dress reform, aesthetic dress may be categorised loosely with other efforts that justified themselves by reference to universal, aesthetic or rational principles, as 'anti-fashion'. Whether appealing to hygiene, health, women's emancipation or the liberation from the constraints of civilisation, attempts at liberating and mobilising the female body in particular, continuing into the twentieth century, participated in the emancipation of women from the sartorial regime of bourgeois respectability. Writing in 1882 about the lack of suitable dress for the ordinary domestic employments of wives and mothers and deploring the 'fatal predisposition' among English women towards black alpaca, which invariably resulted in their 'voluntary adoption', upon reaching middle age, of this 'symbol of doom', Oscar Wilde nonetheless predicts that women's dress will be the first to express the spirit of modernity. 'For women, as a rule, are always trying to show their sympathy with the movement and tendencies of the age, by the symbolism of dress, since they are prohibited from taking any part in the actual work of life' (Wilde 2004: 237). Besides the new

modes of thought and social intercourse advocated by an elite of eman-
cipated women, Wilde points to economic and material factors in the
imminent democratisation and simplification of sartorial codes, not least
the pressure enforced by the crowd and the 'fifty tons of soot' allegedly
suspended above London's 85,000 streets (ibid.: 238). More than thirty
years later, however, the achievements in dress reform among English
women were still modest, as observed by Katharine Anthony in 1915.
The loose-fitting, one-piece dress pioneered by German dress-reformers
has been adopted and made fashionable by Paris couturiers such as
Poiret, but 'the main want of the woman of to-day . . . a practical street
dress and a "business" dress', remains to be met (Anthony 2004: 124).
With a feminist understanding of the significance of everyday practice,
Anthony defines the struggle of feminism as 'remold[ing] for woman's
use the ordinary symbols of society', the most familiar of which are
'dress, money, and the vote' (ibid.: 118), concluding that: 'To recon-
struct woman's dress for woman's use requires a crusade against the rule
of a fashion which lays upon her all the outward marks of an inferior
sex. Her external appearance is the most concrete, and the least assail-
able, symbol of her subjection' (ibid.: 118).

The importance of clothing to reconfigured gender relations may be
gauged by comparing Virginia's specimen day at Hyde Park Gate in
1900 with the domestic arrangements of Thoby, Vanessa, Virginia and
Adrian at 46 Gordon Square four or five years later, where life, as she
recalls it in 'A Sketch of the Past', was carried on in 'abstract argument,
without dressing for dinner' (*MOB*: 190–2). It has been demonstrated
in detail by art historians like Christopher Reed and others how life in
Bloomsbury was redefined on modern terms through a reconfiguration
of the actual rooms in which it was lived, by reorganising and redefining
domestic interiors and spaces. Equally important in constituting not only
the look of modern identities but in providing the conditions for modern
life as embodied practice, however, was the flouting and reinventing of
sartorial codes. More than a superficial statement, unconventionality
of dress provided freedom from a set of material (economic and corporeal) as well as symbolic constraints. In an atmosphere of intellectual
argument – 'abstract in the extreme' – with a group of young men (Bell,
Strachey, Sydney-Turner among others) who 'had no "manners" in the
Hyde Park Gate sense . . . [who] never seemed to notice how we were
dressed or if we were nice looking or not', all that 'tremendous encum-
brance of appearance and behaviour which George had piled upon our
first years vanished completely' (*MOB*: 190–1). 'When I looked round
the room at 46 I thought . . . that I had never seen young men so dingy,
so lacking in physical splendour as Thoby's friends' (*MOB*: 192). To

the conventional-minded the impression may have been deplorable. To Woolf, however, 'it was precisely this lack of physical splendour, this shabbiness! that . . . meant that life could go on like this, in abstract argument, without dressing for dinner' (*MOB*: 192).

It is not coincidental that the emergence and availability of alternative sartorial practices at this time should be connected with Bloomsbury as locality. Recent scholarship, notably by Anna Snaith and Sara Blair, has stressed the social and institutional importance of this area from the 1890s onwards as a location for numerous cultural and political reform projects and associations aligned with the capital's progressives, radicals and New Women, from labour associations to societies for food and dress reform. Significantly, Bloomsbury was also a prominent site of suffrage politics, and as such the natural location for Woolf's fictional representations of the suffrage campaign in *Night and Day* and *The Years*. Though, as Anna Snaith observes, it was not until 1910 that Woolf became directly involved with the campaign through her work for an NUWS society, her move to Bloomsbury coincided with a time of increasing public visibility, on the streets and by media coverage, of constitutional suffragists as well as militant suffragettes. All the major suffrage organisations, several of which were located within Bloomsbury, participated in what Barbara Green refers to as 'the street theatre of suffrage' through public demonstrations and deputations, mass meetings and carefully choreographed marches through the streets of London (Green 1996: 194). Lisa Tickner's history of the representational strategies of the suffrage campaign in the years 1907–14 details how activists refashioned available images of femininity to create an iconography that would be both strikingly new and immediately recognisable to a mass audience. In the visual modes of agitation – campaign posters and postcards, photographs of campaign leaders, and, most importantly, the highly spectacular and theatrical marches mobilising thousands of participants – dress, complemented by a range of sartorial accessories from badges to hat trimmings and scarves in any combination of the suffrage colours (white, green and purple for the WSPU; red and white for the NUWSS), played an important part as symbols and reminders of the cause. 'Suffrage modes have become the topic of the moment', wrote the *Daily Chronicle* on the occasion of the June 1908 Woman's Sunday Procession:

and the suggestion that all should wear white has been eagerly taken up. To expedite shopping several drapers have arranged to make displays of the suffrage colours . . . . White frocks will be prominent in the windows, with a plentiful supply of dress accessories in violet and green. (Quoted in Tickner 1987: 93)

The sartorial politics of suffrage was strategically varied, however, producing a polysemous and even contradictory feminine iconography that balanced, as both Tickner and Green observe, between activism and Edwardian fashionable femininity. The choreography of the mass spectacles combined historical costume with contemporary dress, academic robes with quasi-military uniforms. 'The signs changed in the feminist semiotic system', argues Jane Marcus, with suffrage activists and artists 'play[ing] every aspect of public attitudes toward women', 'costum[ing] themselves for each occasion' (Marcus 1989: 142–3):

> The smashing of . . . Bond Street windows by women dressed exactly like the mannequins on the other side of the glass is a telling example of feminist semiotics in the service of an attack on commodity fetishism. It also doesn't take a Freudian to explain the effect of feminine sexual solidarity in those masses of huge, flower-bedecked Edwardian hats as they marched in the West-End, smashing the icons of their oppression while wearing them as emblems of class and gender. (Marcus 1989: 145)

Woolf includes neither suffrage pageants nor any other of the more spectacular instances of feminist sartorial politics in her fiction, though suffragist dress codes do figure in *The Years* and *Night and Day* as embodiments of an alternative modernity to that of bourgeois fashion, consumer culture and department stores. In *The Years* street scenes from 1880 to the Present Day (1937) represent an evolving modernity through fashion and shopping, from ladies in flounced Victorian dresses shopping at Whiteley's and the Army & Navy Stores in 1880, to Sloane Street shop windows full of summer dresses, 'charming confections of green and gauze', 'flights of hats stuck on little rods', in 1914, to the painted faces and bright shawls, white waistcoats and smoothed back hair crowding the brightly illuminated West End streets of the present (*TY*: 5, 172–3, 256). In conspicuous contrast to such scenes Red Rose, addressing suffrage meetings in Bloomsbury, campaigning in the North, or throwing bricks through windows, relishes the freedom of being a defiantly shabby dresser: 'Always reach-me-downs, coats and skirts from Whiteley. But they saved time . . . the hat she stuck on without giving a look in the glass. If people chose to laugh, let them. She strode on' (ibid.: 125). The history of suffrage, however, and Woolf's ambivalence towards some of its (militarist, nationalist, autocratic) aspects, is contained in a more striking sartorial iconography: a compound of a pink frock, a knife and a red ribbon bringing together in visual shorthand the changes, contradictions and compromises in the life of an individual as well as a society. The child in the 'stiff pink frock' with 'a green smudge on her pinafore, as if she had been climbing trees', occupies Martin's memory thirty years later – '"I can see you," said Martin. "Wearing a pink frock, with a knife in your hand"'; returning even after five decades to dominate the present, as Rose brandishes a knife in Martin's face at Delia's party: '"Let us talk about pink frocks," he smiled.' '"A pink frock; a pink frock," she repeated, as if the words recalled something' (ibid.: 11, 122, 317). In between there is Sara's image of her in 1914, '"Sitting on a three-legged stool having meat crammed down her throat!"', and the 'red ribbon', 'some decoration . . . given her . . . for her work in the war' (ibid.: 178, 274). '"She smashed his window,"' jeers Martin at her in 1937, '"and then she helped him to smash other people's windows. Where's your decoration, Rose?" "In a cardboard box on the mantelpiece," said Rose. "You can't get a rise out of me at this time of day, my good fellow."' (ibid.: 320). Rose, with her knife and her ribbon, is toasted and hailed with rose petals, and yet, as Kitty asserts, '"Force is always wrong"' (ibid.: 320) – Rose's pride, in her country as well as her sex, recalling the uncomfortable alliance between militant suffragettes, nationalism and imperialism that came to expression in suffragist contributions to the Great War; anticipated years before in the militarist and nationalist aspects of some of its spectacles: armed women with uniformed leaders on horseback; pageants dedicated to Nation and Empire.

Descriptions of clothing do not figure prominently in Woolf's evocation of the suffrage office in *Night and Day* and the liberal/radical Bloomsbury milieu of which it is part, though to Katharine Hilbery's eyes the suffragists are 'queer-looking' (*ND*: 80), and the incongruity of dress between her and them is repeatedly brought out. The activist Mary Datchett feels herself 'shabby and slovenly' beside her, with the 'ruffled appearance' of 'a Russian peasant girl' compared to Katharine's immaculate 'blue silk and pearl-sewn shoes' (ibid.: 143, 302–3). Strikingly, the moment of deepest intimacy and attraction between the two is focused on Katharine's clothing: the furred hem of her dress which Mary fingers, as if all the sensual promise of a 'personal life' were contained in this line of fur (ibid.: 232, 235). Mrs Seal's appearance – of plum-coloured velveteen, short grey hair, and 'two crucifixes, which got themselves entangled in a heavy gold chain upon her breast' – sums up her missionary zeal and dedication to the Cause, and yet Mary finds herself 'looking at the odd little priestess of humanity with something like admiration' (ibid.: 64, 141). Like *The Years*, *Night and Day* confronts the ambivalences involved in believing in the justness of a cause on the one hand – its unquestionable alignment with modernity, progress and the future – while fearing the consequences of Causes, Conviction and Conversion, on the other; what seems to be their inevitable alignment with Pride and Force. In *The Years* this ambivalence is given visual expression in the frock/knife/ribbon image; in *Night and Day* it occurs through a juxtaposition of Mary – shown in what is in effect a scene of investiture – and Mrs Seal. Assigning herself to service, to 'the impersonal life', Mary arrays herself in the 'silver chains and glowing brooches' of office, finding satisfaction in 'making herself not only tidy, but seemly and ornamented'; 'adorned with the dignity' of 'a serviceable human being' (ibid.: 378–9). When at the end of the novel Katharine and Ralph seek out the illuminated blinds of Mary's window in tribute to 'the spirit of the woman within, working out her plans [for the good of the world] far into the night', Mrs Seal with her chain of tangled crucifixes turns up in her wake, heading that 'procession' of figures in 'queer combination' – 'fragments of belief, unsoldered and separate' – which the modern lovers find themselves 'trying to piece together in a laborious and elementary fashion . . . lacking the unity of phrases fashioned by the old believers'. '"It's all so easy – it's all so simple," Katharine quoted, remembering some words of Sally Seal's'. The effect is ironic: for Sally Seal what is 'simple' is to see what is right; for the modern lovers (and the modern writer) what is 'difficult' is to envisage a society 'made up of many different things in cohesion . . . an orderly world' (ibid.: 431).

In Bloomsbury (as place as well as aesthetic and social project) the sartorial embodiment of the modern went beyond deliberate shabbiness as an anti-fashion statement, protesting against the assumptions of class and gender inherent in bourgeois fashion. Following upon the years of suffragist sartorial politics, though with no pronounced political agenda, from 1914 the Omega Workshops incorporated clothing into their wider aesthetic project of proclaiming modernism as an overall experience; as look and as a set of corporeal possibilities. In doing so, the Workshops were continuing the connection that had become established between art, design and theories of dress reform by British Aestheticism and the Arts and Crafts Movement, and seen in the 'Aesthetic dress' of the Victorian avant-garde. Dress-making at the Omega was initiated and supervised by Vanessa Bell, according to her biographer Frances Spalding, under the inspiration of a visit to the Galeries Lafayette in Paris which provided 'gay and fashionable' yet inexpensive off-the-rack clothing to customers of considerably lower social standing than that of Vanessa. As Judith Collins writes in her book on the Omega, however, hand-dyed fabrics had been sold at the Workshops from the beginning, and a few hand-painted dresses and silk evening cloaks were listed in the *Omega Workshops Descriptive Catalogue* in the autumn of 1914. By this time, as Collins also writes, linen tunics were being made to measure from Omega printed linens. Photographs exist which show Nina Hamnett in one made from 'Maud' and Joy Brown in one made from 'Margery' (Collins 1983: 106). Fry himself made a painted shirt, 'a large cubist design in blue, orange, and black', worn by Nina Hamnett at the fashionable Closerie des Lilacs in Paris: 'No one in Paris had seen anything quite like it and although Sonia Delaunay was already designing scarves, this was more startling. It was made and designed for the Omega Workshop by Roger Fry' (Hamnett 1932: 66–7).

Collins agrees that Vanessa Bell had the idea of a line of dresses suitable for Omega clients like Lady Ottoline Morrell, Iris Tree, Marie Beerbohm and Marjorie Strachey, proposing to advertise the dresses at various social functions: something like a 'dress parade, perhaps in Ottoline's drawing room and have a party to see them' (Collins 1983: 106; letter from Vanessa Bell to Roger Fry, quoted in Anscombe 1981: 61). Roger Fry approved the scheme and various dressmakers were considered, including a 'Miss Joy' who, Vanessa wrote, is 'much more in sympathy with us about colours and very anxious to carry out my ideas about cut' (letter to Roger Fry, May 1915, quoted ibid.: 61). Vanessa's idea was to 'make dresses that would use the fashions and yet not be like dressmakers dresses' (letter to Roger Fry, March–April 1915, quoted in Collins 1983: 106). A photograph shows Nina Hamnett and Winifred Gill posing in Omega clothes in front of a painted screen by Vanessa Bell. According to Quentin Bell, Winnie Gill, who, like Nina Hamnett, worked in the Omega, recalled that

> the cloak Nina is wearing was a sort of oyster-coloured satin painted by Duncan Grant, the skirt I am wearing is simply made up of a length of some rather heavy striped silk. The photograph was made at a press view, Nina and I put on the clothes to show them off better . . . if you look you will see Nina's walking shoes and the collar of my woollen jumper . . . . Our rather soppy poses and smiles to order were not of our choice. (Bell 1968: 56)

Yet a surviving press photograph shows an empire-line dress designed by Vanessa, another version of which is seen in a full-length portrait of Nina Hamnett painted by Roger Fry in 1916. Here the geometric design on the fabric of Hamnett's dress matches the Cubist pattern of a cushion also shown in the painting, covered in one of the characteristic Omega textiles.

The first Omega exhibition of garments and accessories opened on 10 June 1915. Isabel Anscombe describes it as showing a collection that included dresses, coats, waistcoats, evening cloaks, parasols, and printed and dyed fabrics. Fabrics were hand painted or designed by Omega artists in a process which allied textile design to experiments in the fine as well as applied arts. Such textiles, as Anscombe writes, 'were a vital part of the overall 'look' of [the Omega]' (Anscombe 1981: 28). Valerie

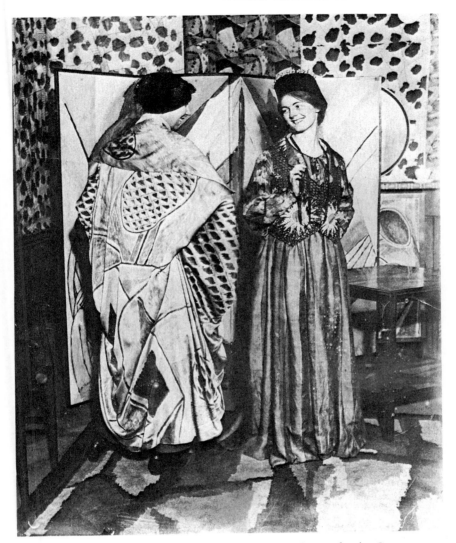

Figure 2   Winifred Gill and Nina Hamnett modelling dresses for the Omega
Workshops

Mendes points to the strong influence by developments in contemporary
painting: far in advance of their time, Omega textiles set a fashion for
abstract and geometric patterns, bright bold colouring, emphatic black
lines and undyed grounds (Mendes 1992: 11). The textiles included
printed linens, silks and batiks. Linens were printed in a special technical
process aimed at preserving 'the freedom and spontaneity of the original drawing', according to Mendes; true pattern freedom was achieved

when the artists painted with dyes directly on the silks and linens (ibid.: 11). As the photograph of Hamnett and Gill suggests, the designs were too avant-garde to be successful beyond a daring minority. For such buyers, however, Omega textiles were dual purpose, to be used as dress materials as well as furnishings (ibid.: 11). A less enthusiastic description of Omega's sartorial experiments is provided by Woolf in a letter to Vanessa:

> My God! What clothes you are responsible for! Karin's clothes wrenched my eyes from the sockets – a skirt barred with reds and yellows of the violent kind, a pea-green blouse on top, with a gaudy handkerchief on her head, supposed to be the very boldest taste. I shall retire into dove colour and old lavender, with a lace collar and lawn wristlets. (*L* II: 111)

Besides showing abstract and geometric patterns, Omega prints and garments also exhibited that playfully allusive iconography of pastoral and myth familiar from Bloomsbury interiors and objects. As such, dress was invested with the same 'spirit of fun' that characterised much other work by Bloomsbury artists and thus included in a modernist project of playful allegorical defamiliarisation and reinscription of visual culture – a working-through, it might be argued, that in many ways centred on Pre-Raphaelite and Symbolist iconography. Woolf's inclusion of a contemporary description of an Omega dress in her biography of Roger Fry captures the nature of this allegorical project:

> 'a radiantly coloured dress of gossamery silk' designed by a French artist . . . . Upon this one the artist had designed 'a mass of large foliage and a pastoral scene, and maidens dancing under the moon, while a philosopher and a peasant stood by'. (*RF*: 195)

The style of this dress is clearly allusive and quotational, part of a playful and ultimately defamiliarising aesthetic, reinventing a traditional symbolic fabric or weave of allusions. With (at least some) Bloomsbury experiments, it seems, fabric becomes the site, and dress the performance, of such reinscription.

Omega's sartorial venture exemplifies the avant-garde's need for distinction from mass culture, which is in turn the very driving force of fashion. As Gutzov observed, the modern and fashion share the quality of uniqueness, of always wanting to be ahead of the mass. What is particularly interesting in the Omega's case is that the quality of being 'ahead' is achieved through a fusion of high with low (fine with applied arts), and, in part, of old with new. Rather than being at odds with the modern understood as a negative moment, a break with the past, the playful citation of old styles corresponds to Gutzov's conceptual definition of the modern as a moment of return. Omega's clothing project, then, is modern not only in its contribution to the construction and projection of modern identities, but in its affirmation of the defining principle of modernism, which is also the principle of fashion.

Besides the opportunities for self-fashioning offered by the Omega and other alternatives to mainstream fashion, the 1910s and the years following the First World War represented a time and an atmosphere, at least among the cultural vanguard, which celebrated the carnivalesque, and which seems to have been unusually conscious of dress not only as a way of practising culture, but as a visual register for exploration and critique. The famous *Dreadnought* Hoax, the most audacious and public of Bloomsbury's carnivalesque adventures, may have begun, as Hermione Lee suggests, as 'a frivolous trespass inside the bulwarks of the establishment', but has long since become established as a signal moment of anti-establishment satire performed through costume (Lee 1997: 283). The story is well known. On 7 February 1910, Virginia Stephen and five accomplices, disguised as the Emperor of Abyssinia and his suite, paid a royal visit to HMS *Dreadnought*, the proudest and

Figure 3   The *Dreadnought* Hoax (Virginia Woolf (seated); Guy Ridley; Horace de Vere Cole; Adrian Stephen; Anthony Buxton (seated); Duncan Grant) by Lafayette (Lafayette Ltd), 7 February 1910

most impregnable battleship of His Majesty's Fleet, of which Virginia's cousin, William Fisher, was flag commander. The joke was organised by Adrian Stephen and his friend Horace Cole. The revellers were dressed by a theatrical costumiers. Virginia, as 'Prince Mendax', was blacked up, with a moustache and beard, and fitted out in suitably 'Oriental' garb, including an embroidered kaftan, a turban, and a gold chain hanging to the waist. The other Abyssinians were similarly dressed. The attempt at impersonation was deliberately and nonchalantly amateurish. Adrian, as the bearded and bowler-hatted interpreter, was hardly disguised at all, while Duncan's moustache came off at a critical moment and had to be hastily reattached. Miraculously, their cousin failed to recognise them. The royal entourage, conversing in an improvised mixture of Latin, Swahili and gibberish, was received with all due courtesy, including a guard of honour, a red carpet, a launch and a naval band, and shown round the ship by one of the Admirals and Commander Fisher himself. The company eventually left the ship without being unmasked, and it was only after one of the jokers leaked the story to the newspapers that the royal visit was exposed as a hoax. The papers gave the story full coverage, and huge embarrassment ensued. The Navy's attempts at retribution involved ceremonial taps of canes 'on the hindquarters', though the greatest source of indignation, apparently, arose from the fact that one of the Abyssinians was a woman (Lee 1997: 282–6).

The subversive aspects of the incident and its connections with many of Woolf's abiding concerns, have been noted by numerous commentators. Quentin Bell fastens on 'the theme of masculine honour, masculine violence and stupidity, of gold-laced pomposity, [that] remained with her for the rest of her life' (Bell 1972: 161). Hermione Lee sees the hoax as combining 'all possible forms of subversion: ridicule of empire, infiltration of the nation's defences, mockery of bureaucratic procedures, cross-dressing and sexual ambiguity' (ibid.: 283). Kathy Phillips and Jean Kennard emphasise the connections between gender and race set up by Virginia's double cross-casting, as African/Oriental and male. Phillips claims that the event shows Woolf's early recognition of the parallels between women in patriarchy and the colonised other (Phillips 1994: 248–9), while Kennard describes the hoax as a power game played through costume 'in which the traditional emblems of superiority, masculinity, and whiteness were the counters' (Kennard 1996: 151). At the most fundamental level, as Kennard also notes, the costumes mimicked the fancy dress aspect of the naval uniforms, thus trivialising and effeminising the officers (ibid.: 151).

This was a story, as Hermione Lee says, which Woolf loved to tell. She wrote an account of the incident which she read for the Women's Institute in Rodmell in the summer of 1940, and again to the Memoir

Club in the same year. The three surviving pages of this talk are included as an appendix in Bell's biography. Adrian Stephen wrote his own account, *The 'Dreadnought' Hoax*, published by The Hogarth Press in 1936. Woolf also writes of the incident in fictional form, in the short story 'A Society' (1921), in which a society of women resort to undercover research in order to determine the state of a world 'civilised' by men: one disguises herself as a charwoman to gain access to the bastions of Oxbridge, another dresses as a (male) reviewer to examine the state of modern literature, a third masquerades as 'an Aethiopian Prince' to gain access to one of His Majesty's ships (*CSF*: 125–6). What is at issue in this story are the thoughts which Woolf pursues in *A Room of One's Own* and *Three Guineas*: the questions about the nature and value of civilisation, and the ridicule of ceremony. With the exploits of Rose's 'Ethiopian' at the centre of the story, ceremonial dress and uniforms as cultural signifiers – the external signs of establishment values – are subjected to carnivalesque appropriation and redeployed in a strategy of theatricalisation and parody.

Virginia and Vanessa's appearance as 'indecent Gauguin girls' at the 1910 Post-Impressionist Ball brings yet a dimension to Bloomsbury's sartorial practice: the connections and intersections between aesthetic and socio-cultural domains. As Vanessa recalled the costumes, they consisted of brightly coloured lengths of fabric 'made for natives in Africa' which they draped around their bodies: 'we wore brilliant flowers and beads, we browned our legs and arms and had very little on beneath the draperies' ('Memories of Roger Fry', quoted in Lee 1997: 291). Thus the costumes combined the double affront of nudity and primitivism that had proved so disturbing to the critics of the Post-Impressionist show. Here were real bodies, redoubling the challenge of the painting by breaking out of the aesthetic domain and into the social one of embodied practice and performance, translating the artist's conception into a proclamation for modern modes of life. As Lee points out, there are some striking resonances between the *Dreadnought* escapade, the Post-Impressionist exhibition, and Virginia and Vanessa's appearance at the ball. The rhetoric of outrage provoked by the three events is similar in terms if not in scale or degree of publicity, expressing public fears about sexual identity, racial and national survival. In the case of the exhibition, 'the reactions ran together the defence of the realm, the purity of women and the mental health of the nation, in a confused and emotional alignment' (ibid.: 291). In a parallel move, Woolf's (and Bloomsbury's) sartorial crossing of boundaries of 'civilised' and 'primitive', man and woman, English and Oriental, brings out similar reactions by enacting the shock of the new in the social domain.

It seems to be the hybridity of clothing – its dual nature as system and event – that makes it the signature of the modern for Woolf and many of her contemporaries. Bloomsbury parties at this time were mostly fancy dress, with theatricals and impromptu performances as part of the entertainment (George Rylands in Noble 1972: 140–1). A diary entry from 1923 records Woolf's thoughts on a costume party at Gordon Square, confiding her childish delight in recycling her mother's clothes. What had once seemed an inheritance of all the pomp and weight of the Victorian Mother's 'ceremonial robes' (*MOB*: 53), has been refashioned as costume:

> Let the scene open on the doorstep of number 50 Gordon Square. We went up last night, carrying our bags, & a Cylonese sword. There was Mary H. in lemon coloured trousers with green ribbons. & so we sat down to dinner; off cold chicken. In came Roger & Adrian & Karin; & very slowly we coloured our faces & made ready for number 46. It was the proudest moment of Clive's life when he led Mary on one arm, Virginia on the other, into the drawing room, which was full, miscellaneous; & oriental for the most part. Suppose one's normal pulse to be 70; in five minutes it was 120; & the blood, not the sticky whitish fluid of daytime, but brilliant & prickling like champagne. This was my state, & most peoples. We collided, when we met: went pop, used Christian names, flattered, praised, & thought (or I did) of Shakespeare . . . Gumbo distorted nursery rhymes; Lydia danced; there were charades; Sickert acted Hamlet. We were all easy & gifted & friendly & like good children rewarded by having the capacity for enjoying ourselves thus. Could our fathers? I, wearing my mothers laces, looked at Marys soft Jerboa face in the old looking glass – & wondered. (*D* 2: 222–3)

George Rylands remembers 'a marvellous party, called the Sailor's Party, in which we all had to go wearing naval costume. I went as a lower-deck type and Lytton went as a full Admiral of the Fleet' (Noble 1972: 140). Lydia and Maynard Keynes also gave regular theatrical parties at this time: 'Keynes used to appear as the Prince Consort and his wife, Lopokova, as Queen Victoria' (ibid.: 140). Barbara Bagenall recalls the influence of the Russian Ballet on costumes and décor as well as the manner of dancing. People would come to the parties straight from Covent Garden, 'everyone dancing madly together, probably still influenced by the ballet' (ibid.: 145).

Different, though clearly related sartorial strategies are being deployed in these examples. The satiric masquerade of the *Dreadnought* Hoax takes the form of absurd impersonations that travesty by their deliberately amateurish mimeticism, seeming to flaunt its carelessness. In the theatricals and fancy dress parties hierarchies are staged and unsettled in carnivalesque manner, the remains of the past recycled as pastiche and parody. Through costume, performance and sartorial practice, the participants speak to each other about the past, about the present moment, and about the future, laughing at authority and pomposity, at unthinking adherence to institutions, conventions, social and sexual mores, at the euphemisms and hyperboles of the nineteenth century and those who were still clinging to them.

More than a local, Bloomsbury phenomenon, the predilection for costumes and dressing up seems to have coincided with a wider sense that sartorial play with identities and self-fashioning constituted a social practice and a mode of thinking that was particularly modern. Christopher Reed refers to the culture of *Vogue* and the Sitwells, costume parties and camp, in defining play with gendered roles and costumes as characteristic of the 'modern' sexuality of the 1920s (Reed 2004: 242). Most radically such gender reconstruction was signified in the early twentieth-century image of the cross-dressed lesbian as, in Havelock Ellis's words, 'terribly modern & shingled & monocled' (Farfan 2004: 85). In Benjamin's reading of Baudelaire, nineteenth-century lesbian dress becomes symptomatic of modernity's protest against technological development (Benjamin 2006: 144). Reed's point, however, is that by the 1920s such sartorial styles of sexual nonconformity have been overtaken by fashion. Thus, for a time, under the editorship of Dorothy Todd and Madge Garland, British *Vogue* 'embodied the experimental ethos of the twenties', the centre of a new culture of sexual nonconformity whose style was 'androgynous in both the extravagant fancy-dress of its parties and its everyday mode of unisex woolen [*sic*] "jumpers" and short hair, a style Woolf adopted at this time' (Reed 2004: 242).

Woolf of course subjects androgyny to further twists in *A Room of One's Own* and *Orlando*. By the mid-1920s, however, there is no doubt that she was herself 'overtaken by fashion'. *Vogue*, as Nicola Luckhurst puts it, was 'making the highbrow chic' through a fashionable blend of de rigeur intellectuals and society figures, avantgarde and mass culture (Luckhurst 1998: 8). Luckhurst, Jane Garrity and Aurelia Mahood have written about *Vogue*'s interweaving of high culture and fashion, especially during the years of Dorothy Todd's editorship, and the role played by Vanessa and Clive Bell, Duncan Grant, Vita Sackville-West, Maynard Keynes, Woolf herself, and a host of others more or less closely connected with Bloomsbury, in lending intellectual and cultural legitimacy to the magazine's promotion of cutting edge styles of life and appearance. The look of Bloomsbury was exhibited in photographs of artists and intellectuals in their homes, while their cultural capital served to promote the idea of modernism not only as high art, but as essential 'fashion accessory' (Mahood 2002: 38–40, 46–7). Woolf, despite criticism from younger writers, found herself defiantly 'whoring after Todd',

Figure 4   Virginia Woolf, 27 April 1925. Photographers: Maurice Adams Beck and Helen Macgregor, Marylebone Mews, London, for *Vogue*

writing five articles for the magazine between 1924 and 1926, sitting for its photographers Maurice Adams Beck and Helen Macgregor, and even for Man Ray, himself consciously crossing boundaries between avant-garde art and fashion. One photograph by Gisèle Freund shows Virginia and Leonard Woolf in their sitting room at 52 Tavistock Square, which had been decorated by Vanessa Bell and Duncan Grant, and illustrated in *Vogue*, early November 1924 (Reed 2004: 224–5). Another famous example is the picture of Virginia wearing her mother's dress with an incongruity that seems citational; thoughtful more than playful – as if to see what happens. In April 1925 she has been sitting for the *Vogue* photographers and reflects that

> people have any number of states of consciousness: & I should like to investigate the party consciousness, the frock consciousness & c. The fashion world . . . is certainly one; where people secrete an envelope which connects them & protects them from others, like myself, who am outside the envelope, foreign bodies. (*D* 3: 12–13)

Virginia may have balked at Vanessa's dresses, and been riven by contradictions in her encounters with the world of fashion, but there is little doubt that her understanding of the discursive, performative and imaginary range of clothing went far beyond that of her Bloomsbury contemporaries. In an age which is particularly aware of clothes and fashion as social, aesthetic and intellectual phenomena, Woolf stands out as a perceptive analyst and a writer who works the sartorial into her writing to an extent that one may argue it constitutes much of its character. Clothes are included in her analysis as a material fact in economies of class, gender and power. As shown in *Three Guineas*, where the second letter, asking for the second guinea, comes as a request for cast-off garments for 'women whose professions require that they should have presentable day and evening dresses which they can ill afford to buy' (*TG*: 179), the need for proper clothes to enter the professions is both as real and as symbolic as the need for an income of £500 a year and a room of one's own. Within the same logic of necessities, Helen Dalloway's estimation of her husband's chances of being made a professor at Cambridge concludes that 'the difficulty would be his clothes' (*VO*: 87). Woolf's interest is also focused on how social organisation is signified and represented visually; naturalised and embodied through clothing as system and practice. Her reading notes for *Three Guineas* show her taking particular note of ceremonial dress and uniforms of all types, whether service or work uniforms or military ones, containing notes and newspaper cuttings on a range of topics from official orders regulating dress for royal funeral and coronation ceremonies, to reports of committees appointed to consider 'smarter walking-out uniforms' for army soldiers, as well as demands for 'smartly cut uniforms for postal workers' (Monks House Papers, Notes and Cuttings, B16f). While Woolf's research extends to the signifying, regulatory and performative force of ceremonial dress in general, the historical urgency of this topic becomes fully evident only in light of the rise of political uniforms and their increasing visibility in ceremony and spectacle during the 1920s and 1930s, with the blue military-looking uniform ('Blueshirt') adopted by the party of British Fascists from 1927, and the black uniforms ('Blackshirts') worn by members of Oswald Mosley's Union of Fascists from 1932. The discomforting presence of boys in uniform, carrying guns, is registered in *Mrs Dalloway* (*MD*: 56), but it is *Three Guineas* of course which addresses the connection between military and political uniforms and other types of ceremonial dress (academic, ecclesiastical and judiciary), making evident a logical continuum that the culture was eager to repress.

With much less urgency, though still of importance in Woolf's exploration of cultural practice, a group of eight stories, written after *Mrs Dalloway* and set at Mrs Dalloway's party, explore the 'party-consciousness' (*D* 3: 12), which is very much a consciousness of dress. Self-fashioning as a characteristically modern project is noted by the elderly Mrs Vallance in 'Ancestors', whose father would never *think* of noticing what a woman wore, and whose mother 'never seemed to dress differently summer or winter'; 'always looked *herself* in lace' (*CSF*: 182). This is in great contrast to the young people at the party who avail themselves of the language of fashion with much fluency, revelling in its individualising potential and in its possibilities of erotic display. Subtle yet incontrovertible messages of distinction are signalled among the arbiters of fashion, to the exclusion of those who have to be content with dressmakers of the less fashionable kind. In 'The New Dress' a woman's projection of self is painfully exposed, turning to negative introjection as she sees herself in the image of a wretched fly, stuck in a saucer, among dragonflies and butterflies. The dress in 'The Introduction' is the visual symbol which 'proclaims' one a woman, the materialisation – in fabric, frills and colour – of the familiar metaphors of femininity: 'frail creature', 'butterfly' and 'flower'. This 'being as a flower', the female protagonist finds, comes with a whole world and with the seductiveness of 'all the little chivalries of the drawing-room' – all the naming and proclaiming of the woman as the poet's muse, the object of masculine worship, 'a cloak for him to trample on', 'a rose for him to rifle' – mild ironies which point forward to the more pronounced sarcasm that fuels *Three Guineas* on the same issue: the seductive interpellations of sartorial practice; of ties and dog-collars, ribbons and badges.

Another pendant to *Mrs Dalloway*, the short story 'Mrs Dalloway in Bond Street', brings into view the socio-economic implications of the sartorial commodity by substituting 'gloves' for the novel's 'flowers' in the famous opening sentence: 'Mrs Dalloway said she would buy the gloves herself'. Clearly, with the change in the object of transaction a change is brought about in the nature of the transaction itself, foregrounding its relations of class, of server and served, their inscriptions and conscriptions as sartorial bodies. Faced with the shop-woman, 'in her place', fetching and carrying, Clarissa adopts the matter-of-factness of Simmel's economic-psychological relation: 'Selling gloves was her job' (*CSF*: 157). Gloves of the kind Clarissa Dalloway wants, white or grey, with pearl buttons, are not made for work. Their function, as historians of dress will tell us, is to 'gentle the hand', to 'draw attention to the hands while making the hands useless, or useful only for putting on or taking off a glove, or for holding gloves or handkerchiefs or fans or flowers' (Stallybrass and Jones 2001: 118). On this background, finding the right glove, proper to the occasion, with the perfect individual fit, poses no threat of infringement; it is class practiced through everyday ritual. Correspondingly, the received wisdom of bodily practice – ' A lady is known by her gloves and her shoes' (*CSF*: 157) – is given prominence as people interpellate themselves and others, bolster faith in the reality and continuity of their existence at times of transition and crisis. Fastening one's hem, buttoning one's gloves, keeping one's head high and body upright – this is the embodiment, the corporeal practice of faith, we are shown: faith in the values of one's class and past generations, the dignity of sacrifice, loyalty to the flag. Lady Bruton's dress may have a shabby look, one white glove loose at her wrist, but her bearing – raised, regal, upright – embodies the discipline of class instilled by bodily practice, the inscription of '[c]haracter, . . . something inborn in the race', 'against the contagion of the world's slow stain' (*CSF*: 153, 158).

Similarly true to the character of *habitus*, Doris Kilman, 'lurching among the commodities' in the Army & Navy store in *Mrs Dalloway* (*MD*: 145), wears her green mackintosh coat as a stamp, a reminder to herself and others of the indignities inflicted upon her by gender, age and class, of being a woman, over forty, and poor (*MD*: 145). Unable to afford the protection of fashion's 'levelling cloak', dress to her takes the form of painful exposure of the wound. Her less than successful performance in the commodity spectacle is foregrounded by the object of transaction, a petticoat, which she chooses 'portentously', an act that is revealing more than trivial in its public display of intimacy and the contrast between her 'unlovable body', which no clothes will ever suit, and the luxurious garments on offer (*MD*: 141).

Woolf, as is well known, was conscious of writing at a time of transition in the conception and representation of character in fiction, advocating a turn towards interiority and modes of depiction interpreted by many commentators in analogy with Post-Impressionist formalism in painting. Rather than a simple dismissal of the significance of clothing, however, her famous renunciation of 'the fashion of the hour' down to its 'last button', is to be understood as a polemical attack on an overly detailed realism still caught up in the physiologies of the previous century and their 'infallible' tests of appearance. Simmel draws attention to *das Gewebe* as a defining figure of the metropolis and its mental life, and, inextricably connected with it, the interface of clothing as that which signifies, and thereby upholds, individual freedom – by protecting us against other bodies, preserving anonymity, and making us into signs, should we so wish, of our 'character'. As already suggested, Woolf has a sophisticated understanding of clothing as a trope of the interface and the place where the contingencies and precariousness of negotiating a visual field are visually represented.

Figures of the interface have a wider expressive range connecting them with modernity and modernism, however. Benjamin writes about the nineteenth century's double fascination with physiologies and with the contours of *étuis*, containers and coverlets of various kinds as related bourgeois attempts at guarding against the alienation and dehumanisation of metropolitan dwelling. Physiologies were exemplifications, in written or visual form, of physiognomic types, hence popular guides to reading character from facial features. For Benjamin they were complicit with the metropolitan phantasmagoria, by suggesting to the individual that he possesses a knowledge of the other that is in fact inaccessible. Within the same logic, Benjamin suggests, bourgeois interiors and objects were designed to humanise the modern condition, in compensation for the fact that the private life leaves no trace in the big city. To dwell means to leave traces and imprints. In recognition of this fact *Jugendstil* interiors were designed as imprints or signatures of their inhabitants, while a range of coverlets, cases and *étuis* were devised to take the traces of objects, thus to humanise the commodity sentimentally: to give it, like the human being, a home (Benjamin 2006: 39–40, 69–70, 148–9). The physiologies, as Benjamin observes, and Woolf's 'Character in Fiction' confirms, were soon outmoded. The fantasy of the trace, however; the fascination with contours, imprints and interfaces, remains, not least in its spectral, allegorical dimension, a characteristic feature of twentieth-century modernism – recognisable in modern materialism as in Woolf's speculations on the manifestations and readability of character.

Clothes figure in these speculations from Woolf's earliest attempts at 'character'. Following the relative modernism of *The Voyage Out, Night and Day* is usually read as something of a false start, a detour around the conventional novel. Even if we take seriously Woolf's claim that she was teaching herself how to write by copying from plaster casts, however, this is a novel which can be seen to thematise modern identities, not so much in the sense of self-fashioning or -staging, as of resisting the stamp of character of one's gender and class – being allowed to develop and express an individual, authentic character, and recognising the character of the other, outside the frames of social and discursive convention. As part of this thematisation, Woolf experiments with the expressive range of dress, using clothing to represent character at a point of transition. Thus the representative of fashion in the novel is Rodney, whose attire is always immaculately correct, and whose wish to dress Katharine (he is upset when a box of clothes he has selected especially for her to wear goes missing) is matched by his fondness for the over-dressing of conventional literary metaphor. His clothes intercept Katharine's attempts at judging his character, nonetheless she finds that he is not entirely represented by his appearance (*ND*: 268–9).

More profound in nature, Ralph and Katharine's relationship traces a route towards mutual recognition where each begins by misrepresenting the other's character by false recourse to convention, Romance, or simply by inattention. On this journey, clothing, with its many languages, serves both to assist and deflect their purpose. To some extent, Ralph's shabbiness and Katharine's carelessness of clothing ('her beauty saved her from the worst fate that can befall a pedestrian; people looked at her, but they did not laugh' (ibid. *ND*: 265)) are indexes of their authenticity and intentions. Katharine's animated dress – 'her skirt had blown, her feather waved' – is indicative, like the sound of her voice, of the real body with which Ralph needs to negotiate his romantic fantasy (ibid.: 256). Yet clothing as allure intercepts his gaze: 'romance seemed to surround her from the floating of a purple veil' (ibid.: 280). By the end of the novel, however, recognition of the other comes not as an awareness of the other's phenomenal presence, but in moments of intuitive, synthetic glimpses of the other as abstraction or figure. As any reader of Woolf's fiction knows, however, such abstraction is not the last word in Woolf's experiments with character. Positioning itself on the interface between interiority and exteriority, her work continues to explore surfaces and interfaces in their phenomenal, semiotic and allegorical dimensions, as clothing and physiognomy, sartorial imprints, and the character cut on a face.

Lily Briscoe's prolonged meditation on the secrets of Mrs Ramsay's character in *To the Lighthouse* contains a sartorial image which is particularly striking for its suggestion of the power of the imprint even in its separation from an animating presence: 'What was the spirit in her', Lily thinks, 'the essential thing, by which, had you found a glove in the corner of a sofa, you would have known it, from its twisted finger, hers indisputably?' (*TTL*: 9). Retaining not only the contours of the hand itself, but of its work, the glove for Lily is neither an inorganic other nor a container of absence, but a manifestation of truth – like an allegorical sign if only one knew how to read its language. One might compare it to the 'steel engravings' appearing on Mrs Ramsay's brow as she sits reading: both are engravings of character, though differently so. Where the lineaments of what one may take as melancholy are inseparable from physiognomy, the glove, like marks of writing, continues to signify apart from the body. As such it becomes a figure of the power of the *tupoi* – the imprint – over death.

Mrs Ramsay's glove is unpaired, gesturing not only towards the absent hand but also towards its absent other. Derrida's *The Truth in Painting* contains some reflections on pairing and unpairing which are suggestive in this context. Writing on Van Gogh's painting *Old Shoes with Laces*, he observes that a

> pair of shoes is more easily treated as a *utility* than a single shoe or two shoes which aren't a pair. The pair inhibits, at least, if it does not prevent, the 'fetishizing' movement; it rivets things to use, to 'normal' use. (Derrida 1987: 332)

Where Mrs Ramsay's glove takes on the mystery of an unreadable sign because it appears by itself, it seems to be the pairedness of the shoes displayed as the concluding image of *Jacob's Room*, that allows them to represent character in terms of everyday, habitual usage: '"What am I to do with these, Mr. Bonamy?" [Mrs Flanders] held out a pair of Jacob's old shoes' (*JR*: 155). The novel's suggestion is that these contours are all we have, because of the unrelenting interpellations of the social machine, the institutional and discursive dressing of character. In Jacob's case, the gowns and boots of the academic procession; Cambridge's 'plaiting of the garland of manliness'; friends and admirers dressing him as the classical 'Greek type' – all serve to hollow out, to displace what may have existed of an 'unknown and uncircumscribed spirit' (*JR*: 24, 33, 63). Thus the shoes are more poignant than the circumscribed absence of the empty room itself or any of its memorabilia for precisely not being what Benjamin would call a souvenir or *Andenken* but rather *Spur* – trace, imprint – and also waste; things, as well as objects for the ragpicker.

As a last indication of the many dimensions involved in the modern consciousness of clothes, I want to bring in briefly a connection that will be explored further in subsequent chapters: the connection between dress and an anthropomorphising tendency in Woolf's fiction. Draped, veiled and garlanded figures – suggestive of Greek sculpture or Pre-Raphaelite iconography – keep turning up in her narratives at moments of heightened significance, gesturing towards a temporality other than the present and a domain one might think of as other-worldly. Appearing against the phantasmagoria of the metropolis, these draped apparitions suggest not so much the speaking other of the commodity or a material spectrality, however; they seem rather to be implicated with depictions of an anthropomorphised, allegorical Nature. Thus *The Waves*, as Woolf's most complex handling of clothing, alternates between a vision of auratic veiling and unveiling, giving us the alienation and serialisation of the modern city in a procession of hats – 'the aimless passing of billycock hats and Homburg hats and all the plumed and variegated head-dresses of women' – circumscribed by the cloths of water and sky, of meaningful, creative nature (*TW*: 70).

The modern clothes-consciousness that this chapter has begun to explore can be seen to mediate and focus some of the most pressing concerns of modernity. Metonymically or metaphorically, fashion is seen to signify the constitutional character of modern temporality and social organisation, with clothes representing the threshold where the modern subject/object relation plays itself out in a series of encounters and ruptures. Clothes are the place where character becomes image, the place where one's inscriptions in culture and the system of exchange become visible. They also circumscribe and mediate the body as thing, the materiality-effect of the corporeal. Precisely because they exist on and as a boundary, clothes are experienced at once as quasi-objects and quasi-subjects, as chiasmic figures interstitially inhabiting/invoking the organic and the inorganic, life and death. As signifiers liberated from historical bodies and a system of signification, clothes may enter into a Benjaminean archaeology of the imaginary or into quotational play with the past; in both cases, it seems, clothes serve to render the relations between *then* and *now* particularly and graphically clear. Finally, clothes are deployed in modern projects of self-fashioning, visual proclamations of new aesthetics and, not least, bodily practices opening up for new relations between habitus and field. Woolf's writing, as we have seen, is cognisant of all these dimensions of modern clothes-consciousness. In addition, as I have suggested, it introduces a tropology of garments – of dressed figures and what I propose to designate a poetics of investiture, of apostrophe and prosopopoeia – which seems to mediate, within a Woolfian but also more generally modernist, materialism, between people and things, human beings and nature, life and after-life. It is the modern habit of 'seeing through clothes' in all these dimensions – and Woolf's writing as both a generic and particular modern gaze in this respect – which will be at the centre of inquiry in the chapters that follow.

Notes

1. The term 'mnemotechnological' is Ulrich Lehmann's. See *Tigersprung: Fashion in Modernity* (2000).
2. *Seeing Through Clothes* is the title of Anne Hollander's influential 1978 study of costume, nudity and fabric in art (see Hollander 1988).

Chapter 2

From Symbolism in Loose Robes to the Figure of the Androgyne

Looking at Woolf's writing through its clothes brings out some striking intertextual dialogues, one of which takes place among three texts written within a decade of each other: the play *Freshwater*, begun in 1923 and performed in a revised version in 1935; *Orlando*, Woolf's 1928 mock-biography of the fashionable writer and sapphist Vita Sackville-West, and *A Room of One's Own*, her genealogy of women's writing, also written in 1928 (published 1929). The target of *Freshwater*'s satire is a late Victorian sartorial practice based in ideals of authenticity and truth of expression; aligned with a Carlylean sartorial semantics in which clothes are emblems proclaiming the allegorical nature of life. *Orlando* participates in a related idealist send-up, most outrageously by substituting a playful and performative vestimentary practice for the nineteenth-century discourse of authenticity. Both texts introduce the modern moment as a fashionably androgyne woman, developed into a figure of modern writing through the reflections on the literary mind contained in *Orlando* and *A Room of One's Own*.

Though much of Bloomsbury's sartorial practice was directed against the authority and constrictions of their parents' generation, it both continued and departed from the practices of the previous century, as the introductory chapter suggested. Sandra Gilbert was among the first to observe that the clothes-consciousness which defines modernist writing continues and intensifies a heightened awareness of the theatricality of clothing and the potential of vestimentary self-fashioning that came to effect in the nineteenth century, partly in consequence of the increasing availability of photography (Gilbert 1980: 393–4). For writers, painters, and others within the circumference of 'art', clothing was a means of publicly proclaiming anti-bourgeois identities that would be immediately visible (Jones 1995: 18–20). The Victorian avant-garde (Aestheticism and the Arts and Crafts Movement) connected art, design, and theories of dress reform in several radical departures from established dress codes, the Pre-Raphaelites providing one of the first alternative vestimentary movements in nineteenth-century England. As D. M. Mankoff writes, most of the women in the Pre-Raphaelite circle dressed 'with an unorthodox flair' (Mankoff 2000: 85). Contemporaries cited by Mankoff record their impressions of 'odd-colored gowns with long trains', 'contrary to all the fashions of the day' (ibid.: 85–6). Such 'aesthetic' dress became emblematic of the freethinking, 'artistic' woman, devotee of the Aesthetic Movement and its aestheticisation of the everyday as a counter-strategy to mass-production, advocating organic, true relations between spirit, body and dress in opposition to the corporeal stylisation and restriction of commercial bourgeois fashion.

Closer to Bloomsbury, though still with links to the Pre-Raphaelites, the Cameron circle employed clothing in their own idealist aestheticism which Woolf parodies in *Freshwater*. What is particularly interesting about this practice, providing the primary target of Woolf's satire, is its connection to a sartorial semantics: the visual and verbal vocabularies and tropes by which this avant-garde expressed its ideas about truth, reality, and the possibilities of knowledge. In praxis dress was used to signal an anti-philistine, if not strictly anti-bourgeois, individualism based on contempt 'for the ways of the world – at any rate, for the conventions of Putney' (Woolf 1973: 15). The Cameron sisters were known for their eccentric dress sense based on flowing gowns, Indian shawls and exotic jewellery. In a biographical essay introducing Julia Cameron's photography, Woolf imagines her 'dressed in robes of flowing red velvet . . . stirring a cup of tea as she walked, half-way to the railway station in hot-summer weather', or pacing the lawn with her husband, the latter 'wearing a coned hat, a veil, and several coats' (ibid.: 15, 18). Closely connected to such proclamations of individualism, was the group's idealist commitment to art, also expressed in sartorial terms. As Roger Fry writes in another essay, Cameron's photographs reveal an 1860s and 1870s England 'given over to art to an extent which we find it hard to understand': 'The cult of beauty was a religion . . . a violent . . . aversion from . . . Philistinism . . . . The devotees of this creed cultivated the exotic and precious with all the energy and determination of a dominant class' (Fry 1973: 24). Such cultivation involved the aestheticisation of the quotidian; perceiving the symbolic and transcendent meanings of everyday things, events and persons. Critics have pointed to the connections existing between the Camerons and the Christian aesthetics of Keble and Newman. Mike Weaver argues that Cameron regarded her photographs as theophanies – iconic and indexical 'manifestations of God in terms of living persons' – quoting from Newman's 'Poetry' (1829) in support of his view:

> With Christians, a poetical view of things is a duty – we are bid to colour all things with the hues of faith, to see a divine meaning in every event and a Superhuman tendency. Even our friends around are invested with unearthly brightness . . . beings . . . stamped with His seal. (Weaver 1986: 24)

Whether Weaver is right or not in evoking Keble and Newman, it remains that the idealist integration of art and life, as well as the symbolic invest-ments of objects and people, both in Cameron's photographs and the mode of life of this avant-garde, occurred predominantly through a sartorial register. To a considerable extent it was the costumes, the veils, draperies and other sartorial items that proclaimed the symbolic and allegorical nature of the subjects and objects of a photograph, paint-ing or tableau. Along with the blurred, differential focus, the poses and expressions of the models, and the title of the picture, the sartorial items were instrumental in identifying the allegorical nature of the represen-tation; gesturing towards other worlds; giving the unsubstantial and invisible mystical presence. In elaborately arranged group compositions, 'Annunciations', 'Holy Families', 'The Kiss of Peace', 'Venus Removing Cupid's Wings', and the like, improvised and fanciful costumes were relied upon to turn 'boatmen . . . into King Arthur; village girls into Queen Guenevere':

> Tennyson was wrapped in rugs; Sir Henry Taylor was crowned with tinsel . . . . The carpenter and the Crown Prince of Prussia alike must sit as still as stones in the attitudes she chose, in the draperies she arranged, for as long as she wished. (Woolf 1973: 18)

Draperies, as in the other visual arts, had particular significance, invested with centuries of allusive and symbolic meaning. With some reservations Fry comments on Cameron's composition 'Mary Mother' as an example of her control of 'the disposition of the drapery':

> No doubt a great painter . . . would introduce almost unconsciously certain changes. The rhythm of the drapery would have been more completely brought out by slight amplifications here and retrenchments there, by a greater variety and consistency of accents, and by certain obliterations. In particular the awkward direction of the fold seen in the penumbra behind the profile would have been suppressed and changed . . . but none the less few could have surpassed the beauty of modelling. (Fry 1973: 26–7)

That such extended concern with the composition of the drapery was more than purely pictorial, we shall see below.

Not surprisingly, it is the sartorial symbolism that strikes Woolf's imagination and her satiric vein in *Freshwater*. As observed by many com-mentators, Bloomsbury's relations with the inheritance of the Cameron circle were far from straightforward.[1] In *The Art of Bloomsbury*, Richard Shone writes about Fry, Bell and Grant's extension of certain nineteenth-century preoccupations, arguing that their connection with High Victorian art and the Cameron circle in particular, hinges on the importance to the younger group of imagination, fantasy, and the spiritual (Shone 1999: 24–5). Bloomsbury art and design show a tendency to return to the iconographic and allegorical semantics of their predecessors: textiles are given mythical and allegorical names such as 'Maud', 'Amenophis', 'Daphne and Apollo'; Bell and Grant's decorative schemes of the 1920s show variations on classical myths – 'Narcissus and Echo', 'Psyche and Cupid'; and it is difficult, as Shone writes, 'not to see a curious continuity between Cameron's fantastic, contrived, and mood-pervaded figure-groups . . . and the later artists' propensity to create just such tableaux on their own, whether in fine or applied art or in family theatricals' (Anscombe 1981: 28–9, 108; Mendes 1992: 73; Shone 1999: 27–8). Vanessa Bell's photograph of a tableau based on *Antony and Cleopatra* from the late 1930s (reproduced in Shone 1999: 28) shows a clear example of the abiding interest in this visual vocabulary. As in Cameron's photographs, arrangements of draperies, curtains and other textiles are at the centre of the composition. In Bell's photograph, however, the ambiguity that defines Bloomsbury's appropriation of this aesthetic semantics is clearly present. Throughout the group's recycling of the nineteenth-century iconography and allegorical modality, the satiric alternates with the serious, parody with pastiche, to distinctly equivocal effect. In Shone's words, these various modes, the satiric and the serious, 'form a single tissue, so that it is impossible to make fast distinctions between genres of Bloomsbury art in terms of imagery' (Shone 1999: 28).

The ambivalence of attitude apart, there is no doubt that the Bloomsbury artists were fascinated by the sartorial practice and tropology of the Cameron circle, and that for Woolf and her immediate artistic community this entered into a visual and verbal inventory in such a way that particular sartorial items or tropes would immediately conjure up an entire idealist aesthetic, a mode of life which was consistently 'symbolic', and a spirituality which was as high-minded as it was earnest, far removed from the almost reckless playfulness that informed the sartorial games of the next generation. This, evidently, is how the satire of *Freshwater* works. Perhaps the main target of this satire is what Woolf perceives as the previous generation's symbolic over-investment in life and the world, considered from the perspective of what she called 'the modern distaste for allegory' or 'symboli[sm] in loose robes' (*M*: 27; *D* 3: 230): an aesthetic in which capital letters proclaimed the allegorical content of a poem; while tags, allusions and painterly conventions – not least of dress and drapery – proclaimed the content of narrative and allegorical painting. In Cameron's circle, it seemed, such over-investment went on to the extent that, in *Freshwater*'s parodic rendition, everything stands absurdly for something else, while all things of substance seem to be unreal.

At the centre of Woolf's comedy is G. F. Watts's painting 'Mammon', for which Ellen Terry is posing as 'Modesty at the Feet of Mammon' draped in white, in the 1923 version specified as 'white veils which are wrapped around her arms, head, etc.' (*FR*: 69). The painting in question may be a reference to Watts's 1884–5 oil study *Mammon*, subtitled 'Dedicated to his Worshippers' (Wilton 1997: 169). In this painting Mammon sits enthroned as the embodiment of greed and cruelty. Money bags fill his lap, a naked youth lies crushed beneath one of his feet, while a beautiful girl, also nude, crouches at the other. The idealised nudity of these youths presents them as emblematic of purity and innocence, while Mammon's corrupted nature is shown by his 'gorgeous but ill-fitting golden draperies, [falling] awkwardly about his coarse limbs' (Spielmann 1886, cited in Wilton 1997: 169). A painter of expressive allegories such as 'Love and Death', 'Love and Life' and so on, Watts was a central figure in the Cameron circle and clearly influential on Cameron's photography, especially in its representation of spiritual and allegorical dimensions. Cameron's blurred focus resembles Watts's characteristic muted picture surfaces, intended as a suggestive membrane through which the world 'parallel to Nature' could be perceived, while Cameron's preoccupation with draperies and veils corresponds to Watts's Symbolist pronouncements on 'the veil that covers the mystery of our being', and the connections between the veil and a 'visionary' style of painting (Wilton 1997: 27, 73). In Woolf's play he is absurdly preoccupied with 'the problem of the drapery':

> That indeed is a profoundly difficult problem. For by my treatment of the drapery I wish to express two important but utterly contradictory ideas. In the first place I wish to convey to the onlooker the idea that Modesty is always veiled; in the second that Modesty is absolutely naked. For a long time I have pondered at a loss. At last I have attempted a solution. I am wrapping her in a fine white substance which has the appearance of a veil; but if you examine it closely it is seen to consist of innumerable stars. It is in short the Milky Way. (*FR*: 17)

The relative degree of 'truth' to be ascribed to body, dress and drapery has hardly remained stable through the history of painting, though neoclassic aestheticians such as Joshua Reynolds separate drapery from clothing on the basis that clothes are contingent, bound to style and

Figure 5   Angelica Bell as Ellen Terry in *Freshwater*, 8 Fitzroy Street, 18 January 1934

finite time, while the generalised texture of antique drapery transcends the finite to signify universal truths. Moral judgements concerning the appropriate pictorial rendering of cloth and the dangers of being seduced by the materiality of the cloth itself, abound.[2] In the Renaissance allegories that inspired Watts, drapery approximates the status of the idealised nude body as the embodiment of celestial (as opposed to worldly) truths (Hollander 1988: 75–6, 448). Watts's drapery in *Freshwater*, however, represents the moment when symbolic investment spins out of control. Consulting the dictionary of symbols Watts finds that he has been 'most cruelly deceived':

> 'The Milky Way among the ancients was the universal token of fertility. It symbolised the spawn of fish, the innumerable progeny of the sea, and the fertility of the marriage bed.' Horror! Oh Horror! I who have always lived for the Utmost for the Highest have made Modesty symbolise the fertility of fish! (*FR* 19)

As it turns out, however, the Symbol always knows its meaning. Mermaid-like, on a rock in the sea, Ellen Terry is discovered kissing John Craig, causing Watts to declare: 'Modesty forsooth! Chastity! Alas, I painted better than I knew. The Ancient Egyptians were right. This veil did symbolise the fertility of fish' (*FR*: 42).

To equally satiric effect, Julia Cameron is seen frantically searching through her sartorial inventory for a pair of wings to fit the Muse in one of her many compositions (and 'the Muse must have wings'): 'Towels, sheets, pyjamas, trousers, dressing gowns, braces – braces but no wings. Trousers but no wings. What a satire upon modern life!' (*FR*: 10–11). Resolutely, the modern poverty of spirit is counteracted with a pair of turkey's wings straight off the bird. The turkey, Mrs Cameron decides, is happy to be 'part and parcel of my immortal art' (ibid.: 14). Meanwhile Mr Cameron, the philosopher, elucidates his wife's idealist aesthetic in philosophical and distinctly Carlylean terms:

> All things that have substance seem to me unreal. What are these? [*He picks up the braces.*] Braces. Fetters that bind us to the wheel of life. What are these? [*He picks up the trousers.*] Trousers. Fig leaves that conceal the truth. (ibid.: 14)

Where Mike Weaver evokes Keble and Newman to contextualise the aesthetic practice of the Camerons, one may safely argue that Thomas Carlyle's thoughts in *Sartor Resartus* are equally close at hand – not least in light of the constant interplay observed between the work of Carlyle and that of Watts. As Andrew Wilton points out, for instance, Watts's *Mammon* is a direct response to Carlyle's attack, in *Past and Present* (1843), on 'Midas-eared Mammonism' as one of the evils of modern life (Wilton 1997: 131). Beyond specific allusions, Carlyle's thoughts on the essentially symbolic nature of events, objects and lives, and the idea of symbols as clothes, are closely consistent with the thought and practice both of Watts and the Camerons. In the theory of the symbol

Carlyle elaborates in *Sartor Resartus*, 'man . . . everywhere finds himself encompassed with Symbols, recognised as such or not recognised; the Universe is but one vast Symbol of God'; 'Nay, if you consider it, what is Man himself, and his whole terrestrial Life, but an Emblem; a Clothing or visible Garment for that divine ME of his, cast hither, like a light-particle, down from Heaven?' (Carlyle 1869: 49).

Carlyle's theory of clothes in *Sartor Resartus* pursues two lines of argument that are closely connected and that seem to have caught the imagination not only of the Cameron circle but to some extent of Woolf herself: one, that clothes are symbols; the other, that symbols are clothes. The first concerns the semiotic function of clothes within a cultural system of signification, inscribing a range of social relations, beliefs and assumptions. This is where we find the 'clothes philosopher' railing against empty clothes and soulless cloth: Church-Clothes that have become 'mere hollow Shapes, or Masks', or bodies which 'appropriate what was meant for the Cloth only!' (Carlyle 1869: 149, 166). In both cases, what is at stake is a lack of correspondence between inside and outside, introducing a dangerous duplicity into the system, or falsely appropriating the meaning that rightly belongs to the clothes. The other part of Carlyle's argument, 'that all Symbols are properly Clothes' (ibid.: 187), involves an understanding of the proper function of linguistic mediacy and the relation of individual symbols to a universal allegory of the divine, a meaningful scheme in the universe. This scheme – the 'Living Garment' of which all nature and life are part (ibid.: 141) – is not vouchsafed by means of Romantic translucence; by the spirit shining through nature. For Carlyle, if 'all visible things are emblems', then 'all Emblematic things are properly Clothes, thought-woven or hand-woven' (ibid.: 49). Language as he understands it is predominantly metaphoric, a weaving which illuminates relationships and reveals connections. By 'the wondrous agency of Symbols', revelation comes as concealment: 'In a Symbol there is concealment and yet revelation: here, therefore . . . comes a double significance' (ibid.: 151).

Carlyle's argument, Michael Carter suggests in *Fashion Classics from Carlyle to Barthes*, may be read as a manifesto for authenticity, for a truthful relation between the spirit and its corporeal and sartorial manifestations (Carter 2003: 11). 'In all [man's] Modes, and habilatory endeavours', writes Carlyle, 'an Architectural Idea will be found lurking: his Body and the Cloth are the site and materials whereon and whereby his beautified edifice, of a Person, is to be built' (Carlyle 1869: 23). Carlyle's 'architectural idea', as Carter also shows, corresponds to the *Geist* of German Romantic thought (Carter 2003: 11). Clothes, in other words, are manifestations of spirit and spiritual bonds: emblems in a divine allegory and in an idealist (German Romantic) *Geistesgeschichte* whereby *Geist*, or spirit, manifests itself as sartorial style.

It is the Carlylean deployment of emblematic clothes in a mission of earnest spiritualism Woolf stages with such impudence in *Freshwater*. Where Carlyle insists on authenticity and truth, the play opts for satire. Divesting herself of veils and draperies, 'Modesty' is seen leaving with her lover for Bloomsbury, 'painted, powdered – unveiled' (*FR*: 47). In the 1923 version Woolf gives Terry a fashionably androgynous look, dressing her as a young man in checked trousers (apparently an allusion to a costume worn by the real Terry in a boy's role). Such corruption of femininity's spirit, Watts finds, is beyond forgiveness: 'Had you gone to meet him as a maiden, in a veil, or dressed in white, it would have been different. But trousers – no – check trousers; no.' Ellen, however, calmly pulls a long veil out of her trouser pocket: 'Here's your veil. I intend to wear trousers in future. I never could understand the sense of wearing veils in a climate like this' (ibid.: 81).

As we shall see in Chapter 3, the pictorial context for Charles Baudelaire's elevation of the fashion plate in his essay 'The Painter of Modern Life' was the conventional, allusive depiction of dress in late Romantic painting – careful arrangements of folds and drapes alluding to antique, medieval or Renaissance sources – Baudelaire's point being that immutable truths are accessible only through the historical mediacy of contemporary dress. Truth, Baudelaire argues, is to be found neither in nude nor draped bodies, but in the contingency and transitoriness of fashion. There is a link from this argument to Woolf's preoccupations in *Freshwater* with the smothering weight – the near-compulsive allegorisation – of nineteenth-century (sartorial) symbolism. Like Baudelaire, Woolf lets fashion – and significantly the fashionable woman – represent the modern: stylised and made-up, or cross-dressed and androgynous. *Orlando*, in similarly playful and parodic mood, turns from the sartorial discourses and practices of the past to those of the present, though still with an edge against the Carlylean symbolism of the previous century. In this combination of mock-biography and parodic history of writing, Woolf not only substitutes performativity for authenticity in a modern theory of clothes, but thinks about the past through a parodic *Geistesgeschichte* which rewrites Carlyle's emblematic clothes as frivolous and mutable fashion. Bloomsbury as a cultural avant-garde was known not only for its eccentric clothing styles, its fancy-dress parties, masquerades and theatricals, but also for the fashionable cross-dressing of some of its members. It is this vestimentary practice that Woolf both celebrates and gently parodies in *Orlando*. Where *Freshwater* stages the sartorial semantics and claims to authenticity of the Victorian avant-garde, *Orlando* looks at the past through the lens of fashion – a move which effectively liberates style from *Geist*, present from past, clothes from spirit and body.

Orlando's biographical subject Vita Sackville-West, an arbiter of fashion as well as literary modishness, was a well-known lesbian and cross-dresser whose register of self-presentation ranged from English nobility to Spanish gypsy, from breeches to satins and pearls. Whether glamorously 'grape clustered' and 'pearl hung' (*D* 3: 52); arrayed 'more than ever like a Guards officer in bearskin & breeches' (Lee 1997: 497); or turning up to receive the Hawthornden Prize wearing a black Mexican hat and a knotted red tie (Glendinning 1983: 177), Vita's appearance suggested the theatrical, a manner of self-performance, as D. A. Boxwell rightly observes, which aligns her with the style and sensibility of camp (Boxwell 1998). Victoria Glendinning's biography comments on Sackville-West's narcissism, her myths and fantasies of herself, her fascination, not least, with 'projections of her masculine aspect' (Glendinning 1983: 202). This particular avenue of exploration was begun in 1918 when, for the first time, Vita put on men's clothes to reinvent herself as the young gentleman 'Julian', soon to be seen dining and dancing and strolling around the streets of London and Paris in the company of his girlfriend 'Lushka' (Violet Trefusis) (ibid.: 99). Reputedly descending from gypsies (by way of her Spanish dancer grandmother, Pepita de Oliva), Sackville-West also enjoyed projecting this aspect of herself. Neither mode of self-presentation was unique to Vita, however. Representing modern fantasies of exoticism, primitivism, eroticism and nature, costumes based on gypsy style were popular in the 1920s, at a time when writings in anthropology, travel and fiction were establishing a discourse on the gypsy as the embodiment of such features. More specifically, as Kirstie Blair notes in an article on 'Gypsies and Lesbian Desire', gypsy dress also entered into the inventory of lesbian self-fashioning and cultural performance at this time (Blair, K. 2004). While associated in the popular imagination with female sexuality rather than sapphism per se, the extravagance and flamboyance of gypsy costume fitted well with the artifice and camp of homosexual performative styles. To English eyes, gypsy dress was also associated with a wider range of exotic 'Oriental' fashion, among them a fashion for 'Turkish trousers' which seemed to be doubly invested with the erotics of gender ambiguity and of the 'Far East' (Garber 1992: 310–15). Having experienced the Orient at close hand during her husband's postings to Constantinople and Teheran, Vita included Turkish dress in her repertoire of performative styles, a fantasy which of course Woolf reinvents as one of the core episodes of *Orlando*.

Though the photo purporting to represent "Orlando around 1840" is as far from this performative inventory as one could possibly get (showing a rather demure female figure in hat, shawl and checked skirt), his/her personae both before and after this low point exhibits the stylishness, the ambiguity, and the polymorph sexuality of fashionable avant-garde sartorial performance. The relationship between sex, gender and sexuality is shown as capable of near-endless permutations; so is the relationship between people and their clothes. Depended on to explore and assert these fundamentally unstable and mutable relationships, clothes are cast in a variety of roles, sometimes representative of anatomy, sometimes of gender; sometimes repressive, sometimes liberating. Orlando, though ambiguously gendered by clothing, is a man until the age of thirty, when he becomes a woman. As a man he is heterosexual, though attracted to sexually ambiguous figures; as a woman she is bisexual. The change from man to woman goes virtually unnoticed by Orlando herself, invested it seems, with no more consequence or permanence than an actor's change of clothes. Thus Orlando

> found it convenient at this time to change frequently from one set of clothes to another. . . . She had, it seems, no difficulty in sustaining the different parts, for her sex changed far more frequently than those who have worn only one set of clothing can conceive; nor can there be any doubt that she reaped a twofold harvest by this device; the pleasures of life were increased and its experiences multiplied. For the probity of breeches she exchanged the seductiveness of petticoats and enjoyed the love of both sexes equally. (O: 152–3)

Throughout the biographer's attempts to keep track of these permutations, Woolf remains facetious, seeming to throw ideas in the air – odds and ends; old and new thoughts on sex and gender, self and appearance, habitus and field – while keeping ironically aloof from all of them. Thus, on the one hand,

> there is much to support the view that it is clothes that wear us and not we them; we may make them take the mould of arm or breast, but they mould our hearts, our brains, our tongues to their liking. (O: 132)

On the other hand, there is relief in being able to conclude that 'the difference between the sexes is, happily, one of great profundity' (O: 132). 'Clothes are but a symbol of something hid deep beneath', asserts the biographer with Carlylean conviction, only to find himself face to face with a dilemma:

> Different though the sexes are, they intermix. In every human being a vacillation from one sex to the other takes place, and often it is only the clothes that keep the male or female likeness, while underneath the sex is the very opposite of what it is above. (O 132–3)

Woolf's history of styles renders the Elizabethan age chic and the Victorian age hopelessly out of fashion, with the Renaissance emphasis on modishness, ornamentation and erotic display for both male and female aristocratic dress anticipating to some extent the transgender, self-conscious, and self-fashioning identities *Orlando* asserts. Considering the restrictiveness of Renaissance sumptuary law it is perhaps paradoxical that this period should come to stand as one of comparative freedom in Woolf's mind. According to Marjorie Garber, more royal orders were issued in this area of life during the Elizabethan age than at any other time in English history, prescribing in great detail the particular materials and items of dress permitted for each rank (Garber 1992: 26). The emphasis on regulation came in response to growing tendencies towards indecorous excess in clothing, though the main threat of such behaviour was perceived to be against social and economic, rather than sexual, distinctions (ibid.: 26–7). Reconstructing Elizabethan fashion from the modern perspective, however, *Orlando* represents it as a precursor for the artifice, self-conscious display, and gender ambiguity that figures the modern. The 'fashion of the time', as the biographer points out even in the opening sentence, tends towards ambiguity. Dressing for the Queen's visit at the age of sixteen, Orlando tosses stockings and jerkin to don 'crimson breeches, lace collar, waistcoat of taffeta, and shoes with rosettes on them as big as double dahlias' (O: 16). The effect may be studied by turning to the 'illustration' provided, 'Orlando as a Boy'; the effect may also be observed in the impression made on the ageing queen – of innocence, 'manly charm', and 'a pair of the finest legs a young nobleman had ever stood upright upon' (ibid.: 17). Correspondingly, the 'extraordinary seductiveness' to Orlando's eyes of the Russian Princess issues both from the flamboyant exoticism of her appearance – 'dressed entirely in oyster-coloured velvet, trimmed with some unfamiliar greenish-coloured fur' – and the uncertain nature of her gender: 'for the loose tunic and trousers of the Russian fashion served to disguise the sex' (ibid.: 26).

The seventeenth century in *Orlando*'s historiography offers a similar freedom from restrictions, though projected onto another locale: a fantasmatic Orient. Here the fantasy of self-fashioning across lines of gender and class is enabled by the imagined ambiguity of oriental dress and, as in the previous century, by recourse to disguise. During the Elizabethan age, Orlando's use of disguise allows him to indulge his liking for 'low company': 'wrapped in a grey cloak to hide the star at his neck and the garter at his knee', he is free to listen to stories told by sailors and loose women in beer gardens (O: 21). In Constantinople we see him alternately at the window, wrapped in a long Turkish cloak, gazing at the city with its 'multi-coloured barbaric population'; a few hours later, 'properly scented, curled, and anointed' he performs his dip-lomatic tasks to admiration, while late at night, it is rumoured, he passes out of his own gates 'so disguised that the sentries did not know him', to mingle with the crowds in the streets and bazaars or 'throw aside his shoes to join the worshippers in the Mosques' (ibid.: 85, 89). Orlando's adventures with the gypsies show ambiguity extending from gender and class to ethnicity, as, having discovered herself a woman, she proceeds to dress 'in those Turkish coats and trousers which can be worn indif-ferently by either sex', to take off with a band of gypsies among whom 'her dark hair and dark complexion bore out the belief that she was, by birth, one of them' (ibid.: 98, 100).

Interestingly, this is also the episode where *Orlando*'s parodic project most clearly overwrites the celebratory. More than a simple pointer to Vita's 'gypsy' identity, this episode presents itself as a parody of such self-presentational strategies and the acquisitive logic of their sartorial inventories which appropriate the 'oriental' as easily as the 'gypsy'. In Woolf's parodic version, Orlando's 'English disease', her compulsive and excessive symbolisation, inscribes *her* – not the gypsies – in a dis-course of extravagance and flamboyance; a symbolism in loose robes in which everything 'is something else'. Similes turn into baroque figures as Orlando

> liken[s] the hills to ramparts, to the breasts of doves, and the flanks of kine
> . . . compares the flowers to enamel and the turf to Turkey rugs worn thin
> . . . pray[s] that she might share the majesty of the hills, know the serenity of
> the plains,

imagines the eagle's raptures her own, and salutes 'each star, each peak, and each watch-fire as if they signalled to her alone' (O: 101). The English disease – the cultural compulsion to appropriate, to inscribe eve-rything with meanings and symbolic value in one's own private drama – is opposed to the gypsies' pragmatic and practical recognition of the nature of things, while Orlando is exposed as camp performer in fancy dress, regarded with understandable suspicion by the gypsies.

The eighteenth century has Orlando returning to England dressed in a complete outfit suitable for a young Englishwoman of her rank and day:

> It is a strange fact, but a true one, that up to this moment she had scarcely given her sex a thought. Perhaps the Turkish trousers which she had hitherto worn had done something to distract her thoughts; and the gipsy women, except in one or two important particulars, differ very little from the gipsy men. At any rate, it was not until she felt the coil of skirts about her legs and

the Captain offered, with the greatest politeness, to have an awning spread for her on deck, that she realised with a start the penalties and the privileges of her position. (*O*: 108)

A lengthy meditation on the nature of this position and its connection with clothing ensues. Her skirts, she finds, 'are plaguey things to have about one's heels', making it impossible, if need be, to leap overboard and swim. On the other hand, 'the stuff (flowered paduasoy) is the love-liest in the world'. Gloom falls upon her at the realisation that wearing a skirt and not being able to swim compels her to 'respect the opinion of the other sex, however monstrous' (*O*: 110). And as if this corporeal and mental discipline imposed by dress were not sufficient, her time, from now on, will literally be ruled by the clock of fashion and all its 'staying and lacing', 'washing and powdering', and 'changing from silk to lace and from lace to paduasoy' (ibid.: 110).

Not surprisingly, Woolf's representations of the fashions of the past become most dismissive when approaching the sartorial regimes of the nineteenth century. The overdress presented here is not that of baroque display but of claustrophobic concealment and totalitarian gender seg-regation. Here Woolf's historiography, though exuberantly parodic, is not far off the mark, as the clear sartorial definition and demarcation of gender is a primary characteristic of Victorian fashion. While as late as the 1830s and 1840s, as Valerie Steele's history of nineteenth-century fashion shows, men's fashion still emphasised the wearer's physical attractions, typically by means of tight trousers or pantaloons, worn with 'short tight tail-coats, cut high in front, nipped in at the waist and with broad shoulders', male dress of the second half of the century, con-sisting of coat, trousers and waistcoat of looser fit, created a more solid, boxy shape (Steele 1985: 57–8). Luxury and modishness were essentially features of women's dress, with women of the middle and upper classes carrying on the aristocratic code of decoration, display and novelty. The dome-shaped structure of the cage-crinoline changed women's dress from the 1850s, writes Steele, producing a visual definition of gender – the 'box' and the 'hourglass' – which marks men and women as not merely different but radically and absurdly incompatible (ibid.).

The hallmark frock-coat and sponge-bag trousers compose Woolf's image of Victorian male costume; for women it is the crinoline and the many layers of clothing that are subjected to parody. At the approach of the new age the 'pyramid' of Victoriana in 'plaid-like juxtaposition' supported on one side by a gentleman in 'frock-coat and sponge-bag trousers', and on the other by 'a female figure clothed in flowing white', draws Orlando's attention to the fact that she herself is inappropri-ately clad in breeches while the Queen is in crinoline and the maids are wearing 'three or four red-flannel petticoats, though the month [is] August' (O: 160–1). Yielding to the age and fitting herself out in suitably black bombazine, Orlando finds herself

> dragged down by the weight of the crinoline . . . heavier and more drab than any dress she had yet worn. None had ever so impeded her movements. No longer could she stride . . . or run . . . her skirts collected damp leaves and straw. The plumed hat tossed on the breeze. The thin shoes were quickly soaked and mud-caked. Her muscles had lost their pliancy. (O: 168)

In line with such rigid demarcations, the 'Spirit of the age' is at no time more pervasive than in the nineteenth century, when, given literal rendition in the climate, *Geist* infects every cultural expression with the consequences of one phenomenon: damp. In Woolf's absurd *Geistesgeschichte*, 'Rugs appeared; beards were grown; trousers were fastened tight under the instep . . . furniture was muffled; walls and tables were covered; nothing was left bare . . . sentences swelled, adjectives multiplied, lyrics became epics', with the consequence that 'Love, birth, and death were all swaddled in a variety of fine phrases' (O: 158). Attempting to write, Orlando finds to her alarm that the pen begins to write insipid nineteenth-century verse of its own accord (ibid.: 164). It is only under cover of marriage that she manages to smuggle her 'contraband goods' – the poem 'The Oak Tree' with its seductive 'Egyptian girls', 'Scarfed in dull purple' – past the watchful gaze of the spirit of the age (ibid.: 183).

Orlando's historiography is conducted through outrageous and deliberate mismatchings between writing and illustration, in an iconology that rejects any logic and lets all the seams show. What is striking is the degree of care taken in the assembling and production of these illustrations, and at the same time the fun that was obviously generated by the fancy dress and the staging involved – photographic sessions conducted in an atmosphere of childish pranks and general unruliness with Virginia as queen of misrule. No consistent strategy is apparent either in the selection or the production of images. Some, like 'Orlando as a Boy' or 'Orlando as Ambassador', reproduce paintings of Sackville forebears, selected by Woolf from the collection at Knole. Others, like the portrait of 'Orlando on her return to England' or the Grant and Bell photograph of 'The Russian Princess as a Child' seem to represent playful takes on various styles. The latter shows an angelic Angelica Bell wrapped in painted silks and decorated with pearls, posing against a studio set piece which has evidently been painted on to the photographic surface after the fact as announced pastiche – a wink in the direction of Julia Cameron's 'draping and arranging' more than a picture one would be likely to find in a history of Russian dress. (The original photo, reproduced here, was

Figure 6   Angelica Bell as the Russian Princess in *Orlando*

taken in the garden of La Bergere and shows the subject seated, her hands tucked away under her arms.) Sandra Gilbert lists the picture of Orlando on her return to England as probably taken by the society photographer Lenare, though intended to suggest the somewhat baroque style of Lely, the most fashionable portrait artist in England in the mid- to late seventeenth century (Gilbert 1993: xlviii). In the end it looks very much like a 1920s society portrait depicting Orlando, all feminine vulnerability in satins and pearls. Vita, posing for the picture, was 'miserable', she later told her husband, 'draped in an inadequate bit of pink satin with all my clothes slipping off', while Virginia as the stylist 'was delighted and kept diving under the black cloth of the camera to peep at the effect' (cited in Glendinning 1983: 182). Glendinning also recounts a photo session with Bell and Grant as the photographers. On that occasion Virginia spoilt the photographs by reading aloud from *The Times* obituary notices, interlarding them with her own comments and making everyone laugh (ibid.).

The 1840 portrait was taken by Vanessa Bell and Duncan Grant in their studio, and shows Vita posing in a fancy-dress outfit of checked wool skirt, an eastern shawl and a garden hat, and as Glendinning puts it, 'not looking 1840 in the least' (Glendinning 1983: 205). The photo of Vita in country clothes, the last one in the illustrated edition, was taken either by Leonard Woolf or by Virginia herself. Ironically, as Glendinning observes, Vita looks very much herself, 'conventionally dressed in skirt, blouse and cardigan' (ibid.: 205), though she looks nothing like the Orlando described in the text, ambiguous and outrageous as ever in breeches and a gigantic set of fluorescent pearls. In its visual form, then, *Orlando* does not end with a photographic image of fashion. The most contemporaneous style, as Steele asserts, was youthful; with young women as society's trendsetters, embodying chic would be to combine a boyish look with soignée sophistication (Steele 1985: 240). The photograph, on the other hand, represents a mature femininity – casual and relaxed, but still rather respectable and conventional. By comparison, the final textual image is much more radical in its combination of masculine clothing and highly eroticised pearls, repeating the mismatchings of text and illustration and adding to the slipperiness of Orlando's defiance of styles, genres and genders in a process where writing clearly outwits visuality.

The present moment for Orlando combines the definition and distinctness of the eighteenth century with the magic and adventure of the Elizabethan age. Among Marshall and Snelgrove's phantasmagoria of commodities, the 'innumerable coloured stuffs' displayed bring back the scent of Elizabethan treasure ships, while 'perhaps from the fancy goods department' the figure of an aged Sasha appears, as ambiguously seductive as ever in Russian trousers, before magically metamorphosing into a 'fat, furred woman, marvellously well preserved, seductive, diademed, a Grand Duke's mistress' (O: 209). The modern masquerade and mutability of the department store is given a counterpoint, however, in a condition and an aesthetic suggestive of the modernist simplicity of Diaghilev and the Russian Ballet, where 'the shrivelled skin of the ordinary is so stuffed out with meaning . . . that to see Orlando change her skirt for a pair of whipcord breeches and leather jacket . . . was to be ravished by the beauty of movement as if Madame Lopokova were using her highest art' (ibid.: 217). What allows for this condition of simplicity, suggestiveness and implication, seems to be an awareness of the foldings and unfoldings of memory. Like the twentieth century, Orlando is approaching maturity – Orlando is 36, the century 28 – a time when memories tucked away among the folds, the scents in the fabrics, the memory of a lover magically returning in fancy dress, alternately unfold and refold, layer upon layer, lining, interweaving, and 'plumping out' the simplest everyday words and acts. In Orlando's mind the modern condition at the end of the third decade of the twentieth century is figured by fashion – the turn towards the future – complicated, implicated and explicated by the fold.

The idea of women's dress as a screen for projections of modernity is a prominent feature of late nineteenth- and early twentieth-century culture, and takes several different, even opposing, forms. On the one hand, as discussed in Chapter 1, the politicising of women's dress was an important part of the suffrage movement in England as well as America. To some extent fashion and the new reproductive technologies of photography and film aligned themselves with such developments, turning the 'New Woman' or the 'Flapper' into marketable commodities, often associated with urban spaces and 'new' sexual relations (Goody 2000: 269; Fillin-Yeh 1995: 33). Feminine images also entered, or at least made some impression on the mainstream from various avant-garde circles, in many cases with the effect of suspending boundaries between high art and bourgeois consumer culture. As Brigid Doherty has shown, Dada's celebrations of fashion, seen for instance in photomontages like Raul Hausmann's *Fashion* and *Fiat Modes* or Hannah Höch's *Da-Dandy* (all c. 1920), assert not only the avant-garde's alignment with mass culture, but more specifically the proliferating images of fashionable women as signifiers of modernity (Doherty 1995). *Fiat Modes*, for instance, is a collage of fashion illustrations predominantly made up of cut-outs of women's legs, creating an impression of chic, eroticism, movement and, above all, contemporaneity, the here-and-now pointing towards the future. Much more resistant to fashion, associated with individual restraint and convention, the essentially conservative regimes of male bourgeois dress were thought of (both by a Dadaist like Hausmann and a social reformer like Flügel) as irreversibly inscribed in the outdated aesthetic and social order of an establishment looking towards the past (ibid.: 46–8).

While the artistic avant-garde proclaimed their allegiance to fashion, other subcultural, 'eccentric' or 'inverted' femininities had already made their impact on the fashionable mainstream, at least to some extent. Esther Newton writes of 'the mannish lesbian' as a 'New Woman', by the early years of the century public, partial cross-dressing among bourgeois women had turned into a public symbol of the new social and sexual category 'lesbian' (Newton 1984: 558–60). The most recognisable image of the lesbian circulating in so-called 'decadent' or avant-garde circles of Paris, Berlin and London, was that projected by the woman with cropped hair, dressed in a man's tuxedo, posing with a cigarette and the signature monocle also employed as a defamiliarising accessory by the Dadaists. The quotational and highly stylised aspects of this practice clearly point in the direction of camp, drag and other types of sartorial performance, though, as we shall see, contemporary sexologists were quick to inscribe such cross-dressing within a discourse of authenticity; as signs of an authentic, if inverted, sexuality. Radclyffe Hall, perhaps the most public of British lesbians, dressed flamboyantly in garments from a London theatrical costumier that included a cape and a sombrero (Farfan 2004: 85). As Penny Farfan argues, it was the public outrage at such flamboyant visibility of lesbians, 'flaunt[ing] themselves in public places with increasing effrontery and more insolently provocative bravado', in the words of a *Sunday Express* editorial, which caused the most damning attacks on Hall's *Well of Loneliness* in the press in 1928 (ibid.: 85).

While public anxieties over confused genders, effeminate men, androgynous flappers and mannish women may have been particularly strong as a consequence of the social and demographic changes following the Great War, ambiguity or hybridity as figures of the modern were also a phenomenon of the years before the war, and even of the previous century. In Benjamin's typology, the lesbian, the androgyne, the prostitute and the dandy are images of nineteenth-century modernity, or rather of 'the ambiguity peculiar to the social relations and products of this epoch' (Benjamin 2006: 41). What is common to these figures in Benjamin's analysis is precisely a degree of ambiguity – the ambiguities of masculine/feminine, human/commodity, organic/inorganic, subject/object – ambiguities, moreover, which are proclaimed visibly, through the style of their appearance. Above all, it is the stylisation of fashion in its various forms that renders these figures allegorical, makes them readable as de-idealised bodies, ruins of nature, dialectical images. The standardising effect of cosmetics makes the prostitute appear 'not only as a commodity but, in the most graphic sense, as a mass-produced article' (ibid.: 165). In her, the '"triumph of allegory" – the life which signifies death' – is present in its most inalienable form (ibid.: 144). Correspondingly, the androgyne and the lesbian displaying masculine

Figure 7   Marguerite Antonia Radclyffe-Hall ('Radclyffe Hall') by Howard Coster

traits signify modernity's processes of production; their bodies overwritten by industry as a force that moves the world. Hence, 'the motif of androgyny, the lesbian, the unfruitful woman, should be treated in connection with the destructive power of the allegorical intention . . . the rejection of the "natural"' (ibid.: 139). To Benjamin, Baudelaire's idealisation of the dandy and the lesbian as heroically resistant to modernity represented a phase of modernity which, from Benjamin's twentieth-century perspective, history had rendered obsolete. When Baudelaire depicted the lesbian in terms of a spiritual ideal from Greek antiquity this was no more than an indication of his ambivalence towards modernity and a retreat from its material and economic processes.

Orlando, too, has been criticised for its evasions of history and a properly materialist basis, proposing a performative 'strategy' that would be available only to a privileged elite. It is true that the cultural avant-garde which fuelled Woolf's imagination, supplying the mood and to some extent the cast for *Orlando*, were both fashionable and privileged: they were the Bloomsbury that was showcased in *Vogue* as trendsetters in writing, art, design and sartorial fashion, embodying for a time all the chic and potential of performative self-fashioning. At the same time, Woolf's playfulness may be considered from another perspective. Presenting history as a sequence of fashions, and sexual identity as mutable and performative, may be understood as a strategy directed partly against a nineteenth-century idealist discourse of authenticity and *Geist* (as featured in *Freshwater*); partly against what seemed like a contemporary recasting of such discourse in putatively scientific and liberal terms. The literal visibility of the sexual 'invert' – their immediate recognisability through dress – had already contributed to the taxonomies of contemporary sexology and psychology, most prominently in the works of Krafft-Ebing, Havelock Ellis and J. C. Flügel, which, in different ways, were attempts to regulate and codify ambiguity by making it signify within a system. In Krafft-Ebing's *Psychopathia Sexualis*, for instance, the lesbian was known by her strong preference for male garments (Newton 1984: 566; Garber 1992: 135). Ellis and Flügel, too, categorised dress among sexual symptoms; as symptomatic behaviour indicative of sexual typologies and inversions. If Woolf was aware of writing at a historical juncture when typologies and taxonomies were mobilised in concerted efforts to codify practice within an inventory of 'inversions' and identities, for the most part presented as 'authentic', genetic and immutable, clothes seemed to represent a strategy for returning discourse to its origin in practice by theatricalising the relations between inner and outer selves.

Havelock Ellis treats transvestism, or what he prefers to call eonism, in Volume VII of *Studies in the Psychology of Sex: Eonism and Other Supplementary Studies* (1928). Interestingly, one of the case stories Ellis presents in elucidation of this phenomenon is that of Lady Hester Stanhope, taken from Lytton Strachey's *Books and Characters* from 1922. The story, as told by Strachey and recounted by Ellis, is that of a lifelong exile, begun in 1810 when Lady Stanhope sailed from England to Athens and Constantinople, 'lodged with governors and ambassadors', lost all her clothes in a shipwreck on the coast of Rhodes, and 'was forced to exchange her torn and dripping raiment for the attire of a Turkish gentleman' (Strachey 1922: 284). 'It was', as Strachey observes, 'the first step in her orientalization' (ibid.: 284). 'Her transvestism was thus apparently due to an accident,' observes Ellis,

> but the significant fact was that she clung to it for the rest of her life and also adopted many other male habits, though there seems no reason to suppose that she was sexually inverted. So that, as sometimes happens, an accident had served to reveal an innate disposition. She dressed sometimes as an Albanian Chief, sometimes as a Syrian soldier, sometimes a Beduin, sometimes like a Pasha's son. For the Moslems she became a prophetess, almost a queen. (Ellis 1928: 6–7)

In Strachey's account, Lady Hester died in old age, an 'unaccountable figure', 'inexplicable, grand, [and] preposterous' (Strachey 1922: 289–90).

The inclusion of this sketch among Ellis's medical cases is interesting for a number of reasons. First, as a story it has many points of resonance in *Orlando*, anticipating the latter's connections between orientalism and ambiguities of gender, and Woolf's casting of the Orient as a phantasmatic locality for such ambiguities. Further it exemplifies what one may see as a transition from practice to discourse. Lady Stanhope and her transvestism represent the type of eccentric femininity Woolf was interested in; the rather fantastic life lived in the margins and against the grain that she made the subject of some of her anti-traditional biographical sketches. Ellis's presentation of this as a typological case, by contrast, represents the moment when eccentric behaviour becomes identity; part of a medical taxonomy, however liberal and descriptive. Lastly, however, Ellis's case story presents a theory of eonism as aesthetic empathy or *Einfühlung* – a theory which he adapts from contemporary aesthetic philosophy and which, as we shall see, also approaches quite closely to Woolf's thoughts on androgyny and its representation through dress. In both cases what is involved is a type of emotional identification that is symptomatically or symbolically signified as transvestism.

A significant point to Ellis's case stories, and his argument for substituting the term 'Eonism' for what he used to refer to as 'Sexo-Aesthetic Inversion', is that the cross-dressers he describes 'are not sexual inverts and seldom even tend to become inverted' (Ellis 1928: 11). The earlier term was useful for pointing out the correspondence between the emotional identification with the beautiful object that is the essence of artistic creation, and the 'aesthetic emotion' – 'the impulse to project themselves by sympathetic feeling into the object to which they are attracted' – which motivates the transvestite (ibid.: 27). 'Inversion', however, is too apt to arouse suggestions of homosexuality, which may be quite absent, and must consequently be rejected. The type of erotic empathy that manifests itself in the assumption of the garments of the desired sex originates in feelings of admiration and affection; it does not as a rule imitate the sexual desires of the other sex (ibid.: 27). For the eonist, unlike the fetishist, garments are the outward symbols of the inner spiritual state, having their supreme attraction when worn by the individual him – or herself (ibid.: 52–3). In its most developed form, however, eonism is affective and emotional, with cross-dressing manifesting itself as merely a minor symptom. 'Transvestism', consequently, is an inaccurate term. Eonism, in Ellis's taxonomy, is 'an abnormal and perhaps pathological exaggeration of the secondary component [of the sexual impulse]', which is to say the element of sympathy and identification which is connected with an aesthetic attitude:

> In his admiration of the beloved [the eonist] is not content to confine himself to the normal element of *Einfühlung*; he adopts the whole aesthetic attitude by experiencing also the impulse of imitation. He achieves a completely emotional identification which is sexually abnormal but aesthetically correct. (ibid.: 104, 107–8)

More consistently than Ellis, the clothes psychology developed by J. C. Flügel during the late 1920s proceeds to establish taxonomies based on sartorial practice. Flügel's theories were published in academic papers and popularised in a series of BBC talks given in 1928, which in turn led to the publication of *The Psychology of Clothes* by the Hogarth Press in 1930. Throughout Flügel's work, clothes are given symptomatic status in individual as well as cultural histories of sexuality, taken to indicate not only individual traits, but sexual difference as such.[3] Flügel's ultimately progressive agenda – as evidenced for instance in calls for male dress reform as an essential strategy in the creation of modern human subjects – does little to change the fact that his theory participates in a moment of discursive regulation which to Woolf must have seemed ridiculous if not highly suspect. Interestingly, however, in one instance the unruliness of sartorial practice seems to defy Flügel's medical typologies in ways that are reminiscent of *Orlando*. In his chapter on 'Sex Differences' in *The Psychology of Clothes*, Flügel includes a section on 'eonism' where he adheres to Ellis's view that eonism represents an extreme version of the tendencies to identification that play some part in every normal sexual life, and that this process has something akin to aesthetic empathy (Flügel 1930: 119–21). The nature of this identification, however, remains to be fully understood as taxonomies are complicated by the fact that transvestism may or may not coincide with active homosexuality; and may or may not involve a tendency towards the physical characteristics of the opposite sex (ibid.: 120–1). For Flügel and Ellis alike, then, transvestism or cross-dressing is a figure of hybridity; the visual manifestation of an imaginative crossing-over to the place of the other (sex), which belongs to the philosophy of aesthetics as much as to the science of sexology.

Orlando is the biography of a writer, and so, among other things, a history of the writer's progress and of styles of writing, though – literalising the old metaphor of writing as the dress of thought – the writer's progress it depicts is more of a parodic, highly theatrical tour, enabled by masquerade and disguise, through centuries of shifting literary fashions. Not surprisingly, the route it traces goes from ornamentation and overdress to simplicity; from symbolism in loose robes to androgynous writing. Orlando at the age of sixteen in the late sixteenth century is engaged in a plethora of literary projects: writing an allegorical tragedy centred on the personages 'Vice, Crime, Misery'; describing, 'as all young poets are for ever describing, nature'; being frustrated by the 'natural antipathy' seeming to exist between nature and letters; and mobilising a whole repertoire of images to match Sasha's sensuality ('a melon, a pineapple, an olive tree, an emerald, and a fox in the snow all in the space of three seconds' (O: 13, 26)). The seventeenth century shows him still afflicted by 'Ambition, the harridan, and Poetry, the witch, and Desire of Fame, the strumpet', despairing at his own 'manifestly untruthful' metaphors (ibid.: 57, 70). The tour continues, however, as Orlando has his 'floridity . . . chastened' by the age of prose, is infected with the 'English disease' in the Turkish desert, writes insipid nineteenth century verse in the age of Victoria, smuggles 'contraband goods' past the spirit of the age under the disguise of marriage, and makes the discovery that Victorian literature is 'an elderly gentleman in grey suit' (ibid.: 77, 195). Symbolism in loose robes is the target of Woolf's parody throughout. Orlando's compulsive troping in the Turkish desert recalls the mock-allegorical battle that forms the theatrical backdrop to the famous change from man to woman, when the three Ladies of Purity, Chastity and Modesty, equipped with the complete allegorical inventory of robes, veils, mantles and draperies, battle it out with unveiling Truth, Candour and Honesty in a set-piece of sartorial and rhetorical excess as parodic as that of *Freshwater* (ibid.: 96–7).

Shakespeare is a continuing presence in this literary history – though always in the margins, caught in the corner of an eye, while Orlando is busy 'win[ning] immortality against the English language' (O: 56). On his way to be presented to the Queen, extravagantly decked out in crimson breeches, lace collar and waistcoat of taffeta, Orlando is stopped in his tracks at the glimpse, through an open door, of the poet, 'a rather fat, rather shabby man, whose ruff was a thought dirty, and whose clothes were of hodden brown', writing at the table in the servants' room (ibid.: 16). A century later, Memory, the capricious 'seamstress', with 'all her ragtag and bobtail', brings into view that same face, adding 'first, a coarse, grease-stained ruffle, then a brown doublet, and finally a pair of thick boots such as citizens wear in Cheapside' (ibid.: 56). Finally, driving home from Marshall and Snelgroves on Thursday, the eleventh of October 1928, Orlando finds herself stopped short again:

'He sat at Twitchett's table', she mused, 'with a dirty ruff on . . . Was it old Mr. Baker come to measure the timber? Or was it Sh-p-re?' . . . 'Haunted!' she cried, suddenly pressing the accelerator. 'Haunted! Ever since I was a child. There flies the wild goose.' (O: 215–16)

If her life, as she says, has been a wild goose-chase, a flinging of 'words like nets' after the writer's truth; the writer's self, then it seems, in the final image, the goose comes to her of its own accord, 'a single wild bird' springing up over Shelmerdine's head: '"It is the goose!" Orlando cried. "The wild goose . . ."' (O: 216, 228). The ordinary aligns itself with the fantastic, fluorescent pearls with hodden brown, as Orlando in whipcord breeches and leather jacket 'bar[es] her breast to the moon . . . so that her pearls glowed like the eggs of some vast moon-spider. . . . burnt like a phosphorescent flare in the darkness', to receive Shelmerdine and the wild goose in androgynous union (ibid.: 227).

'Let biologists and psychologists determine . . . let other pens treat of sex and sexuality', writes Woolf with mock deference for the sexologists and psychologists (O: 98). The only theory *Orlando* is caught promoting – apart from the mutability of anything human – is that of androgyny, which, in Woolf's version, is not so much a theory of sexual identity as an ethics based in aesthetic theory. The perfect sympathy – the marriage of minds, the openness towards the other – that defines Orlando and Shelmerdine's relationship is represented by the liminality and transcendence of the androgyne and the androgynous union ('"You're a woman, Shel!" she cried. "You're a man, Orlando!" he cried' (O: 174–5)). Unlike the Benjaminean androgyne, then, whose hybridity figures the modern as a break with humanism and man as totality, Woolf's androgyne points towards a human (and humanist) ideal: the mind which comprises entireties; the capacity for imaginative *Einfühlung* which founds an ethics of human relations. Woolf uses transvestism as a metaphor for androgyny; Ellis and Flügel, as we have seen, think of transvestism as the outward expression of aesthetic inversion. The convergence of views here between Woolf and the sexologists is explained by the latter's reference to the philosophy of art. As Woolf's elaborations on androgyny in *A Room of One's Own* make abundantly clear, it is aesthetic theory – not contemporary sexology – that founds her thoughts on this matter.

Orlando ends on the 11 October 1928, the day she sees Shakespeare in hodden brown and when the androgynous lovers are reunited. The 26 October 1928 is the day that completes the essayist's reflections in *A Room of One's Own*. This is also the day when the traffic of the street brings together 'a girl in patent leather boots' and 'a young man in a maroon overcoat', so fusing the divided halves of the essayist's mind in the concluding meditation on androgynous writing, taking her back first to Coleridge (who 'meant, perhaps, that the androgynous mind is resonant and porous; that it transmits emotion without impediment'), then to Shakespeare ('the type of the androgynous, of the man-womanly

Figure 8   Virginia Woolf. Photographer: Man Ray

mind') (*AROO*: 94). The writer whose mind is not blocked by the ego, who does not let 'I' get in the way of expression, is Woolf's model for an ethical writing and an ethical relationship between the sexes, one based on empathy, imaginative and sympathetic identification. This human-ised and humanising androgyny is a figure of modern gender relations and modern writing in *A Room of One's Own* as well as *Orlando*, meta-phorically represented as transvestism and the mutability, flexibility and liminality of clothing.

Freshwater concerns itself with the sartorial as a means of crossing boundaries of 'high' and 'low', but only in the sense of letting 'art' work on 'life', aestheticising and allegorising the quotidian. *Orlando*, too, refers to a moment when sartorial and aesthetic experiments overlap, though with an impetus far from the Carlylean fantasy of transcendence and depth, affirming instead the freedom at the surface of fashion and fashioning. Yet there are moments of retreat from the surface of fashion: a folding back on Shakespeare's hodden brown, which – transformed into the wild goose of writing – finally and fantastically presides over the androgynous couple. If we may say that the androgynous ideal is what anchors *Orlando*'s dehistoricising playfulness; what gives depth to a fantasmatic surface of endless possibilities seemingly without mate-rial, historical or economic restrictions, *A Room of One's Own* is con-cerned precisely with the social and material conditions that will allow an androgynous writing to come into existence. In this project, clothes are indicators both of the restrictions and restraints of tradition, of Woolf's redefined reality, and of the writing she predicts for the future. In a present where women 'sit in the rough and ready-made clothes' of the male writer, where 'football and sport are "important"; the worship of fashion, the buying of clothes "trivial"', clothes become the archives of a reality habitually ignored: the 'dressing in the afternoon [which] must be a ritual, and the clothes themselves put away in cupboards with camphor, year after year' (*AROO* 70, 84–5). For the Mary Carmichaels anticipating the birth of Shakespeare's androgynous sister, reality is to be found in the quotidian as much as the rarefied object: in 'the everchanging and turning world of gloves and shoes and stuffs', along 'arcades of dress material', in shops 'hung, astonishingly beautifully, with coloured ribbons' (ibid.: 86). The choice of dress as signs of a gen-dered (as opposed to 'stridently sex-conscious') reality is not coinciden-tal (ibid.: 94). It is not simply that clothes provide access to a history of woman as capitalist modernity's vicarious consumer and exhibitionist; or that dress represents a silent history of women's work; or that fashion signifies the present in its turn towards the future: Most importantly of all, the garment stands in place of a gendered reality because, in its transformative, transvestite, hybrid modality, it figures modes of being and writing which give women, as individuals and writers, what Woolf has been looking for: room of their own.

Notes

1. Shone and Reed both comment on attempts by Bloomsbury to 'rescue' the older generation by adopting part of their work as symbolist and pictorial, as opposed to allegorical, literary, or narrative, thus aligning them at least in some small measure with the moderns. One such rescue attempt is Fry's 1905 essay 'Watts and Whistler', which takes issue with the view that Watts's paintings were simply didactic and literary, 'a rebus in paint of . . . moral platitudes which could have been put more concisely in words'. There are cases, Fry admits, where Watts 'becomes mystical merely by being misty'; for the most part, however, his paintings 'transcend the material . . . by the discovery of forms which symbolise the spiritual . . . that is to say, by purely pictorial and not literary elements in the work of art' (Fry 1905, in Reed 1996: 34–5).

2. Reynolds' *Fourth Discourse on Art* (1771) repudiates the look of any pictorial cloth that does not share the clarity and universality of antique drapery. As Anne Hollander shows, Reynolds' critique is directed against the excesses of later schools, such as the Gothic and the baroque. Commenting on some sculptures by Bernini, Reynolds writes dismissively about the artist's attempt to make 'drapery appear to flutter in the wind or fly through the air', a folly which 'carries with it its own reprehension' (Hollander 1988: 77, 9–10). One of many examples of moral judgements concerning the appropriate rendering of pictorial cloth, Reynolds' views are echoed a century later by John Ruskin, writing contemptuously about some Venetian seventeenth-century angels where the artist has been seduced by the materiality of the cloth itself, thus creating nothing but the 'flabby flutter, wrinkled swelling, and puffed pomp of infinite disorder': 'Worse drapery than this, you cannot see in mortal investiture' (cited ibid.: 75–6).

3. According to Flügel, among the most important of sexual differences is the tendency for the sexual libido to be more diffuse in women than in men. With women the whole body is sexualised; with men the libido is concentrated upon the genital zone. Women, argues Flügel, have difficulty in a complete sublimation of exhibitionism from body to clothes; the male libido can more easily find a symbolic substitute for the phallus (as seen in the phallic value invested in ceremonial dress, uniforms, and the like). While modern female dress allows for erotic exposure and thus for some harmless and essentially healthy exhibitionism, male dress – for reasons which may be social in origin but nevertheless indicate the operation of very powerful (and gendered) psychical inhibitions – has been brought under the rule of an essentially repressive super-ego. Thus, Flügel concludes, 'It is, indeed, safe to say that, in sartorial matters, modern man has a far sterner and more rigid conscience than has modern women, and that man's morality tends to find expression in his clothes in a greater degree than is the case with woman.

Hence it is not surprising that . . . modern man's clothing abounds in features which symbolise his devotion to the principles of duty, of renunciation, and of self-control. The whole relatively fixed . . . system of his clothing is, in fact, an outward and visible sign of the strictness of his adherence to the social code (though at the same time, through its phallic attributes, it symbolises the most fundamental features of his sexual nature)' (Flügel 1930: 113).

Chapter 3

Fashion and Literary Modernity

If one were to ask three prominent theorists of nineteenth- and twentieth-century modernity – Charles Baudelaire, Paul de Man, and Walter Benjamin – what the presence of sartorial fashion might signify in a modernist literary text, say one by Virginia Woolf, one would be likely to expect at least three different answers. Baudelaire might say that fashion reveals the immutable in the fugitive and contingent, de Man that fashion indicates the modernist's nostalgia for the present, while Benjamin's reply might be that fashion, because of its double connection with the world of commodities as well as with an age-old symbolic tradition, has the potential for performing within two types of allegory: one pre-modern, suggesting transcendence and redemption; the other modern, suggesting rupture and lack.

The difference in views here comes from a difference in the understanding of fashion, most fundamentally its temporality. Baudelaire writes about fashion and its connection to modern art in 'The Painter of Modern Life' (1859), an essay on the work of the fashion illustrator Constantin Guys in which Baudelaire argues that fashion and the fashion plate are paradigmatic of modern art and writing in so far as they bring into play that synoptic or synthetic gaze which Baudelaire thinks of as characteristically modern. This is the gaze that synthesises two temporalities and two aesthetic paradigms: *éternité* and *modernité*, fluidity and form. The fluidity and non-finality of the fashion sketch captures modernity – 'the ephemeral, the fugitive, the contingent' – in the rapid metamorphoses of fashion. At the same time, that 'other half' of art, 'the eternal and the immutable', attain visibility through fashion's 'taste for the ideal', for stylisation, the 'sublime deformation of Nature' – in effect, a transhistorical truth which, without the circumstantial, contingent element that fashion also supplies, 'would be beyond our powers of digestion or appreciation' (Baudelaire 1964: 2–3, 32–3).

Paul de Man's engagement with fashion comes in a section of

Blindness and Insight (1971), a discussion of the relation between literature and modern experience which takes Baudelaire's 'The Painter' as its foundational text – though not without translating Baudelaire's double temporality into a fantasy of an absolute present. First of all, in de Man's argument, fashion is made to illustrate that conscious amnesia which defines 'the authentic spirit of modernity' (de Man 1971: 147), the Nietzschean 'ruthless forgetting' by which 'all anteriority vanishes': 'the radical impulse that stands behind all genuine modernity when it is not merely a descriptive synonym for the contemporaneous' (ibid.: 147). At the same time, the inevitable accompaniment of this insistent amnesia is modernism's 'nostalgia', as de Man has it, 'for the immediacy, the facticity of entities that are in contact with the present' (ibid.: 158–9), a nostalgia which fashion is made to signify. Characteristically for de Man's thinking, however, any literary invocation of the present can only take place in a moment of denial of the ontology and temporality of writing (as repetition and allegory). Thus, whether Baudelaire's subject in 'The Painter' is 'the outer garment of the present, the unwitting defiance of death in the soldier's colourful coat, or . . . the philosophically conscious sense of time of the dandy', the subject in each case is preferred 'because it exists in the facticity, in the modernity of a present that is ruled by experiences that lie outside language and escape from the successive temporality, the duration involved in writing' (ibid.: 159).

What is at issue here are the limitations involved in an understanding of fashion which allows it to signify only the present. Turning to Woolf's engagement with the present moment, which seems so often to be an attempt to understand modern experience against the horizon of an individual and cultural past, an idea of fashion simply as the modernist's fantasy of participation in the immediate world can have little to say about the work that clothes perform in her texts. I mentioned initially that for Walter Benjamin clothes have the potential for performing within two kinds of allegory. So it seems is the case for Woolf. If we think of her work roughly in terms of three interrelated projects – as an engagement with the phenomenal world of commodities and social norms, a working-through of individual memory and cultural archives, and, lastly, as asserting what we may call a modality of transcendence, indexing parts of the world we did not know (we knew) about – we must ask whether clothes perform in all these projects. My answer would be that they do, and that they even have an enabling function which comes from Woolf's awareness (which she shares with Benjamin) of clothing's signifying potential – its capacity, as demonstrated for instance in the complex sartorial fabric that constitutes *Mrs Dalloway*, of interweaving worlds and temporalities, opening the folds of individual and cultural memory to view and connecting with other organic surfaces, webs and fabrics.

Benjamin's work on fashion is a particularly rich source for understanding how clothing and sartorial figures are deployed in Woolf's work because it so consistently moves between and comprises different materialist and mythopoeic meanings. In their thinking on clothes, both Woolf and Benjamin draw on the culturally established knowledge that sartorial items have properties which allow them to oscillate, and so establish connections between, different worlds – one of which is the connection to organic surfaces, webs and fabrics. Clothes and leaves, for instance, share the property of being rustled, blown about, animated by the wind, or made transparent by the sun. Ewa Kuryluk in her book *Veronica and Her Cloth* draws attention to the sense of unity between humans, animals and vegetation established by the fact that textiles were traditionally woven of organic materials (such as wool, hair, cotton, flax and silk) and worn together with animal skins. Kuryluk also comments on the many metaphors inspired by 'analogies between cloth(es), skin, hair, mirrors (including the pupil of the eye), and the surfaces of sky, earth, and water, which lack permanence and are prone to transformations' (Kuryluk 1999: 180). The change of dimensions seems particularly important for such analogies to be established: just as cloth becomes three-dimensional when draped or folded, so does the surface of water as waves form (ibid.: 180). On this symbolic background, then, clothes become relevant and significant not simply to understanding literary modernism's negotiations with modernity, but also to some of its attempts at negotiating alternative rationalities and what may be understood as an alternative transcendence at the end of religion – visible perhaps in mysteries of material presence, in illuminations of the profane, or in the metaphysics of the metropolis.

Benjamin's thinking on fashion has the potential of illuminating Woolf's work because both make use of clothing to say something about the multidimensionality of modern experience, showing that clothes, more than other everyday phenomenal objects and commodities, have a particular way of giving access to such ontological and epistemological modalities as well as to the connections and transformations between them. One dimension folded within another may be unfurled, brought to life, by a change in wind or light, or by the movement of a body. By such unfoldings clothes may take on the appearance of dialectical images or, alternatively, turn into the signals, the banners and veils, of a modality of transcendence. Benjamin, for instance, writes about a lost *vie antérieure* of *Erfahrung* and *Naturgeschichte* whose absence is figured as auratic veils, as webs and fabrics.[1] Similar explorations of modalities and dimensions via sartorial registers inform fictions as different as *Mrs Dalloway* and *Between the Acts*.

In discussions of the relation between literature and modern experience such as de Man's, sartorial fashion comes to represent modernism's nostalgia for the present: its dream of including the phenomenal world in its fleetingness, to grasp the moment with the speed of the fashion sketch. As long as this engagement with the present is predicated on deliberate amnesia, however, there can be no historical awareness involved. Woolf's writing, I would argue, is consistently historiographical in its consciousness of the present as arising from an individual and cultural past. Benjamin's thinking on fashion, too, is imbued with historicity, not only in its understanding of the folds of memory, but particularly in placing fashion at the centre of a dialectical theory. Like de Man, Benjamin writes about the relation between literature and modernity, specifically the lyric and its relevance to modern metropolitan experience, taking Baudelaire's writing on fashion as his foundational text. Where de Man makes fashion describe a present without history, however, Benjamin consistently brings out the historicising dimension of Baudelaire's thinking, developing this into a theory in which fashion actively enables the dialectical, allegorical grasp of modernity as a historical condition.

Through the Baudelairean gaze on fashion Benjamin discovers the changed appearance of the phenomenal world and its subject/object relationships. The key terms by which these changes are elaborated, moreover, are sartorially defined, in a dialectic of veiling and unveiling, dress and nakedness, organic bodies and inorganic fashions. Prescribing 'the ritual according to which the commodity fetish demands to be worshipped', fashion is instrumental to the constitution of the phantasmagoria as semblance or *Schein* (Benjamin 2006: 37). Through the 'agitated veil' of the masses the Baudelairean poet surrenders to 'the intoxification of the commodity', to 'empathy with inorganic things' (ibid.: 15; Benjamin 1999: 448–9). With the same logic the metropolitan phantasmagoria Woolf describes in *The Waves* takes on fantasmatic proportions, colonising even subterranean worlds:

> look how they show off clothes here even under ground in a perpetual radiance. They will not let the earth even lie wormy and sodden. There are gauzes and silks illumined in glass cases and underclothes trimmed with a million close stitches of fine embroidery. Crimson, green, violet, they are dyed all colours. (*TW*: 149)

The 'triumphant procession' of fashion is the new religion, issuing the signals that hail and interpellate, inspiring the believer with commitment and faith: 'This is what has my adhesion. I am a native of this world. I follow its banners. . . . Therefore I will powder my face and redden my lips' (*TW*: 149).

Yet, as both Woolf and Benjamin show, there are moments when 'this veil tears' (Benjamin 2006: 90). Benjamin's famous reading of Baudelaire's 'A une passante' elucidates such a moment of shock in sartorial terms.[2] In the sonnet a woman in the crowd enters and leaves the *flâneur*'s field of vision as a figure of unfulfilled desire. She is in mourning, dressed in 'majestic' black. As she passes the poet she gathers her skirt, in the words of the sonnet, 'with fastidious hand/Raising and swaying festoon and hem;/Agile and noble, with her statue's limbs' (quoted in Benjamin 1998: 169). As Ulrich Lehmann points out, the image of the woman lifting the hem of her dress, revealing a glimpse of shoe, leg and volants in her progress through the crowd, had been depicted in numerous sketches by Constantin Guys, and so established in Baudelaire's consciousness as the very icon of modernity.[3] Here is Benjamin's analysis of the poem:

> In a widow's veil, mysteriously and mutely borne along by the crowd, an unknown woman comes into the poet's field of vision. What this sonnet communicates is simply this: Far from experiencing the crowd as an opposed, antagonistic element, this very crowd brings to the city dweller the figure that fascinates. The delight of the urban poet is love – not at first sight, but at last sight. It is a farewell forever which coincides in the poem with the moment of enchantment. Thus the sonnet supplies the figure of shock, indeed of catastrophe. But the nature of the poet's emotions has been affected as well. What makes his body contract in a tremor . . . is not the rapture of a man whose every fiber is suffused with *eros*; it is, rather, like the kind of sexual shock that can beset a lonely man. [These verses] reveal the stigmata which life in a metropolis inflicts upon love. (Benjamin 1998: 169)

What is shown here is the shock of the death of love, the unveiling moment of Spleen that 'exposes the passing moment in all its nakedness' (Benjamin 1998: 185), rending the veil of phantasmagoria and revealing the lost aura. Significantly, the shock effect arises from the fact that the female apparition brought to the poet by the crowd is dressed in mourning, a manner of attire which corresponds to that of the modern hero. 'Regarding the attire, the covering of the modern hero,' writes Baudelaire in 1846,

> [i]s this not an attire that is needed by our age, which is suffering, and dressed up to its thin black narrow shoulders in the symbol of constant mourning? The black suit and the frock coat not only have their political beauty as an expression of general equality, but also their poetic beauty as an expression of the public mentality: an immense cortège of undertakers . . . . We are all attendants at some kind of funeral. (Benjamin 2006: 106)

Benjamin cites Baudelaire and concludes: 'These mental images are part of the profound fascination which the *femme passante* dressed in mourning . . . exerted upon the poet' (Benjamin 2006: 106). Moreover, the crowd which supplies the figure of shock and through which Baudelaire saw Paris, Benjamin figures in sartorial terms as a veil: 'The crowd is the veil through which the familiar city beckons to the flâneur as phantasmagoria'. 'Because of it, horrors have an enchanting effect upon him' (ibid.: 40, 90). The point here is that the sartorial metaphors are not coincidental, nor are they necessarily to be understood as metaphors. It is the material effect of clothing which creates the veil which 'billows in the twisting folds of the old metropolises', and it is fashion in its 'perceptible presence' (as poeticised and fetishised commodity) which produces both the urban phantasmagoria and the moment of shock (ibid.: 90).

To Benjamin's thinking the historicising, allegorical effect of fashion also resides in its temporality of repetition and citation, its 'eternal recurrence of the new' (Benjamin 2006: 155). The playful recycling of costumes in Bloomsbury theatricals and fancy-dress parties, or the allusive fabrics produced by the Omega Workshops may have had the effect for the most part of innocent pastiche. When Benjamin speaks of fashion as having 'redemptive features', however, what concerns him are the potential dislocations and ruptures brought by fashion's irreverent quotations from the past: 'This spectacle, the unique self-construction of the newest in the medium of what has been, makes for the true dialectical theater of fashion' (Benjamin 1999: 64). As Ulrich Lehmann demonstrates in his book, *Tigersprung*, it is the leap out of linear historicism that Benjamin speaks of here, making capitalism's primary commodity paradigmatic, through its aesthetic process, of a political one. By the *Sprung* of the title, fashion detaches itself both from the eternal ideal (*éternité*) and the continuous progression of history (*fugitivité*), bringing into play a temporality which is not the moment waiting to become *passé*, but the continuous generation of a series of antiquities, and thus of a perspective of estrangement. As with the dialectical force Benjamin attributes to obsolete artifacts in general, fashion's radical potential – the allegorical mode of vision – appears most clearly in the 'outmoded,' in 'the dresses of five years ago' (Benjamin 2007: 181): 'Thus, the confrontation with the fashions of previous generations is a matter of far greater importance than we ordinarily suppose' (Benjamin 1999: 64–5). Turning to Woolf one is reminded of the 'dismal foreboding' felt by Ralph Denham at the antiquated and even inorganic appearance of Katharine Hilbery's aunts in *Night and Day*. Not only are both 'so apparelled with hanging muffs, chains and swinging draperies that it [is] impossible to detect the shape of a human being in the mass of brown and black'; there is 'something fantastically unreal in the curious swayings and noddings of Mrs Cosham, as if her equipment included a large wire spring': 'What remark of his', Ralph wonders, 'would ever reach these fabulous and fantastic characters?' (*ND*: 122).

In part, it is the connection between fashion and the inorganic that attains visibility through the strangeness of the outmoded. Where the modern world works by mystification, by appearances and simulacra, fashion's allegorical vision reveals it as an exchange market which habitually conflates the organic and the inorganic, setting the stamp of merchandise on both:

> Every fashion stands in opposition to the organic. Every fashion couples the living body to the inorganic world. To the living, fashion defends the rights of the corpse. The fetishism that succumbs to the sex appeal of the inorganic is its vital nerve. (Benjamin 1999: 79)

The standardisation of fashion, moreover, causes the woman in particular to appear 'not only as commodity but, in a precise sense, as mass-produced article' (Benjamin 1999: 346). *The Waves*, with its processions of headgear in eternal recurrence, gives us the negative aspect of such serialisation, a condition of melancholic alienation in which faces become interchangeable with hats and soup plates. The 'dwarf' woman in 'Street Haunting', however, clearly relishes the standardisation that fashion provides. For the brief space in the shoe-shop, her deformed body is metonymically defined by her foot, the shoes she tries on prosthetically supplying the sex appeal that genders her:

> She sent for shoe after shoe; she tried on pair after pair. She got up and pirouetted before a glass which reflected the foot only in yellow shoes, in fawn shoes, in shoes of lizard skin. She raised her little skirts and displayed her little legs. She was thinking that, after all, feet are the most important part of the whole person; women, she said to herself, have been loved for their feet alone. (*E* 4: 483)

For the essayist, however, this exhibition of the inorganic in its uncanny encounters with the organic, introduces the defamiliarising, detotalising gaze of the allegorist:

> [The dwarf] had changed the mood; she had called into being an atmosphere which, as we followed her out into the street, seemed actually to create the humped, the twisted, the deformed. . . . Indeed, the dwarf had started a hobbling grotesque dance to which everybody in the street now conformed: the stout lady tightly swathed in shiny sealskin; the feeble-minded boy sucking the silver knob of his stick; the old man squatted on a doorstep as if, suddenly overcome by the absurdity of the human spectacle, he had sat down to look at it – all joined in the hobble and tap of the dwarf's dance. (*E* 4: 484)

The 'mnemotechnology'[4] of sartorial fashion enables not only the ruptures and leaps of modern allegory, but may also establish correspondences between conscious and unconscious, individual and collective memories. The discoveries held by a sartorial image are central to Woolf's autobiographical 'A Sketch of the Past',[5] as in her first memory: 'of red and purple flowers on a black ground – my mother's dress . . . she was sitting either in a train or in an omnibus, and I was on her lap' (*MOB*: 64), which leads directly to the next memory, 'the base on which my life stands' – lying in bed in the nursery at St Ives, listening to the waves and watching the blind, translucent in the sunlight, being blown in and out by the wind. A third, related memory is of 'the looking-glass shame' which has lasted all her life and which means that 'Everything to do with dress – to be fitted, to come into a room wearing a new dress – still frightens me' (ibid.: 68). Woolf does not dwell on the mnemonic properties of cloth or clothing in her account of these memories – what it is that makes dress take on particular poignancy in recollection, causing memory to unfurl or unfold – she simply offers us three fundamental memories in which items of cloth or clothing figure. What interests me is not the origin or the biographical facticity of these memories, but the recurrence of similar images across Woolf's fictional and autobiographical writing. Thus, what enters into a process of individual recollection in 'A Sketch of the Past', intertextually comes close to that gathering of unconscious data which Benjamin refers to as *Gedächtnis* – a mode of memory connected to the *Erfahrung*, as opposed to the isolated moments pertaining to *Erlebnis* – and which he elaborates through a tropology of fabrics, webs and threads.

Benjamin writes about several kinds of memory, but the sartorial tropology and the connection to webs, fabrics and thread are constant features. Proust's *mémoire involontaire* is figured as a forgetful weaving that inverts the classical Penelope myth, taking place by night rather than by day.[6] What is 'loomed for us' (Benjamin 1998: 202) by this nightly forgetting are the *correspondances*, the resemblances whose most familiar terrain is the world of dreams:

> The similarity of one thing to another which we are used to, which occupies us in a wakeful state, reflects only vaguely the deeper resemblance of the dream world in which everything that happens appears not in identical but in similar guise, opaquely similar one to another. Children know a symbol of this world: the stocking which has the structure of this dream world when, rolled up in the laundry hamper, it is a 'bag' and a 'present' at the same time. And just as children do not tire of quickly changing the bag and its contents into a third thing – namely, a stocking – Proust could not get his fill of emptying the dummy, his self, at one stroke, in order to keep garnering that third thing, the image which satisfied his curiosity. (Benjamin 1998: 204–5)

Benjamin is writing here about Proust's 'universe of convolution': 'the world in a state of resemblances, the domain of the correspondances' which attains visibility 'in our lived life . . . [w]hen the past is reflected in the dewy fresh "instant"' (Benjamin 1998: 211). The rolled-up stocking is the figure of that opaque similarity as well as of the unfolding, the work of the *mémoire involontaire* (emptying the 'bag' of its secret gift), which opens convoluted time to view in the image. Once more Benjamin's choice of image – the stocking – testifies to the symbolic and imaginary force of everyday sartorial objects. This particular image draws on the fold, the covering, the outside which harbours an inside, and the idea of 'invagination' by which the inside comes to harbour (become the outside of) another inside. The stocking is the image of the surrealist appearance of the world, the image which assuages Proust's homesickness for 'the world distorted in the state of resemblance, a world in which the true surrealist face of existence breaks through' (ibid.: 205).

In light of what has been said so far about fashion and the sartorial – what it allows one to understand about a condition of alienation, serialisation and the hypertrophy of the inorganic, but also about connections between temporalities and worlds – one may usefully consider *Mrs Dalloway* as a novel where the sartorial serves to bring together two topographies: On the one hand, life in the metropolis with its exhilarating modernity, though also its aspects of reification and alienation; on the other hand, a world of mystery and transcendence, of correspondences and convolutions. Mrs Dalloway's decision to buy gloves, in the story, and flowers, in the novel, sets in motion two different metonymic chains, the decision to buy flowers issuing 'weaver's notations' which interweave organic and inorganic tissues and filaments into a mnemonic fabric of mesh, muslins, leaves, flowers, trees, veils, the roses in Mulberry's the florists, 'fresh, like frilled linen clean from a laundry laid in wicker trays' (*MD*: 13–14), and so on. Clarissa's mind weaving surmounts her momentary consciousness of her hat (at seeing Hugh Whitbread's 'perfectly upholstered body'), her sense of her own middle-aged woman's body, 'invisible, unseen'; surmounts even the returning oppressiveness of Doris Kilman's green macintosh coat (ibid.: 6, 11–12). The fabric continues to extend though Clarissa is no longer the consciousness in which the weaving occurs, interweaving the quotidian and the profound: 'glove shops and hat shops and tailors' shops on both sides of Bond Street', ladies '[c]hoosing a pair of gloves – should they be to the elbow or above it, lemon or pale grey?', 'girls buying white underlinen threaded with pure white ribbon for their weddings'; 'well-dressed men with their tailcoats and their white slips . . . standing in the bow window of White's with their hands behind the tails of their coats';

'shawled Moll Pratt with her flowers'; and finally Septimus, 'connected by millions of fibres' to the elm trees, 'rising and falling with all their leaves alight and the colour thinning and thickening from blue to the green of a hollow wave, like plumes on horses' heads, feathers on ladies' (ibid.: 19, 20, 24).

Peter Walsh on his walks through the city is struck by its modernity, the achievement of civilisation, inscribed with the letters of fashion in dress and paint: a silk-stockinged, feathered girl alighting from a car, well-dressed young people passing, 'pink stockings; pretty shoes', flowered shawls, 'coats blowing open', 'floating off in carnival' (*MD* 60, 177, 180):

> There was a freshness about them; even the poorest dressed better than five years ago surely; and to his eye the fashions had never been so becoming; the long black cloaks; the slimness; the elegance; and then the delicious and apparently universal habit of paint. Every woman, even the most respectable, had roses blooming under glass; lips cut with a knife; curls of Indian ink; there was design, art, everywhere; a change of some sort had undoubtedly taken place. (*MD*: 78)

His adventure with the young woman he follows in the street – 'black, but enchanting', shedding 'veil after veil, until she became the woman he had always had in mind' (*MD*: 57) – suggests Baudelaire's 'Passante' in its evocation of phantasmagoric desire. Her gloves and cloak seem to address him in an equivocal language combining with the fringes and laces and feather boas in the shop windows to suggest both erotic adventure and maternal comfort, allure and nostalgic aura: '"You", she said, only "you", saying it with her white gloves and her shoulders. Then the thin long cloak which the wind stirred . . . blew out with an enveloping kindness, a mournful tenderness, as of arms that would open and take the tired' (ibid.: 58). Unlike Baudelaire's hero, however, Peter Walsh (though disappointed in love) is not subjected to the melancholy nakedness of the spleen: '"no matter", his boots on the pavement struck out' (ibid.: 59). On a bench in Regent's Park, guarded by an elderly nurse in a grey dress, 'muffled over' by 'the plumes and feathers of sleep', he sinks into a series of visions of maternal figures composed of sky and branches, fluttering leaves, flowing streamers, a white apron blowing, outlines 'soft with light' (ibid.: 62–4) – figures of comfort, absolution, the lost maternal home and its restitution in the afterlife.

For Septimus, however, clothing functions neither as the herald of modernity nor as allure. Unlike Rezia, who looks with the milliner's professional understanding at 'every hat that passed . . . and the cloak and the dress and the way the woman held herself' (*MD*: 95–6), Septimus does not seek the protection of propriety. His shabbiness of dress nettles Sir William's 'natural respect for breeding and clothing' (ibid.: 106). Septimus aligns himself instead with Shakespeare's loathing of 'humanity – the putting on of clothes' (ibid.: 97). Looking at the world unveiled with the gaze of Benjamin's melancholic, he sees men 'plastered over with grimaces . . . waxed moustache, coral tie-pin, white slip . . . all coldness and clamminess within', 'Toms and Berties in their starched shirt fronts oozing with thick drops of vice': 'They never saw him drawing pictures of them naked at their antics in his notebook' (ibid.: 98). Trimming Mrs Peters' straw hat with Rezia is a moment of pride and happiness at which, Rezia later reflects, 'he had become himself': 'It was wonderful. Never had he done anything which made him feel so proud. It was so real, it was so substantial, Mrs Peters' hat. "Just look at it," he said' (ibid.: 158). Here is the opposite of the nakedness of the spleen: the aesthetic of the gift, the transformation of the quotidian – which Clarissa's mermaid dress also suggests as,

> lolloping on the waves and braiding her tresses she seemed, having that gift still; to be; to exist; to sum it all up in the moment as she passed; turned, caught her scarf in some other woman's dress, unhitched it, laughed, all with the most perfect ease and air of a creature floating in its element. (*MD*: 190–1)

Against such affirmation, for Septimus, stand the invasive forces of reification and serialisation, the melancholia of alienation: 'the doom pronounced . . . when he came into the room [in Milan during the war] and saw [the milliners] cutting out buckram shapes with their scissors; to be alone for ever' (*MD*: 159).

Beyond the fabrics of modern experience – the weaving of individual and trans-individual consciousness – clothes and sartorial discourse figure prominently in Woolf's various attempts at historiography, partly by supplying a visual inventory of the past. Sometimes this takes the form of a convenient, often parodic, shorthand; the past evoked and dismissed with the deliberate amnesia recalled by de Man. At other times, as in *Between the Acts*, clothes enable considerably more complex meditations on the relations between the present and a historical past, supplying the material as well as the method for such reflections. Beyond the perspective of the present, the temporal structure of fashion seems particularly inducive of that Now of Recognisability (*Jetzt der Erkennbarkeit*) by which, in Benjaminean archaeology, the past enters into legibility through the image as historical index.[7] Against the background of Benjaminean dialectical materialism what is at stake in each case may appear with greater clarity.

From one perspective, the 'garish erection' of Victoriana announcing the arrival of the nineteenth century in *Orlando*, displays the principle of Benjaminean *Lumpen*-historiography, a deconstructing and detotalising tradition in which the past appears as given, but also constructed from the present, capable of revealing sudden correspondences and constellations. To Orlando, however, this is less a case of active remembrance than the insistence of the present in a 'conglomeration . . . of the most heterogeneous and ill-assorted objects, piled higgledy-piggledy in a vast mound': 'widow's weeds and bridal veils; . . . military helmets, memorial wreaths, trousers, whiskers, wedding cakes . . .' – the indication being that here is a wish for Nietzsche's 'active forgetting', the deliberate amnesia recalled by de Man, rather than Benjamin's revolutionary nostalgia. For Orlando, the 'incongruity of the objects, the association of the fully clothed and the partly draped, the garishness of the different colours and their plaid-like juxtapositions' causes 'the most profound dismay' (O: 160). The erection takes the uncertain form of a 'pyramid, hecatomb or trophy', a monument-as-funeral pyre. It is supported 'on the right side by a female figure clothed in flowing white; on the left by a portly gentleman wearing a frock-coat and sponge-bag trousers' (ibid.: 160) – both of which suggest a past which is usable to the modern writer only as material for parody and pastiche, otherwise calling for active forgetting.

Significantly the frock-coat which appears here is not the covering of the modern hero dressed in black; the mourner in the writings of Baudelaire and Benjamin; or the agent of political reform in F. T. Vischer's 1861 analysis of the deformations and dehumanisation of male clothing, upon which Benjamin draws (Vischer 1861: 117). Vischer's critique of men's fashions arrives at insights similar to those of Baudelaire, writes Benjamin, though there is a significant difference in emphasis: 'What provides a hue for the dusky prospectus of the modern in Baudelaire is a shiny argument of political struggle in Vischer' (Benjamin 2006: 106). Where the condition of the modern hero is expressed metaphorically, however, these opposite views meet. Thus Baudelaire's recognition of himself in the image of a captured albatross ('The Albatross') resounds in Vischer's political critique of male clothing, the dark frock-coat whose wide sleeves render arms '"not arms any more but the rudiments of wings – stumps of penguin wings and fins of fishes. And the movements of the shapeless appendages when man walks look like foolish, silly gesticulating, shoving, rowing"'. 'The same view of the matter', Benjamin concludes, 'and the same image' (ibid.: 107).

This is not Woolf's view of the matter in *Orlando*, however, where the frock-coat suggests the antiquated habit of a pre-modern past, its associations of mourning pointing back to a culture of conventionalised sentimentalism rather than any heroic modernity. Nor does the female apparition – the figure clothed in flowing white – suggest anything but a parodic invocation of the past. The garments indicate the type of conventionalised allegorical figure – Love, Chastity, Reason, and the like – whose allegorical status is signified through modes of dress, draperies, veils and mantles, drawn from classical sculpture and painting, and endlessly recycled in literary representations. In Woolf's writing, as shown in Chapter 2 of this volume, such figures recur in many cases as objects of fun, a collection of cultural representations paraded as the detritus of the outmoded. The place for them here is the funeral pyre, indicating the conscious amnesia that defines modernity.

As Benjamin's practice of revolutionary nostalgia shows, however, such radical forgetting is neither possible nor desirable. Far removed from *Orlando*'s playfulness, *Between the Acts* explores Benjaminean modes of cultural memory at a time of crisis – the beginning of war – when the future is radically uncertain and questions of the value of a cultural past appear both extremely urgent and hopelessly irrelevant. Thus Woolf's concern in the novel is essentially the same as Benjamin's in his writings on Baudelaire: the changes in the structures of human experience that have made literary experience lose its validity and relevance. As in Benjaminean historiography, clothes function as an organon of history both in their representation as material presence and as tropes. Woolf poses her questions about the value of culture throughout the novel, in as well as between the acts of the pageant-play at its centre, investigating the possibilities for establishing a common ground for cultural survival and resistance on what is in effect an archaeological site: the remains of an ancient landscape, inscribed with centuries of human life, folkloric and literary tradition. In the balance against such efforts are the designs cast on the past by a chokingly patriotic, nationalist and imperialist rhetoric, as well as the general social marginality of literature and the arts, the growing sense that, at the end of civilisation, 'culture' does not matter.

Connecting with the questions of memory and historiography, the relation of past to present, is that of 'modern' versus 'old' modes of rationality. The 1930s may perhaps be thought of as a time when the crisis in Enlightenment rationality and bourgeois humanism, with the consequent modernist explorations of other rationalities, have given way to an urgent concern with distinguishing between critiques of classical reason which might be potentially progressive, and those which are irrationalist in the worst (fascist) sense. The time when Woolf was writing her last novel was hardly one for pondering such distinctions. Yet this is a question Woolf does not give up on, continuing to put forward and ironically withdraw claims for transcendence. As we shall see, clothes figure prominently in both areas of concern: that of the connection between present and past, and that of the connection between this world and potential others.

Ironically, the form which Woolf picks on for her explorations of cultural memory has become associated with a type of historical amnesia – though one which is diametrically opposed to Nietzsche's radical forgetting, designed to hermetically preserve, rather than eradicate, the past. The traditional pageant-play, as Jed Esty observes in his book *A Shrinking Island: Modernism and National Culture in England*, displaces history by heritage, and memory by 'amnesia in fancy dress' (Esty 2004: 59). Woolf's turn to the pageant-play may be understood, as Esty does, as involved with a late modernist revival, also seen in Forster's *Abinger Pageant* (1934) and *England's Pleasant Land* (1940), as well as Eliot's *The Rock* (1940), of one of the 'ur-genres' of English literature, suggestive of a cultural tradition of communitarian ethos, inherited folk consciousness, and an organic embeddedness in the land. The modern (Edwardian) pageant, as described by Esty, combined impulses from late Victorian interest in authentic village culture and traditional English pageantry with Wagnerian opera and German folk festivals, turning local history into massive outdoor spectacles involving elaborate sets and costumes, a large number of props, and large casts of amateur actors, builders, painters, seamstresses and the like. The props for one pageant, staged at Colchester in 1905, included 'hundreds of suits of armour, thousands of weapons, shields . . . thrones, biers, chariots, triumphal cars, and a thousand and one items', which, as the pageant-master writes, 'only the patriotic work of the ladies and gentlemen of the Committee could furnish' (Parker quoted in Esty 2004: 56–7).

The historical scheme for these spectacles was episodic but chronological, designed to instil a sense of continuity and absence of change, especially at the most fundamental, and important, level of chtonic communion with a nativist 'Deep England' (Esty 2004: 80). The effect of a properly conducted pageant, as described by one of its Edwardian proponents, would be to 'kill' not only the 'modernising spirit' but historicity as such. This is where, 'in the place of memory, amnesia swaggers out in historical fancy dress' (ibid.: 59, 244). As argued by Esty, *Between the Acts*, like the other 1930s pageant-plays and pageant-novels mentioned here, turns to the possibilities embodied in the genre at a time of international crisis and re-orientation to problems of national self-representation, attempting to recover a ground for an alternative 'Englishness' outside nationalist and imperialist narratives. Woolf's appropriation, however, more than Forster and Eliot's, parodically rewrites the genre, effectively restoring its historicity. The costumes are highly significant to this move. Functioning as an organon of history, the 'reconstructions' of historical dress play an important part in ironising and undercutting the claims made by the genre. At the same time, to the extent that the scenes and tableaux are still invested with performative power vis-à-vis the audience, in the sense of moving the spectators to assent and identification, this is also an effect of the costumes.

'Anon' and 'The Reader', Woolf's last and unfinished texts, written alongside the final stages of work on *Between the Acts*, give us a clear indication that Woolf's interest in clothes and costumes at this time far exceeds the parodic. Concerned with many of the same ideas as *Between the Acts*, these essays serve among other things to demonstrate the range of Woolf's thinking on dress and historicity at this time. It is obvious that clothes catch Woolf's imagination, that she is fascinated by their history, psychology and semiotics, what they mean and what they do. At this time her interest turns particularly on dress as a form of visual archive, a visual mode of access to the past and its modalities of being in the world. She also develops an idea of the connection between dress and historicity, understood as consciousness of the past and of oneself as inhabiting a present moment. The essays share the novel's concern with the relation between art and society, cultural inheritance and the demands of a present moment. In them Woolf traces the changes in modes of production and reception of literature, from oral to written transmission, anonymous to individualised authors, communal to solitary audience, reflecting on the role of the artist in articulating the communal and collective – shared emotions and experiences – as in 'the common voice' of Anon, the anonymous ballad singer of the past: 'Everybody shared in the emotions of Anons song, and supplied the story' (Woolf 1979: 382). Thinking through clothes, Woolf is particularly concerned with the moments when the communal gives way to the individual, and when an experience of temporal continuum is replaced by historicity. She describes the ancient rituals at which the peasants were led to worship of the old Gods by Anon, dressed in 'coats of green leaves, bearing swords in their hands, dancing through the houses, enacting their ancient parts' (ibid.: 384), and she describes the moment when the ritual garment is reinvented as costume (or even fancy dress): the masque at Kenilworth in 1575 where the old-fashioned mummer, hung with green leaves, was 'presented before Elizabeth . . . as an interesting anachronism', 'a revival'; 'already time had given those green leaves their mystery' (ibid.: 417).

Writing about the Elizabethan period as a time when the printing press had 'brought the past into existence', along with 'the man who was conscious of the past; the man who first sees himself and shows himself to us' (Woolf 1979: 385), yet has no language in which to express his individuality, Woolf speculates at length on Elizabethan dress, as if the mystery of the past were hidden in the folds, woven into its fabric, sewn into the shapes of collars and sleeves:

> When we look at them we see them in their farthingales and ruffs; young mens bodies are stiffly sewn into doublets and school boy's faces are raised above starched collars; young women serve only to display heavy quilted dresses stuck about with huge pearls. (Woolf 1979: 413)

'They [wrap themselves] about in cumbrous garments when they try to talk' (ibid.: 389). 'They can say nothing simple, nothing intimate' (ibid.: 413). If their clothes seem as resistant to reading as their prose, Woolf connects their mode of display to a sense of individuality as well as a consciousness of the past – the man brought into existence by the printing press:

> What desire was it that prompted this extraordinary display? There must have been some protest, some desire to affirm something, behind the slashed cloaks; the stiff ruffs; the wrought chains and the loops of pearls. The cost was great; the discomfort appalling; yet the fashion prevailed. Was it perhaps, the mark of an anonymous, unrecorded age to enforce the individual; to make ones physical body as bright, as definite, as marked as possible? Fame must be concentrated in the body; since the other kind of fame, the publicity of the paper, of the photograph, was denied them. Did the eloquence of dress speak, when the art of verbal speech was still unformed? (Woolf 1979: 388)

For a moment the communal spirit resurfaces as Anon the ballad singer is reborn as Anon, the Elizabethan playwright, and the creative audience in the participatory, ritual aspects of the performance event. Thinking about the role of the actors' costumes in this establishment of a community, Woolf clearly separates theatrical costumes from the clothes of individuals. On stage, the 'taffetas and tinsels', the 'satin doublets and hose laid thick with gold lace', and the 'cast off robes of the nobles', have nothing to do with individual awareness: they function in the performative embodiment, the making 'visible, audible tangible in the light of the present moment' a 'vast universe', 'great names, great deeds, simple outlines, and not the single subtlety of one soul' (Woolf 1979: 393–4). To the extent that the play is 'the work of the undifferentiated audience' (ibid.: 394) and the 'anonymous playwright has like the singer this nameless vitality, something drawn from the crowd in the penny seats' (ibid.: 398), this derives precisely from the act of embodiment, the visual and phenomenal impact of the actors on stage, much of which resides in the costumes. This impression of bodies, however, is a part of the Elizabethan play that is 'sunk beyond recall'; any reenactment always imports something of the present (ibid.: 432).

Turning to the costumes and clothes of *Between the Acts*, we find that it elaborates in more sophisticated terms their connections with the collective imagination as well as their function as a visual archive or memory bank, the signs and the organon of history. The costumes used for the pageant are described both in the material origin of their appearance and as performance effect. With the exception of some original pieces of clothing (like the major's old frock coat), the costumes are not obsolete objects as such, not the surrealists' *objets trouvées*, rather they are (re)constructed obsolete objects, made from cheap material, artifacts and fabrics inscribed with other purposes: crowns are made out of cardboard, swords of silver paper, turbans of sixpenny dishcloths. The point of this is not simply ironic – a parody of the pageant-genre, exposure of the illusion or the conventionality of the audience's response. What we see in these rag-tag costumes is in effect the inversion of the dialectical theatre of fashion: rather than the construction of the newest in the medium of what has been, or the discovery of the obsolete in the 'dresses of five years ago', what takes place is the (potentially paradigmatic) construction of what has been in the medium of the now. What is more, the medium is the waste, the rags and tags, odds and ends, of the now. This places the past at yet a remove from the present, imbues the objects of the present with performative, historiographical force.

If what is performed is nostalgia, it is revolutionary nostalgia, in the sense that it occupies a line between fancy dress and rag-picking, amnesia and dialectical recollection, pointing towards the cultural potential for both. To the extent that the play stages the novel's investigation of the possibility of establishing a ground for cultural action on an archaeological site, one may describe it as a theatricalised archaeology. However, this is not an archaeology which makes manifest the repressed from a collective past, or a cultural Imaginary, on the contrary, it parades and theatricalises the culture's most familiar representations. Through the theatricalisation – the banal pictography and improvised costumes of the amateur pageant – these representations, like the costumes they wear, become the rags and tags, the waste and trivia of what were once the proud narratives of enlightenment, nationalism and imperialism.

The costumes alternately function as the visual shorthand of a stock cultural register, as dialectical material, as aesthetic performance, and as things separated from use-value. Much of the complexity of their effect derives from the impression that they are not *either* this or that, that they move between different registers and that the audience's response moves accordingly. There are moments when the costumes appear separate from all use-value – everyday and dramatic: strewn on the grass or flung on the bushes as the actors change, the clothes attract the butterflies: 'Red and silver, blue and yellow gave off warmth and sweetness. Red Admirals gluttonously absorbed richness from dish cloths, cabbage whites drank icy coolness from silver paper. Flitting, tasting, returning, they sampled the colours' (*BTA*: 57–8). The connection here is with orders other than the human, a connection that the sartorial is habitually drawn upon to suggest.

Presenting their 'Scenes from English history', which Mrs Manresa, well-versed in the conventions of the genre, translates as 'Merry England' (*BTA*: 74), the actors are recognised by the audience as themselves, but also as 'wonderfully made up', 'the very image' of the figures they are meant to depict (ibid.: 113). In the Elizabethan scene Queen Elizabeth is played by 'Eliza Clark, licensed to sell tobacco,' of the village shop:

> She was splendidly made up. Her head, pearl-hung, rose from a vast ruff. Shiny satins draped her. Sixpenny brooches glared like cats' eyes and tigers' eyes; pearls looked down; her cape was made of cloth of silver – in fact swabs used to scour saucepans. She looked the age in person. (*BTA*: 76)

With Brechtian discrepancy between the phenomenal and the semiotic body, her arms emerge from the sleeves of her dress just as 'swarthy' and 'muscular' as when 'reaching a flitch of bacon or hauling a tub of oil with one sweep in the shop' (*BTA*: 76–7). This constructed Queen is met with joyful recognition. She *is* the part. Even when the wind tugs at her headdress and unpins the 'Elizabethan' ruff, the audience laugh so loud that it doesn't matter. Another symbolical figure greeted with the approval of familiarity and representativeness is the Victorian policeman,

> Budge the publican; but so disguised that even cronies who drank with him nightly failed to recognize him . . . . He wore a long black many-caped cloak; waterproof; shiny; of a substance of a statue in Parliament square; a helmet which suggested a policeman; a row of medals crossed his breast; and in his right hand he held extended a special constable's baton . . . . It was his voice . . . issuing from a thick black cotton-wool beard that gave him away. (*BTA*: 144)

Once more the costume emerges from a stock iconography, a visual shorthand that immediately suggests the representative of Her Majesty's Empire, the laws of God and Man (*BTA*: 145–6). Once more, too, the seams of the illusion are exposed, the rag-tag *making* of a cultural past by which a wad of dyed cottonwool comes to represent a historical moment as well as its historicising re-presentation.

Costumes also function prominently in the conventionalised pictography of allegorical figures like Love, 'in white satin', and Reason, whose 'grey satin robe (a bedspread), pinned in stone-like folds, gave her the majesty of a statue' (*BTA*: 82, 110). As with the Victorian constable, this draws upon the visual inventory of traditional sculpture; here particular garments and sartorial conventions – flowing robes, drapes, and folds – define the allegorical figure qua allegorical figure. The song played on the gramophone picks up on the same allegorical iconography as it 'gently state[s] certain facts which everybody knows to be perfectly true', how 'Eve, gathering her robes about her, stands reluctant to let her dewy mantle fall', then 'lets down her sombre tresses brown and spreads her lucent veil o'er hamlet, spire and mead' (ibid.: 120). The view 'repeat[s] in its own way what the tune was saying', and the cows say 'the same thing to perfection'. 'Folded in this triple melody, the audience sat gazing . . . gently and approvingly without interrogation, for it seemed inevitable . . .' (ibid.: 121). The allegorical figure and its iconography are related to the topos and vocabulary of 'Deep England': the oneness of land, people and ancient lore. The audience, appropriately, are enfolded in the reverie of auratic nostalgia, oblivious of the narrative's spoofing of the dream as well as its conventionalised pictography.

The proclaimed moderns, Isa Oliver and William Dodge, whom Isa, evoking Baudelaire's 'hypocrite lecteur', thinks of as 'her semblable, her conspirator, a seeker like her after hidden faces' (*BTA*: 187), are as engaged by the costumes and the sartorial tropology as their fellow spectators, it seems. To William the effect of dancing, fantastically dressed actors is of 'an entrancing spectacle . . . of dappled light and shade on half clothed, fantastically coloured, leaping, jerking, swinging legs and arms. He clapped till his palms stung' (ibid.: 84). Isa's musings affirm the allegorical iconography that connects Eve to an originary condition of organic wholeness: seen against this auratic horizon the future appears as a 'harvestless dim field where no evening lets fall her mantle', while the present figures as a condition of untying of bonds, of being undressed and stripped naked: '"The thongs are burst that the dead tied. Loosed are our possessions. . . ." "It's a good day, some say, the day we are stripped naked. Others, it's the end of the day"' (ibid.: 139–40).

To the extent that the pageant has an unsettling rather than amnesic effect on the audience, this is largely dependent on the sartorial register. It is the actors' costumes which make historicity available to reflection, and it is the consciousness of one's own outer covering as somehow lacking which raises the question of modern subjectivity in the midst of amnesia:

Yet somehow they felt – how could one put it – a little not quite here or there. . . . Not quite themselves, they felt. Or was it simply that they felt clothes conscious? Skimpy out-of-date voile dresses; flannel trousers; panama hats; hats wreathed with raspberry-coloured net in the style of the Royal Duchess's hat at Ascot seemed flimsy somehow. 'How lovely the clothes were,' said someone, casting a last look at Flavinda disappearing. 'Most becoming. I wish . . . (*BTA*: 134)

What the wish is, we are not told, but one might guess it has something to do with the sense of the wholeness and completeness of the past set against the impression of fashion as flimsy, ephemeral, in- and out-of-date with hardly a moment's notice. The paradox is that the costumes, themselves flimsy and improvised, fancy-dress versions of period costume, are still capable of bringing about this sense of incompleteness, of loss and nostalgia for the past. Between the acts, the talk is on clothes; the audience, for all their conventionality, picking up on the costumes as indicators of historicity and identity: '"Dressing up. That's the great thing, dressing up. . . . D'you think people change? Their clothes, of course . . . But I mean ourselves . . . Clearing out a cupboard, I found my father's old top hat . . . But ourselves – do we change?"' (*BTA*: 108–9).

With the staging of the Victorian scenes, nostalgia gives way to travesty. After the actors have foraged through the archives – the rag-bag with the eighteenth-century jack boots, the Victorian whiskers and the mantle with the bead fringe – 'The Picnic party. About 1860. Scene: A Lake', exhibits a young man in peg-top trousers and side whiskers, a young lady in crinoline and mushroom hat, a stout lady in black bombazine, an elderly gentleman in a deer-stalker's cap (*BTA*: 147–9). The chorus of villagers, who until this moment have appeared in shirts of sacking, affirming that despite the passage of time history has not really happened, now appear in Victorian mantles, side whiskers and top hats, to take part in the send-up. For the audience, being transported from the amnesia of heritage to the history of the immediate past, proves 'too much, too much'; 'Cheap and nasty' (ibid.: 153, 155). '"Were they like that?"' Isa is prompted to ask. Mrs Swithin muses, '"The Victorians . . . . I don't believe . . . that there were ever such people. Only you and me and William dressed differently." "You don't believe in history," said William' (ibid.: 156).

The present time opens with a tributary moment: a cloth roughly painted signifying '"Civilization . . . in ruins; rebuilt . . . by human effort', flanked by 'black man in fuzzy wig; coffee-coloured ditto in silver turban; [signifying] presumably the League of . . ."' (*BTA*: 163). To the reader this is clearly Woolf's travesty of some of the familiar illusions and self-flattering idealism that infused the contemporary international situation, the belief in civilisation, in rebuilding efforts, and in the frameworks of international arbitration and transnational legislation of which Leonard Woolf was such a strong defender. The spectators, however, take it as a flattering tribute to themselves, a moment of reassurance which is of course radically dissolved in the final Brechtian scene when the cracked mirrors held up by the actors, leaping, skipping, flashing, dazzling, dancing, jumping, catch 'Here a nose . . . There a skirt . . . Then trousers only . . . Now perhaps a face' (ibid.: 165). Selves and truths dissolving, all the contents of the rag-bag are thrown out, up in the air; all the sayings, the epigrams, the poems, the plays, the figures, the folklore, the wit, declaimed as phrases, orts, scraps, and fragments, rags and tags, in complete cacophony. Here is the ultimate fragmentation of heritage, of the comforting fantasy of cultural identity, of organic unity and connectedness.

The very last moments of performance are of interest for their parody of the Carlylean idealism that infuses the play. First a voice speaking through a megaphone berates the spectators in distinctly Carlylean terms, echoing the urgings of *Sartor Resartus*'s attack on vanity and the abomination of empty, soulless cloth – garments of office that hide the hollowness within: 'Don't hide among rags. Or let our cloth protect us', nor 'vanity', 'lipstick and blood-red nails' (*BTA*: 168). Next comes the post-performance address by the Reverend Streatfield which interprets the performance along the same Carlylean lines, resonant with the vocabulary of 'Natural Supernaturalism': '"we are members one of another. Each is part of the whole. . . . there is a spirit that inspires, pervades . . ."' (ibid.: 172–3). There are only a few steps here to Carlyle's 'Man is a Spirit, and bound by invisible bonds to All Men'; and 'all Nature and Life are but one Garment', 'the living visible garment of God' (Carlyle 1869: 41, 141, 37). Fearing public disgrace, the audience are embarrassed for him, 'their representative spokesman; their symbol . . . an irrelevant forked stake in the flow and majesty of the summer silent world' (*BTA* 171) – or 'a forked radish with a head fantastically carved', in Carlyle's own words (Carlyle 1869: 42). 'Must I be Thomas, you Jane?', seems to be their common response, which is to say: must this 'clergyman in the livery of his servitude to the summing up' subject the complexities and profundities of the experience to 'reduction to simplified absurdity', and must we, the audience, be reduced to that Victorian preacher Carlyle and his preached-for wife? (*BTA*: 171).

What is spoofed and presented as cultural waste, however, is also taken seriously in the text, and once more a sartorial register is involved, gesturing towards modalities of transcendence which perhaps have more in common with modern materialism than Christian idealism, but which nonetheless invoke the connectedness of minds and meaningful, emblematic nature. In fact one may identify two opposing movements in the text, one towards rags and tags, the parodic but also dialectical send-up of 'amnesia in fancy dress', the other towards mythological robes, veils, mantles and raiments. Both movements are signalled early on, through the introduction of the two portraits hanging on the dining-room wall: the 'talk-producing' ancestor and the lady who is 'a picture':

> In her yellow robe . . . and a feather in her hair, she led the eye up, down . . . through glades of greenery and shades of silver, dun and rose into silence. The room was empty. . . . The room was a shell, singing of what was before time was; a vase stood in the heart of the house, alabaster, smooth, cold, holding the still, distilled essence of emptiness, silence. (*BTA*: 33–4)

Metonymically and laterally, through recurring epithets, images and phrases attributed to no one in particular, shared by the narrative consciousness and the characters, connections are established between the lady in her yellow robe, green glades, and the 'deep centre', the 'heart of silence': 'It was in that deep centre, in that black heart, that the lady had drowned herself'; the picture 'drew them down the paths of silence'; 'She led them down green glades into the heart of silence'; the silver and dun shades that led to the heart of silence' (*BTA*: 40, 42, 45, 46). The breeze and the sunlight create other connections: yellow curtains, flapping in the breeze, 'tossing light, then shadow' (ibid.: 15), a painting of another anonymous woman draped in 'lengths of yellow satin', lit up . . . with the sun pouring over her' (ibid.: 63), 'a breeze blew and all the muslin blinds fluttered out, as if some majestic goddess, rising from her throne among her peers, had tossed her amber-coloured raiment' (ibid.: 66–7). The breeze ruffles Mrs Swithin's hair and warms 'the wintry blue in her eyes to amber', then goes 'lolloping along the corridors, blowing the blinds out' (ibid.: 67). Later the same breeze flutters Mrs Manresa's skirts, making her seem – to Giles or the narrative consciousness, or both – 'a goddess, buoyant, abundant, with flower-chained captives . . . in her wake' (ibid.: 182).

In 'A Sketch of the Past', as we have seen, clothes work as part of a process of autobiographical *Erinnerung*, but also as tropes related to *Gedächtnis* understood as a gathering of unconscious data: the flowery maternal dress and the moving blinds, translucent, semi-transparent, with which light, shadow and wind play. Such textiles are not so much tabulas of inscription, as material which speaks by movement, animation, seeming to address one in a language one strives to understand. Similar tropes and their unspoken proclamations resonate through Woolf's work. In *Between the Acts* the suggestion of depths, of meaningful silence, and of speaking, emblematic nature, is linked to sartorial figures, either by dressing natural elements such as the wind, or by making natural elements act on sartorial materials or surfaces, as movement or as light and shadow. If this is the silence of *Gedächtnis*, it seems to indicate something the characters have lost, which Isa attempts to articulate through her poetry, and 'old Flimsy', Lucy Swithin, through her religion, and which connects with the 'superstitions' shared by Mrs Swithin and the servants, the dark centre of which remains hidden in the muddy depths of the lily pond. It may also be that we are approaching the type of memory that Benjamin calls *Eingedenken*: the recollection or commemoration of material from a collective past. Thus Isa reflects on the burden of history:

> How am I burdened with what they drew from the earth; memories; posses-
> sions. This is the burden that the past laid on me. . . . That was the burden
> . . . laid on me in the cradle; murmured by waves; breathed by restless elm
> trees; crooned by singing women; what we must remember; what we would
> forget.' (*BTA*: 139)

In similar terms, Benjamin writes about how contents of the individual past combine in memory with material from the collective past:

> Rituals, with their ceremonies and their festivals kept producing the amalga-
> mation of these two elements of memory over and over again. They triggered
> recollection at certain times and remained available to memory throughout
> people's lives. In this way, voluntary and involuntary recollection cease to be
> mutually exclusive. (Benjamin 2006: 174–5)

In the re-enactments of the pageant-play, however, the ritual *Eingedenken* no longer works. Only rags and tags remain, along with the silences and the texts of nature that speak of what has been lost.

'Anon' and 'The Reader', with their focus on the communal and the ritual, elaborate on the nature of this loss. However, as the essay empha-sises, 'Anon' is 'not yet dead in ourselves': 'There never was, it seems, a time when men and women were without memory. . . . That is the world beneath our consciousness; the anonymous world to which we can still return' (Woolf 1979: 380, 385). In so far as we can become anonymous in reading *Le Morte D'Arthur* or the old play, we can re-enter as well the unconscious world that 'still exists in us, deep sunk, savage, primitive, remembered' (ibid.: 380–1).

Intriguingly, Woolf's last essays show some remarkable points of resemblance with Benjamin's essay 'The Storyteller', not only in their history of the changed modes of literary production and reception, but also in their portrayals of isolated present-day experience set against the communities of the past. Where Woolf writes about the end of the anonymous song and the communal drama, Benjamin writes about the end of storytelling as 'the end of the ability to exchange experiences' (Benjamin 1998: 83). The storyteller has counsel for his readers, writes Benjamin – 'if today "having counsel" is beginning to have an old-fashioned ring, this is because the communicability of experience is decreasing. In consequence we have no counsel either for ourselves or others' (ibid.: 86). Benjamin's point is that a person's inner concerns become inescapably private in a historical situation where it is unlikely that one's external concerns will be assimilated to one's experience. This happens when the newspapers and the concept of information serve to isolate events from the realm in which they could affect the reader. Such modern poverty in communicable experience also informs *Between the Acts*, where the newspaper is described as the new book, and where the newspaper's account of the rape of a young woman preys on Isa's imagination, while Giles's anger and frustration come from newspaper accounts of the war – both external experiences which consciousness fails to assimilate in a productive way.

Woolf, like Benjamin, sees the beauty in what is vanishing. Employing Benjaminean terms one might refer to it as *Erfahrung* or *Naturgeschichte*, the 'natural history to which stories refer back' (Benjamin 1998: 94). This natural history seems to concern the way in which events are embedded in the inscrutable course of the world, 'the web which all stories together form in the end' (ibid.: 98). Whether this web is 'the golden fabric of a religious view of the course of things, or the multi-colored fabric of a worldly view', makes no difference: 'The only certain thing is that it is by definition outside all real historical categories' (ibid.: 96–7). It is that fabric within which man exists in harmony with nature, finding himself addressed and counselled by its agents. In *Between the Acts*, as we have seen, the wind and the sun alternately speak and remain silent. There is a sense of the transcendental home speaking in a lost language, and there is homelessness with its rags and tags. The modern novelistic conception – the 'figure in the carpet' which attains visibility through the author's act of creative memory – is no longer available as a possibility; nor is the weaving of stories. At best there are epigrams with the force of proverbs: 'Where there's a will there's a way' (*BTA*: 108). Allegorical figures appear in fancy dress rather than garments of transcendence. Nonetheless, the 'home' towards which Woolf's work gestures exists as more than an auratic horizon for the dialectical theatre of the ragbag. Rather, it indexes an attempt that may be traced through the length of Woolf's writing life: to articulate a belief, a conviction, or intuition. Partly, this is a private, idiosyncratic belief, grounded in personal experience and reading, though, as we have begun to see, it also connects with contemporary articulations of an oscillation which defines some modernist projects: an oscillation between the material and the immaterial, the present and the past, the topography of this world and that of potential un-worlds.

Notes

1. *Erfahrung*, a privileged term throughout Benjamin's work, refers to a condition of harmonious fusion between subject and object, a sense of integral wholeness and plenitude, as well as a mode of knowledge which 'is less the product of facts firmly anchored in memory than a convergence in memory of accumulated and frequently not conscious data', where 'certain contents of the individual past combine with material of the collective past' (Benjamin 1998: 157, 159). This earlier life connects in Benjamin's theory with the *Naturgeschichte*, a natural history outside all real historical categories that seems to concern the way in which events are embedded in the inscrutable course of the world (ibid.: 94–8).

2. To Benjamin the modern *Erlebnis* describes a state of rupture between subject and material reality, and of immediate, isolated experience parried by the defence mechanisms of consciousness. The *Chock*, by contrast, is produced in the violent contact which occurs at those moments when the shock defence fails and excessive stimuli penetrate and deform the subject's unprepared consciousness.

3. See e.g. Constantin Guys' *Woman Lifting Her Skirt* (c. 1850), reproduced in Lehmann's *Tigersprung*, or *Three Women by a Bar* and *Two Courtesans*, in Baudelaire's *The Painter of Modern Life and Other Essays*, ed. J. Mayne.

4. The term is Ulrich Lehmann's.

5. See Carolyn Abbs, 'Writing the Subject: Virginia Woolf and Clothes', for a discussion of the connection between clothes/textiles and memory in Woolf's autobiographical writing, and the influence of this on Woolf's fiction. Abbs reads Woolf in light of Flügel and Bergson, arguing that Woolf's understanding of what Flügel terms 'confluence' (the illusion of identity between body and clothes) allows her to recreate memory as sensory perception and corporeal presence, as for instance in her recollections of her mother. Apart from the autobiographical material, Abbs's focus is mainly on 'The New Dress' (Abbs 2006).

6. 'The important thing for the remembering author is not what he experienced, but the weaving of his memory, the Penelope work of recollection. Or should one call it, rather, a Penelope work of forgetting? Is not the involuntary recollection, Proust's *mémoire involontaire*, much closer to forgetting than what is usually called memory? And is not this work of spontaneous recollection, in which remembrance is the woof and forgetting the warf, a counterpart to Penelope's work rather than its likeness? For here the day unravels what the night was woven. When we awake each morning, we hold in our hands, usually weakly and loosely, but a

few fringes of the tapestry of lived life, as loomed for us by forgetting' (Benjamin 1998: 202).

7. 'It isn't that the past casts its light on what is present or what is present its light on what is past; rather, image is that wherein what has been comes together in a flash with the now to form a constellation. In other words: image is dialectics at a standstill. For while the relation of the present to the past is purely temporal, the relation of what-has-been to the now is dialectical: not temporal in nature but figural [*bildlich*]' (Benjamin 1999: 464).

Chapter 4

Modernism against Fashion

The Apes of God (1930), Wyndham Lewis's 'delayed time-bomb' aimed at the 'gilded Bohemia' of Bloomsburies and Sitwells (Meyers 1980: 160), opens with a characteristically absurd prologue, a lengthy description of 'The Toilette of a Veteran Gossip-Star', during which a lady's maid is engaged in the sacred ritual of adorning her mistress's head with an ornate lace cap appropriate to a lady's standing. The prologue is written in satire of the modernist's (post-Jamesian/post-Bergsonian) 'internalist' method, conveying the 'thought-stream' of Lady Fredigonde's isolated and decrepit mind, whose preoccupation is the passage of time and approaching death, 'the big ruthless question: What would be the last thing alive in that room?' (Lewis 1987: 98; Lewis 1965: 22). In mocking travesty of familiar Woolfian preoccupations and styles the reader is made to follow the stream of consciousness, the flux taking us from the Lady's characteristic answer to the ontological puzzle she has set herself – 'Beyond all doubt things, not PERSONS' – followed by a mental note to herself to bequeath her collection of lace caps to the appropriate museum ('Let her by all means survive as a cap – there were worse things than that, by Jupiter'), and finally, lace caps flashing upon the screen of her mind, the contemplation of a less than flattering future scenario: her head-dresses in their glass cases in the museum 'examined by the hundred bloodshot eyes of a Red Sunday-School'; 'little jumping bolsheviks' smashing the glass of the show-cases and heading off with the caps, each neatly adjusted to a cropped bolshevik skull (Lewis 1965: 24–5).

In sum *The Apes of God* presents Lewis's famous case against the fashionable bohemia of the 1920s. At a time when 'everyone able to afford to do so has become a "bohemian"', the rich indulge in aesthetic experiment rather than offering patronage to the true artist, taking 'quaint' little studios and so ruining the market for the struggling painter or sculptor (Lewis 1965: 127). In this setting Bloomsbury and the Sitwells appear thinly disguised as 'self-advertising gossip-stars' and 'party-lighthouses';

exponents of a culture of dilettante art and fashionable society incapable of distinguishing real artistic experiment from experiments in dress and carnival.[1] This is the culture, as Lewis writes elsewhere, which makes the Russian Ballet its fashionable fetish, and whose adherents fly 'hatless and crimson' whenever they hear an egg is to be broken, 'panting to be *there in time*, punctual at all the dates of fashion' (Lewis 1927: 45). The greatest Ape of all is of course Horace Zagreus, the notorious practical joker who (in all-too obvious allusion to the *Dreadnought* hoax) once 'dressed up as a Guards Officer and disarmed the sentries at the Palace . . . . The idea was to show how easy it would be to kidnap the King' (Lewis 1965: 225). Presumably as a warm-up to the excesses of its second part, Lord Osmund's Lenten party, the novel gives us the details of Zagreus's party costume over several pages, repeating the focus on dress from the opening scene, but this time from a thoroughly externalist rather than internalist perspective. The costume is a satire of the dilettantes who 'fancy themselves as savages', a bizarre concoction 'bristling with emblems' and anthropological allusions, bird's feathers, snake's eggs, goat's ears; the crown of a hat representing 'the beak of the Ibis', 'a pearl upon the front . . . the Urna or third eye of Siva', and so on *ad absurdum*. 'My very fly-buttons are allusive', as Zagreus complacently observes (Lewis 1986: 71; Lewis 1965: 350–3).

As a writer of fiction Wyndham Lewis perceives himself as a satirist, though not a moralist, producing a 'non-ethical satire' (Lewis 1987: 88) whose laughter depends on the externalist aesthetic of the 'personal-appearance' artist which gives us people's thingness, their machinations, in place of the disembodied internalism of the humanist mistake (ibid.: 95–105). *The Apes of God* is his most consistent application of this principle: 'No book has ever been written that has paid more attention to the outside of people. In it their shells or pelts, or the language of their bodily movements, come first, not last' (ibid.: 97). Clothes, as we have seen, have a place in Lewis's externalist satire, a point he expounds upon in *Men Without Art*: 'A naked person is much less a *thing* than is a dressed person', he notes: 'Confronted by Queen Elizabeth, for instance, "dolled-up" as she is shown us in any of her portraits, you would have much more the sensation of being in the presence of a life-size puppet than if you encountered her naked' (ibid.: 128–9). In consequence, he goes on to reflect,

> the particular ritual that dress involves, and the dramatization of the body by dress is, I believe, the reflection of a higher culture in man than is the barren metaphysics of the Naked Body. The body spells the 'naked-truth' . . . art consists among other things in a mechanizing of the natural. It . . . substitutes a thing for a person every time . . . . (Lewis 1987: 129)

Submitted to the gaze of the satirist, in other words, the deformation
of fashion may serve to counteract humanist, evolutionary illusions. By
contrast (as in the '*Nacktkultur* to which every "daring" forward step of
the sportsman or sportswoman tends'), the modern mythology of nudity
aligns itself in Lewis's thinking with an internalist, disembodied writing.
Paradoxically, 'the first great step upon the road of complete disembodi-
ment is to get *unclothed*':

> Already today . . . as compared with any former times, in these parts of
> Europe, we look, from the outside, rather uniform and indeterminate – it will
> be readily conceded the proletarianization does that, science does that. All the
> influences in fact of the machine-age, political and intellectual, are productive
> of this back-to-nature, or *back-to-the-body*, movement, where our persons
> are concerned: an abstracting and abstracting of distinctive marks, of distinc-
> tive dress, until we get back to the puritanic bedrock of the bare body and no
> nonsense. But in one sense . . . *back-to-the-body* means *down-to-the-soul* as
> well. (Lewis 1987: 128–9)

Lewis's concern in these passages is with the logical and actual connections existing between the evolutionary idealism of the nude culture
movement and the post-Jamesian or post-Bergsonian preoccupation
with the stream of internal experience. His point is that both posit the
ideal of an organic relationship between body and mind along with
naive analogies between bodily and political liberation. The materialist
externalism he himself promotes is of an entirely different order: not
back to the corporeality of the 'inveterate humanist' but to 'the *shell* of
the animal': 'the shield of the tortoise . . . the rigid stylistic articulations
of the grasshopper' – or the inorganic deformations of dress (Lewis
1987: 99).

Though fashion in this sense is awarded a critical role in the satirist's exposure of humanist and modernist illusions, Lewis's position
throughout his work is decidedly *against* fashion. 'Art is nothing to
do with the coat you wear', the first issue of *BLAST* announced in
1914, thus giving expression to an anti-fashion sentiment which were
to remain at the forefront of Lewis's confrontations with modernity
and modernism for years to come, and in light of which his attacks on
Bloomsbury in general and Woolf in particular, need to be understood.
As previous chapters have shown, for a modern artist to adopt a stance
against fashion was hardly unique in itself: from one perspective, argu-
ably, this was a position occupied by avant-garde movements from the
Pre-Raphaelites to the Futurists. To the extent that fashion embodied
modern commodity culture, mass production, and the subsumption
of the local and particular under the pressures of centralisation, anti-
fashion initiatives, variously motivated and articulated, attempted to

create alternatives to the commercial, wasteful, and repressive regime of official, bourgeois fashion, crossing boundaries of 'high' and 'low' art in order to act directly on everyday life (Stern 2004: 2–3).

Not surprisingly, such ventures were imbued with contradictions, among them the paradox of being promoted as distinctly modern yet somehow released from the system of fashion and the restless changes imposed by the market. For instance, as Mark Anderson has shown, the cross-European *Jugendstil* movement presented itself as a modern international style appropriate to the new age while founded on the organic composure and unity of a classic plastics perceived as the very embodiment of a formal resistance to change. Even more paradoxically, as Radu Stern argues in her study of European anti-fashion ventures, the garments created by the Italian Futurists proposed an absolute, 'ever-changing' modernity to replace the deceptive modernity of fashion; clothes which were works of art and as such never supposed to become dated, yet 'short-lasting, in order to be able to renew incessantly the pleasure and animation of our body and to favour the textile industry' (Giacomo Ballo, 'Futurist Manifesto of Men's Clothing, 1913', quoted in Stern 2004: 29). Among the techniques used to effect a Futurist dyna-mism of clothing were so called modifiers, appliqué pieces of cloth to be attached to any part of the garment, so allowing its owner to 'not only modify but also invent a new dress for a new mood at an instant' (Ballo, 'Male Futurist Dress', quoted ibid.: 32). In this way, as Stern writes, 'attire became an "open" work of art' in which the wearer was given a collaborative part and the fashion system supposedly evaded (ibid.: 32).

The Omega's ventures in dress, too, were promoted as modern alter-natives to mainstream fashion, though neither the Workshops' methods of production nor their marketing strategies could, or would, gloss over their implication in the mercantile logic of fashion. Among the great selling-points of the Omega, as Fiona MacCarthy observed in her intro-duction to a 1984 Omega retrospective, was the 'custom-design service' which it offered to its customers and which in turn rested on a commit-ment to the impulse of the moment rather than the traditional Ruskinian concern with craft and with things of lasting value. The Workshops, according to the catalogue, were prepared to 'arrange the making up of dresses and evening cloaks from Omega materials and hand-dyed silks to customers' specifications . . . design furniture to suit specific set-tings; hand-dye bedspreads, silks and chair covers to order' and so on (MacCarthy 1984: 9–14). Decorations, like clothes, could be changed at whim, in accordance with the shifting desires and self-fashioning impulses of the buyer. 'If people get tired of one landscape', as Roger

Fry said to a newspaper reporter, 'they can easily have another. It can be done in a very short time' (*RF* 195).[2]

Returning to Wyndham Lewis's case against fashion we find that it is conceptually and strategically different from the alternatives to fashion outlined above. Initially, and somewhat generally, the *BLAST* pronouncement expresses Lewis's disdain for the fashionable infatuation among his fellow moderns with 'the People' or the 'outcast bohemian': 'Art is nothing to do with the coat you wear. A top-hat can well hold the Sixtine. A cheap cap could hide the image of Kephren' (*BLAST* 1). Second, and more specifically, Lewis's target is the fashion experiments of the Futurists: 'We do not want to make people wear Futurist Patches, or fuss men to take to pink and sky-blue trousers. We are not their wives or tailors'. Implied in both statements are the twin targets of Lewis's attacks on his fellow moderns, especially on Bloomsbury: the artist's fetishisation of modishness and the growing tendency for art to occupy itself with trivia. In Lewisian thinking fashion stands in for both and supplies the motivation as well as the means of attack.

One aspect of Lewis's critique of fashion directs itself against anti-fashion stances which, to his mind, thrive on being fashionable while evading or failing to grasp their own implications in the system of fashion, in the market and commodity culture. Much of his polemic against Bloomsbury falls into this category, his case against the Omega, Fry, and Woolf herself resting on a view of them as a fashionable coterie, on the one hand financially independent of the pressures of the market; on the other in a position to actively use their reputation of vanguard exclusivity to promote a modish and marketable modernism. In this respect, Lewis's critique anticipates, though in highly polemical and tendentious form, the recent critical interest in the economies of modernism, in particular the wealth of scholarly material concerning Bloomsbury as a system of production and consumption with rather complex relations to the market, to mass culture, as well as to processes of promotion and commodification.[3] However, where current criticism emphasises the ambivalence in Bloomsbury's relation to capitalism and the culture of the commodity; the distanciation and critical potential compounding the fascination with the high capitalist phantasmagoria, Lewis's perspective categorically denies any such potential. Central to his indictment of Bloomsbury – which is closely involved with his case against fashion – is the view that Bloomsbury's Paterian devotion to the experience of the moment, along with its aestheticisation of the quotidian and the promotion of vanguard self-fashioning through consumption, amount to an aesthetic praxis which is inscribed by mercantile logic in more ways than its exponents were able to oversee, participating in the fetishisation of commodities and the emphasis on fleeting sensations that define commodity culture.

In Lewis's criticism in *The Caliph's Design* (1919), for instance, Roger Fry emerges as 'our indigenous aesthete', the mind which is engrossed not with the (aesthetic) object as such, but 'with himself and his own sensations', who 'gets excited' about pseudo-aesthetic commodities ('stuffed birds and wax flowers' or 'the tiles in the refreshment room in South Kensington') in the exact same way that advertisement urges us to 'get excited' about goods for purchase (Lewis 1986: 131–5). The artist-collector, moreover, derives from such excitement both financial and sexual returns, able to sell his 'treasures' (the collected birds and flowers) 'for *Twenty Times the Price* paid for them' (ibid.: 132). As an agent in the aesthetic marketplace Fry operates at a characteristically modern intersection of fashion, sex and consumption, Lewis's analysis proclaims. With Fry's brand of promotion the 'aesthetic thrill' obtained by French painting resembles that of a pornographic sideshow, imbued with 'naughtiness' and the 'English philandering flapper-sensibility' (ibid.: 134). On the same pattern, though Lewis does not explicitly comment on this, it may be argued that the Omega's marketing strategy, resting quite clearly on the erotic appeal of its particular brand of consumer goods, draws on the mix of sexology and political economy which commentators from Michael Tratner to Douglas Mao have identified as the core of modernism's declared liberation from Victorian constraints.[4] Against a background of Keynesian economics advocating increased consumption, Vanessa Bell's proposal to hold a celebration bohemian dinner to announce the opening of the Omega in June 1913 seems designed to arouse the appropriate 'consuming desire' which binds the pleasures of sexual liberation to those of vanguard consumption:

> We should get all your disreputable and some of your aristocratic friends to come and after dinner we should repair to Fitzroy Square where would be seen decorated furniture, painted walls etc. There we should all get drunk and dance and kiss. Orders would flow in and the aristocrats would feel sure they were really in the thick of things. If properly done it seems to me it might be a great send off for the business. (Letter VB to RF, 6 Feb. 1913, Tate Gallery Archive, quoted in MacCarthy 1984)

Closely connected with Lewis's 'exposure' of Bloomsbury's aesthetic ventures as highly interested, and erotically charged, economies, is his critique of their fashionable concern with trivia and pseudo-aesthetic objects – of which the most trivial of course would be dress. Artists, Lewis announces, may be divided into two groups depending on their attitude to the material world; interpretive or creative, attitudes which also map on to sexual divisions; feminine or masculine. There is the 'Receptive attitude or the Active and Changing one':

> One artist you see sitting ecstatic on his chair and gazing at a lily, at a portion of the wall-paper, stained and attractive, on the wall of his delightfully for-tuitous room. He is enraptured by all the witty accidents that life, any life, brings to him. He sits before these phenomena enthralled, deliciously moved to an exquisite approval of the very happy juxtaposition of just that section of greenish wall-paper and his beautiful shabby brown trousers hanging from a nail beneath it. (Lewis 1986: 123)

The creative act of this passive, receptive mind is essentially reproduc-tive; a decorative assemblage of available material, all the trivial stuff of the world, for which a recurring metaphor in Lewis's critical discourse is that of the dressmaker. Thus, in his note for the 1915 Vorticist exhi-bition catalogue Lewis places Picasso's recent work 'rather in the same category as a dressmaker', someone who 'matches little bits of stuff he finds lying about' and 'puts no life into the pieces of cloth or paper he sticks side by side' (quoted in Mao 1998: 93). Not surprisingly, the 'colour-matching, match-box-making, dressmaking, chair-painting game' carried on at the Omega is of the same feminine mould as Cubist nature-mortism, though the Workshops present a less '"amusing"' kind of 'amateur tastefulness' than the latter's 'assemblings of bits of news-paper, cloth, paint, buttons, tin, and other débris, stuck on to a plank' (Lewis 1986: 124–5).

Predictably, the artists of the dressmaking variety show themselves unable to intervene in the history of art and its dialectic of fashions. In fact, the failure of Picasso and other Post-Impressionists – the degenera-tion of the masculine creator into the feminine dressmaker – stems from a deficiency in their relation to fashion; and fashions in art, like the atti-tude of the community to art, 'the great mass sensibility of our time', 'is not a thing to be superior about', as Lewis demonstrates in two essays, 'Fashion' and 'The Uses of Fashion' published in *The Caliph's Design*. The 'sensibility of the amateur' is always 'at the mercy of any wind that blows', declares Lewis:

> What we really require are a few men who will *use* Fashion, the ruler of any age, the avenue through which alone that age can be approached to get something out of it, to build something in Fashion's atmosphere which can best flourish there, and which is the best thing that therein could flourish. Picasso and the men associated with him seem to have taken their liberty at once too seriously and not seriously enough. They have taken Fashion, too, too, seriously on the one hand, and on the other they have not used it as they might, or done with it what they could. I do not see amongst them all, except possibly in Matisse, a man who is above Fashion, or one unimpressed by it. (Lewis 1986: 96–7)

What Lewis sees in this failed relation to the sensibility of the mass, in other words, is a degeneration of modernism into modishness; called upon to remedy this state of affairs is a strong creative subjectivity able to deflect fashion to the purposes of a vanguard, truly modern art.

That fashion figures the sensibility of the mass, or of mass psychology, in Lewis's thinking, is hardly surprising, not least given the habitual gendering of the masses and mass culture as feminine in contemporary political, aesthetic and psychological discourse, as shown by Andreas Huyssen and Klaus Theweleit, among others. In Lewis's critique fashion as feminine (or effeminate) pursuit sums up the will that objectifies itself, embodying everything that is wrong with modernism and modern society:

> The Will that 'objectifies' itself . . . is a will to what? To nothing . . . . It produces Charlie Chaplin, the League of Nations, wireless, feminism, Rockefeller; it causes, daily, millions of women to drift in front of, and swarm inside, gigantic clothes-shops in every great capital, buying silk underclothing, cloche-hats, perfume, vanishing cream, vanity-bags and furs. . . . It is a quite aimless, and, from our limited point of view, nonsensical, Will. (Lewis 1927: 312)

The real interest of this figuration begins with Lewis's exploration of fashion as a mass discourse capable of altering daily life, a process to which the 'novel pretension of commerce to be romantic', is central: 'the Money-age has created new values. It has incidentally bought the term Romance' (Lewis 1927: 20). In an age of capitalist imperialism, when 'the true grandeur of a nation, its only glory . . . is to sell to neighbouring nations more clothes and calicoes than we purchase of them', cathectic investment in the operations of the market has become second nature: 'there is nothing so "romantic" as Advertisement' (ibid.: 20, 27). Beyond the dangers of fetishisation, however, the romance of commerce (and of fashion as its driving force) has the effect of de-historicising the individual mind and its experience in the interests of large-scale capitalism. 'The spirit of advertisement and boost', writes Lewis, 'has its feverish being in a world of hyperbolic suggestion', a world in which only a single temporality exists. The world of Advertisement and Fashion is a one-day world, a series of de-historicised presents, each temporal entity complete in itself, with no before or after, 'no fundamental exterior reference at all' (ibid.: 28). The influence of this on the structure of human life and on human psychology occurs as the 'average man is invited to slice his life into a series of one-day lives, regulated by the clock of fashion' (ibid.: 28). Reduced to a 'containing frame for a . . . sequence of ephemerids, roughly organised into what he calls his "personality"', the human being experiences life in the form of accentless serial repetition, 'each segment, each *fashion-day* (as the day of this new creature could be called) . . . organically self-sufficing' (ibid.: 28). Predictably, an intellectual, historicising approach is not at all in the interest of Advertisement; on the contrary, the perfect response to the here-and-now of the Fashion-day and its 'giant hyperbolic close-up of a moment' requires '*the perfect sensationalist* – what people picture to themselves, for instance, as the perfect American' (ibid.: 28–9).

Lewis's concern with the fetishisation and romantic investment of fashion has certain points of resemblance to the thoughts of Benjamin discussed in previous chapters. Likewise, a degree of concurrence in their critique of the philosophical underpinnings of fashion's temporality may be observed. For Lewis fashion's close-up on the moment is closely related to the Bergsonian *durée*: 'Time for the Bergsonian or relativist is fundamentally sensation . . . . It is the glorification of the life-of-the-moment, with no reference beyond itself and no absolute or universal value' (Lewis 1927: 27). What the 'pretentious metaphysic' of Bergsonian time-philosophy boils down to, in other words, is no more than the metaphysic of the Money-Age, of advertisement and fashion – a view which is not far from Benjamin's critique of the Bergsonian *durée* as *Erlebnis*, the 'passing moment' that 'struts about in the borrowed garb of experience'. Where Bergson, in Benjamin's critique, rejects any historical determination of mind and thus omits the experience that conditions his own philosophy – 'the inhospitable, blinding age of big-scale industrialism' (Benjamin 1998: 157) – one may argue that what Wyndham Lewis supplies is precisely historical determination, in the shape of modern commodity culture and consumer psychology. Where Benjamin fastens on fashion's redeeming features, however, discovering its radical potential in the way it allows the object world to encroach upon the subject, for Lewis fashion for the most part remains the image of *Schein* and, as we shall see, of the modern collapse of distinctions between subjective and objective worlds.

With reference to what has just been said, one may well point out that what Lewis supplies in his discussion of the modern concentration on the moment of sensation is not historical determination but over-determination. Thus, what he designates in polemical shorthand as the modern 'Time-mind' stands in for a massive epistemological shift the effects of which Lewis discovers through a continuum of discourses and artistic practices. In response to this shift, the project of *Time and Western Man* presents itself as a comprehensive critique of conceptions of time which, to Lewis's mind, are destined to wreak havoc on the individual mind's grasp of the objective world, demonstrating 'how the "timelessness" of einsteinian physics, and the time-obsessed flux of Bergson, merge in each other; and how they have conspired to produce, upon the innocent plane of popularization, a sort of mystical time-cult' (Lewis 1927: 3). In parallel to the way in which advertising and the spectacle of commodities impact upon the individual's mode of perception, the Time-philosophies threaten to alter everyday life and the common-sense conceptions of the external world. With plans afoot 'to teach relativity-physics and the relativist world-view everywhere in our schools', and 'vast propaganda . . . carried on by popular treatises and articles to impose this picture upon the plain-man and the simple common-sense intelligence', the '"common-sense" of tomorrow . . . the one general *sense* of things that we all hold in *common* – is to be trans- formed into the terms of this highly complex disintegrated world, of private "times" and specific amputated "spaces," of serial-groups and "events" . . . in place of "things"' (ibid.: 432–3).

As we have seen, Lewis aligns fashion with mass psychology but also with the high culture of the bohemian avant-garde. His argument in *Time and Western Man* aims to demonstrate that this double alignment is not a contradiction in terms, showing that the internalist aesthetic of the avant-garde and its connections with popular physics, aesthetic philosophy and economic theory (Russell, Bergson, Keynes) have come into being both as a product and a justification of collectivist discourses which include mass democracy and mass capitalism. Michael Tratner's *Modernism and Mass Politics* has shown the connections between modernism's communal or collectivist aesthetic, collectivist political theories, and the theories of the mass mind that emerged in the first two decades of the twentieth century. If modernist experiment aimed to disrupt individual minds and write in the idiom of the mass unconscious, to do so was, as Tratner writes, tantamount to breaking free of the Western metaphysics of individuals and distinct objects (Tratner 1995: 6). Lewis's concern is precisely with the threat posed by such alignment: the coincidence between modernist aesthetics, modern science and mass market advertising strategies. Thus the turn to states of interiority in modern art and writing provides Lewis not only with yet another example of the workings of the Time-mind, but of the coincidence between the Time-mind and the advertising principle of competitive industry: 'the giant, hyperbolic close-up on the moment'. Where the philosophers provide this advertising principle with its metaphysical super-structure, artists and writers translate it into an aesthetic. The sculpture of Auguste Rodin – 'those flowing, structureless, lissom, wave-lined pieces of com- mercial marble' which, incidentally, 'infest the tables and mantelpieces of Kensington and Mayfair, and are to be encountered in great profusion in the shop windows of Bond Street' are 'Bergson's *élan vital* translated into marble' (Lewis 1987: 96). Their equivalents in literature would be the equally decadent internalist methods employed by Woolf, Joyce and Lawrence: 'the romantic snapshotting of the wandering stream of the Unconscious' (ibid.: 104), and the mythology of the moment of *en bloc* intuition experienced by the embodied mind – the mind returned to its 'originary' relationship to the modern 'liberated' body.

What is wrong with modernism, from Lewis's perspective, is that it is under the sway of fashion in more than one sense. Fashion, fashionable art and fashionable time-philosophies are all engaged, to Lewis's mind, on the same project, the same conspiratorial politics: destroying mind and installing in its stead the unconscious, the collective mind, mass-democracy; a sensing in common which is no more than sensationalism and which renders the subject passive in the face of the world, incapable of distinguishing between the subjective and the objective, imbued with a weak, restless will whose image is the female shopper or the aestheti-cist's mythification of the pseudo-object. Advertising supplies the tech-nology, and fashion the practice, that allows the Time-mind to perform its destructive work on daily life, while the art *à la mode* of bohemians and 'party lighthouses' feeds (and feeds on) the fetishising, feminine and dehistoricising aesthetic of the Money-Age (of which fashion is the mechanics as well as the metonym), without seeing that industrial over-production is the historical cause behind imperialism as well as war.[5]

Lewis's anti-fashion critique is extreme, monolithic and conspirato-rial, but not without relevance or interest, providing a context for his attacks on Woolf as well as for Woolf's own writing on fashion, the com-modity culture and the epistemic shift with which Lewis is concerned. In apropos of the recent reappraisals of the relations among modernism, advertising, spectacle and commodification, Lewis's critique helps us think about the particular role played by fashion in these relations, while also raising some pertinent questions concerning the relation between fashions in various fields and the marketplace for art and writing. Previous chapters have shown Woolf critical of fashion's serialisation and standardisation, its hierarchies of gender and class, its processes of interpellation and imposition of corporeal discipline. Equally, she seems to be aware of its performative, historicising and dialectical potential. There are moments in her fiction, as in *The Waves* or 'Street Haunting' when fashion unveils the nakedness of spleen in the midst of phantas-magoria. In light of Lewis's case against fashion, however, it is pertinent to ask whether there are aspects of fashion that Woolf overlooks or fails to engage with; whether her work moves beyond an alternation between phantasmagoria and spleen into more rigorous forms of analysis of the commodity culture and its structures of experience.

There can be no doubt that Lewis's polemics against Woolf grows out of his anti-fashion stance. When Woolf appears in 'Victorian muslins' as the literary snob Rhoda Hyman in *The Roaring Queen* (1936), complete with the 'drooping intellect-ravaged exterior of the lanky and sickly lady' (Meyers 1980: 165), the rhetoric is still the anti-aestheticism of the 1913 'Round Robin' Letter in which Lewis famously washed his hands of the Omega 'Prettiness, with its mid-Victorian languish of the neck' – 'the Post-What-Not fashionableness of its draperies' not withstanding (Lewis 1963: 49). Lewis's reading of Woolf's quarrel with the 'materialists', in 'Mind and Matter on the Plane of a Literary Controversy', was concerned with the economic considerations (to his mind) behind this quarrel and its place in promoting Woolf's brand of fashionable art. His reading of 'Mr. Bennett and Mrs. Brown', as he makes clear in a 1934 letter to *The Spectator*, was deliberately focused on the machinations of Woolf's public self-fashioning: her making as an ultra-feminine icon. His criticism was destructive since it was concerned not with the 'footlight illusion of the prima donna, so much as the latter in process of slimming, voice-production, and make-up' (ibid.: 223).[6] From this vantage point he concludes that the quarrel is not only insignificant – a 'boy and girl' quarrel – but constructed, typical of the advertising strategies of the 'minor personalities' or 'party lighthouses' of Woolf's calibre, who are busy promoting a 'bogus time' in place of common-sense, historical time as a means of accommodating their own *salon* scale work, and who want us to believe in the necessity of a 'season of failures and fragments'; an inevitable condition of tentative and limited output. Thus, Lewis writes, 'just as the orthodox economists have, consciously or not, from interested motives, maintained in its place the traditional picture – that of . . . some *absolute* obstructing the free circulation of the good things in life' – so the people, like Woolf, 'who have been most influential in literary criticism for a number of years now, have been interested in the propagation of this account of things' (Lewis 1987: 138). Moreover, the chief selling-point of Woolf's modernism – its retreat from Bennett's 'last button' of 'the fashion of the hour' towards a spiritual internalism which 'peeps out' at the fascinating spectacles and commodities of the exterior world – is in fact the perfect match of the Edwardian materialist: a feminine excitement at the goings-on of the world which adds nothing to the understanding of the Money-Age propounded by Edwardians or late Victorians (ibid.: 139, 133).

More than a decade before Lewis's attack in 'Mind and Matter', at an early stage of Woolf's career, we find her exploring the possibilities of an internalist approach in a fable about modern writing and character construction which anticipates the discussion in 'Mr. Bennett and

Mrs. Brown'. The story 'An Unwritten Novel' (1920), places Woolf's writer-narrator in a railway carriage opposite an elderly woman of the anonymous Mrs Brown type, for which the narrator – consciousness in full flow – proceeds to imagine a life-story. Intent to uncover the other's truth, the narrator literally incorporates it, 'catching' the woman's most characteristic (and seemingly revealing) symptom, an 'itch' which causes her to twitch and rub her 'stain of sin', to feel plucked and raw 'like the damp chicken's skin in the poulterer's shop-window' (*CSF*: 114–15). Among the narrator's 'choice of crimes' to account for such a permanent stain, she opts for the 'cheapest' of all:

> Passing down the streets of Croydon twenty years ago, the violet loops of ribbon in the draper's window spangled in the electric light catch her eye. She lingers –past six. Still by running she can reach home. She pushes through the glass swing door. It's sale time. Shallow trays brim with ribbons. She pauses, pulls this, fingers that with the raised roses on it – no need to choose, no need to buy, and each tray with its surprises. 'We don't shut till seven', and then it *is* seven. She runs, she rushes, home she reaches, but too late. Neighbours – the doctor –baby brother – the kettle – scalded – hospital – dead – or only the shock of it, the blame? . . . 'Yes,' she seems to nod to me, 'it's the thing I did.' (*CSF*: 115)

From this moment of guilty consumption a host of tragedies ensue – spinsterhood and poverty, the 'shrunken shreds of all the vanishing universe – love, life, faith, husband, children, I know not what splendours and pageantries glimpsed in girlhood' (*CSF*: 120); a life left to finding consolation in bead mats and underlinen, the single muffin and the bald dog. The sartorial both hinges and unhinges the narrative: at the end of the story the truth that was somatically established turns out to be false, 'Mrs. Brown' departs with her mystery intact, leaving the narrator to contemplate 'something queer in her cloak as it blows' (ibid.: 121).

In *The Gender of Modernity*, Rita Felski writes about modern cultural anxieties surrounding the figure of the 'insatiable female shopper', and the fear that such 'consuming desire' (in Lawrence Birken's term) 'would have disturbing and unforeseeable effects, reaching out to subvert the social fabric and undermine patriarchal authority within the family' (Felski 1995: 62–5). The sentimental story Woolf lets her narrator construct in pursuit of elusive characters and storylines, clearly parodies such moralising cultural narratives of the market, of the social consequences of guilty consumption and women's insatiable desire for fashionable dress. Douglas Mao has pointed out how Woolf's novels of the 1920s (*Mrs Dalloway* most clearly) recuperate certain forms of consumption by rewriting them as production, thus supporting a reappraisal of the leisure class and women in general, whose history has been shaped by the idea of non-productivity (Mao 1998: 40–1). What we see in 'An Unwritten Novel' stands in contrast (though not necessarily contradiction) to such reappraisal: here is Woolf undermining society's favourite story about women and the culture of fashion with an irony which both assumes and resists established discourses about fashion and mercantile logic, discourses (of which Lewis is one exponent) which posit fashion as the primary force of the market, acting upon individuals and social structures alike, with the female as its first and natural victim.

Woolf's rejection of such narratives hardly makes her, as Lewis would have it, a player in the market who promotes the aestheticist's precious fascination with the transactions of the world 'out there'. Her analysis of 'trade' and its spectacles around 1930, on commission, ironically, for *Good Housekeeping*, and still a few years before Lewis's public dissection of her 'materialism', shows her an adept and sophisticated analyst of the market and its interactions with bodies and minds. Perhaps the first of these essays, 'The Docks of London', has something of the aestheticist's surprised fascination with commerce's strictly utilitarian temper, by which 'use produces beauty' merely 'as a by-product' (*CDM*: 112): 'Oddities, beauties, rarities may occur, but if so, they are instantly tested for their mercantile value' (ibid.: 110). Mammoth ivory, though it has 'lain frozen in Siberian ice for fifty thousand years', is less durable than elephant tusks, and so of less value. 'One tusk makes a billiard ball, another serves for a shoe-horn – every commodity in the world has been examined and graded according to its use and value. Trade is ingenious and indefatigable beyond the bounds of the imagination' (ibid.: 111). The perspective is clearly different from Lewis's. Where Lewis laments the deterioration in bodily skill and the disappearance of the body-sized experiential world following on the Money-Age, Woolf admires the interaction between commerce, technology and human bodies, the readiness with which 'forethought' (of use- and exchange-value) is translated into 'aptness' (of buildings and machinery), as well as 'dexterity' and skill (of workers). The world she depicts is not a dehumanised world in which the object has taken possession of the subject and the powers of rhetoric have been enlisted by the market. For Woolf, the English language adapts itself to 'the needs of commerce' with the same aptness and dexterity as technologies and bodies, and the subject retains its centrality in the midst of the object world:

> It is we – our tastes, our fashions, our needs – that make the cranes dip and swing, that call the ships from the sea. Our body is their master . . . Trade watches us anxiously to see what new desires are beginning to grow in us, what new dislikes. (*CDM*: 112)

If such humanism in the midst of commerce would strike Lewis as both naive and misguided, the companion piece to 'The Docks of London', 'Oxford Street Tide', handles the question of the subject–object relation in the commodity culture with a sophistication that is more than equal to Lewis's conspiratorial and monolithic theory. How transindividual desires come into being and play themselves out, is the topic of this second essay, written in a tone which is constative and ironic rather than 'fascinated', addressing a reader as much in the know about the goings-on in the marketplace as is the essayist herself. From the beginning consumption emerges as stratified and class-based, with fashion as both the foundation and the driving force of the modern economy. In the 'garishness and gaudiness' of Oxford Street the wife of a 'small clerk in a bank' comes to 'linger and loiter', 'grab and pounce with disgusting greed', while the 'more sublime rites' of fashion are performed discreetly elsewhere (*CDM*: 113, 117). Entrepreneurs and merchants

> are overwhelmingly conscious that unless they can devise an architecture that shows off the dressing-case, the Paris frock, the cheap stockings, and the jar of bath salts to perfection, their palaces, their mansions and motor cars and the little villas out at Croydon and Surbiton where their shop assistants live, not so badly after all, with a gramophone and wireless, and money to spend at the movies – all this will be swept to ruin. (*CDM*: 116)

The give and take of the exchange system has its history, as both the reader and the essayist knows. There is nothing fundamentally new about the system of debts and allegiances that governs the relations between worker and profiteer in the market place, even if the worker is refashioned as consumer and the 'largesse' demonstrated by the present-day aristocracy may take a slightly different form. The modern monument or public building devoted to the sacred transactions of commerce is imbued with the logic of the fashion-machine: pinnacles and façades with the ephemerality of film sets 'made of yellow cardboard and sugar icing' or the restless excess of the baroque,

> crush[ing] together in one wild confusion the styles of Greece, Egypt, Italy, America . . . in their effort to persuade the multitude that here unending beauty, ever fresh, ever new, very cheap and within the reach of everybody, bubbles up every day of the week from an inexhaustible well. (*CDM*: 116)

In the 'breeding ground', the 'forcing house of sensation', that constitutes the commodity spectacle, everything works on the principle of commodification. Human tragedy is sold as sensation, hyperbolically advertised on news-boards in Lewis's 'giant close-up on the moment', instantly consumed by the crowd as with one tongue, one mind; one 'glutinous slab that takes impressions' (*CDM*: 114). The 'constant' and the transitory of human desires are brought together on 'a string of parcels' – as when a shopper adds a tortoise, one of the constant desires of human nature, as constant as that of 'the moth for the star', to her handful of purchases (ibid.: 114). Most ironically of all, in the market-place even self-reflection is refashioned as commodity, the critique of the *flâneur* as an act of consumption. The knowing consumer must await the conclusion to the essayist's reflections 'until some adroit shopkeeper has caught on to the idea and opened cells for solitary thinkers hung with green plush' and equipped with every convenience designed to 'induce thought and reflection' (ibid.: 117). With such knowingness Woolf confronts the specter of the 'moralist' that moves through her essay, a (Lewisian) incompetent reader of culture and its powers of implication and recuperation.

If by 1930 Woolf possesses all the sophistication of analysis that Lewis's critique denies her, returning to some of her early stories serves to re-open the question of the aestheticist's passive (unhistorical and de-politicised) infatuation with the object-world. 'Solid Objects', composed in the years between 1918 and 1920, explores the protagonist John's increasing absorption by the reality of found objects, an obsession which deflects him from a career in politics and eventually from participation in the social world. The objects that grasp his attention are waste prod-ucts emptied of the history of their use as well as the imprints of their user: pieces of china, glass, or iron, broken and transformed – though not 'in some trifling domestic accident, without purpose or character' (*CSF*: 105). The aura they exhibit is not of past lives or civilisations, but of ontological, metaphysical mystery. What possesses the artist-collector is the hope that some agency or pattern behind the objects and the accidents of their shaping will eventually reveal itself.

For Douglas Mao, Woolf's story answers to a socio-economic moment in which art is refigured as solid object and consumption as production (Mao 1998: 39–40). However valid Mao's historicisation, it should be emphasised, first, that 'Solid Objects' explores, rather than simply endorses, the collector's aesthetic project; further, that the par-ticular production and reconfiguration taking place through Woolf's writing at this historical moment also applies to the right to define social and political realities. The political world from which the artist-collector retreats is distinctly and ironically masculine, caught up with the asser-tion of virility and self-importance. Thus, as soon as the word 'politics' is uttered,

the mouths, noses, chins, little moustaches, tweed caps, rough boots, shoot-ing coats, and check stockings of the two speakers became clearer and clearer;

the smoke of their pipes went up into the air; nothing was so solid, so living, hard, red, hirsute and virile as these two bodies for miles and miles of sea and sandhill. (*CSF*: 102)

That Woolf's exploration of orders of reality is fundamentally involved with a critique of a patriarchal politico-epistemic order and its valuations, is further illuminated by an earlier story, 'The Mark on the Wall' (1917), which would seem to be addressing the political implications of the epistemic shift – of relativity-physics and time – of which Lewis was so strongly suspicious.[7] The story is in a related category to 'Solid Objects' and 'An Unwritten Novel' in taking an imagined object, a non-object, as the centre of aesthetic production – the stream of consciousness of a mind sinking away from the surface of 'hard separate facts' to the depths of leisured, experimental speculation (*CSF*: 85); a descent into 'the great River Flux', of which, in Lewis's words, 'both Einstein and Bergson are river officials' (Lewis 1927: 414). In this case the non-object at the source of the stream is a mark on the wall which, at the end of the story, is revealed to be a snail. In *Time and Western Man* Lewis evokes the common-sense object-ness of a wallpaper in defence against the disunity and impermanence consequent upon the relativist view. Where the post-relativist (Bertrand Russell) would have us accept the metaphysics involved in the belief that 'the wall-paper fixed upon the wall in January' is the same entity as 'the wall-paper next December', Lewis, true to form, expounds upon the disastrous consequences of turning 'this simple object hanging on our walls . . . into a very complex temporal "event"-series of discrete and rigidly dissociated "appearances"' (Lewis 1927: 427–30). Woolf's mark on the wall would seem to exists in affirmation of Einsteinian relativity-physics and its structural and political implications, a fuzzy rather than solid object serving to reveal the inaccuracy of perception, the limits of knowledge, the haphazardness of life. In the story, the perspective opened up by relativism is one of anti-patriarchal particularity, as opposed to the absolutism of masculinist (and militarist) 'Generalisations'; the world of Sunday luncheons in which there is 'a rule for everything':

The rule for tablecloths . . . was that they should be made of tapestry with little yellow compartments marked upon them, such as you may see in photographs of the carpets in the corridors of the royal palaces. Tablecloths of a different kind were not real tablecloths. How shocking, and yet how wonderful it was to discover that these real things . . . were not entirely real, were indeed half phantoms, and the damnation which visited the disbeliever in them was only a sense of illegitimate freedom. What now takes the place of those real things I wonder, those real standard things? Men perhaps, should you be a woman; the masculine point of view which governs our lives, which sets the standard . . . which soon, one may hope, will be laughed into the dustbin where the phantoms go . . . leaving us all with an intoxicating sense of illegitimate freedom – if freedom exists . . . . (*CSF*: 86)

Approximately a decade later, while revising *To the Lighthouse* (with its 'subject and object and the nature of reality', *TTL*: 28) in September 1926, Woolf writes a story which picks up on the aesthetising approach to the object world of the earlier stories, while pointing forward to the modern exchange object and its economies in 'The Docks of London' and 'Oxford Street Tide'. What makes this story really interesting, however, is the way in which, like 'An Unwritten Novel' it makes a sartorial object the point on which its analysis turns. 'Moments of Being: "Slater's Pins Have No Points"' is a story which apparently represents all that Lewis detests about fashionable modernism: the internalist method, the close-up on the moment, the 'stream' set in motion by the most inconsequential of objects, and all the unsavouriness of lesbian eroticism.[8] The 'moment' in this short fiction is the time it takes for a pin to fall to the floor and its owner to retrieve it, as well as the time it takes for homoerotic desire to make itself felt. The object in question is the pin used to fasten a rose to a young woman's dress. As a conventionally coded sartorial sign a rose pinned to a dress indicates virginity and marriageability; the currency and value of its wearer within an economy of exchange. A pin by itself is a negligible object, cheap and trivial, yet replete with secrets and intimacies, used to hold together garments and objects in an impermanent fixing always suggesting the possibility of unfixing. The unpinning that occurs in the story as the rose comes unfastened and the pin drops to the floor, as Kathryn Simpson (2005) also argues, is that of story-levels and sexual economies, the movement of currency from a heterosexual exchange system to a homosexual one.

The incident which precipitates the flux of young Fanny Wilmot's mind is not the dropping of the pin itself but the unexpected response of her piano teacher Miss Craye:

> 'Slater's pins have no points – don't you always find that?' said Miss Craye, turning round as the rose fell out of Fanny Wilmot's dress, and Fanny stooped with her ears full of the music, to look for the pin on the floor'. (*CSF*: 215)

The words in fact give Fanny 'an extraordinary shock' which stems from the class of object a pin represents, its mass-produced cheapness, suggesting transactions involving 'coppers', and the implication of a slovenly dresser. Buying pins makes one ordinary, involved in the same sordidly intimate transactions as anyone else:

Did Miss Craye actually go to Slater's and buy pins then, Fanny Wilmot
asked herself, transfixed for a moment? Did she stand at the counter waiting
like anybody else, and was she given a bill with coppers wrapped in it, and
did she slip them into her purse and then, an hour later, stand by her dressing
table and take out the pins? What need had she of pins? For she was not so
much dressed as cased, like a beetle compactly in its sheath, blue in winter,
green in summer. (*CSF*: 215)

The erotic implications of the incident are present from the start, both in
the suggestion of sexual 'deflowering' as the rose falls to the floor, and
in the connotations attaching to the pin as sartorial accessory, slipped
into the purse and taken out, privately, at the dressing table. These are
implications that the fiction continues to tease out, and Fanny naively
and persistently misreads. If the aim of Miss Craye's speech act is to
forge the intimacy that precedes seduction, this is a move which is lost
on Fanny. Speculating on Miss Craye's meaning, Fanny decides that her
words must have been uttered in an attempt 'to break the spell that had
fallen on the house . . . the pane of glass which separated them from
other people': 'None of the Crayes had ever married. She knew nothing
about pins – nothing whatever' (*CSF*: 216). The Crayes, Julia and her
late brother Julius, are what Lewis's naif Daniel Boleyn in *The Apes
of God* would have conscientiously logged as 'minor Apes': a would-
be artist and an archaeologist-collector (of 'green Roman glasses and
things . . . in cases') with a decidedly 'aesthetic' outlook on life. This is
the impression Fanny retains and conveys through the story she imagines for them in her moment of suspended time. The something 'queer'
that attaches to the Crayes, she ascribes to the Aestheticist's dilemma:
the passionate desire for the frozen moment – to arrest time, to possess
beauty; 'the daisy in the grass, fires, frost on the window pane', and
the knowledge of the futility of the attempt – 'you break, you pass, you
go' (ibid.: 216). Even when Miss Craye picks up Fanny's flower and
'crushe[s] it . . . voluptously in her smooth, veined hands' in an erotically
charged moment, Fanny interprets her action in aesthetic rather than
erotic terms, fantasising herself, as flower, in the role of poetic symbol
– the unattainable in art, the impermanence of life – 'like the flower,
conscious to her finger tips of youth and brilliance' (ibid.: 217).

Miss Craye's ouvertures and innuendoes fall to the floor one by one
as Fanny pursues her aestheticist fantasy. Julia's 'odd smile' and the
'extraordinary look' fixed on Fanny as she says that the only use of
men is for protection, has Fanny imagine conventional scenarios of
heterosexual love for her teacher: proposals and rejected suitors, 'her
rose flowering with chaste passion in the bosom of her muslin dress',
while her reason for declining marriage is that of the artist: 'her right

to go and look at things when they are at their best' (*CSF*: 217, 219). The proposal scene Fanny imagines as an offer of marriage interrupting aesthetic contemplation: 'views of rivers were important to her'; Julia's refusal speaks of the artist's frustration: 'I can't have it, I can't possess it' (ibid.: 218). Like Lewis's precious Aesthete, the Ape who refigures life as art (or, in Douglas Mao's terms, consumption as production) by erasing the boundaries between them, Miss Craye's life, in Fanny's idealist construction, is centred on moments of significant being, adorning her as a 'necklace of memorable days, which was not too long for her to be able to recall this one or that one; this view, that city; to finger it, to feel it, to savour, sighing, the quality that made it unique' (ibid.: 219).

Finally retrieving the pin opens up a 'moment' of aesthetic discovery for Fanny too, in which Miss Craye, silhouetted against 'the sharp square of the window', appears as work of art, 'something she had made which surrounded her, which was her', a being dedicated to beauty and the transformation of life into art (*CSF*: 220). The real ending to the fiction, however, comes as a moment of sexual possession:

> She saw Julia open her arms; saw her blaze; saw her kindle. Out of the night she burnt like a dead white star. Julia kissed her. Julia possessed her. 'Slater's pins have no points,' Miss Craye said, laughing queerly and relaxing her arms, as Fanny Wilmot pinned the flower to her breast with trembling fingers. (*CSF*: 220)

Fanny's initial 'deflowering' – the opening disjunction of pin and flower as objects and signs – sets in motion a counter-narrative which runs through Fanny's mythologising reflections, ironically undermining the Aestheticist construction; what she evades the perceptive reader sees – even if the less knowing (less fashionable?) reader (*Forum*'s editor) apparently did not. Fixing the rose to Fanny's dress, the pin is involved in a heterosexual economy of exchange; unpinned it is re-thought as a cheap and mundane object of transaction, implicating Miss Craye in another, materialist and gendered economy, which entails being 'left badly off . . . at her brother's death', and pretending to be taking on 'one or two pupils' merely 'as a special favour' to a friend (*CSF*: 215). As feminine, eroticised use-object the pin is invested with desire, implicated in a scene of same-sex initiation, and implicating the reader in a system of homoerotic exchange. Woolf's pin does not represent sex in the way that a hat represents the female genitals (or a tie the penis) in contemporary surrealist and dadaist experiments, but it does suggest the prick of desire that sets things in motion.[9]

'Slater's Pins', like 'An Unwritten Novel', shows Woolf interested in the work performed by an inconsequential object. In both cases, the sartorial object or accessory opens up for analysis of symbolic and monetary economies, serving to disrupt familiar narratives and mythologies. 'An Unwritten Novel' ironically undermines the popular narrative of female 'consuming desire'; 'Slater's Pins' pricks a hole in the mythology of the Aesthete and the separation of aesthetic from economic and sexual domains. The question opened up by Lewis's anti-fashion critique concerned the nature and complexity of Woolf's understanding of the commodity culture and its structures of experience: whether her approach to fashion as market machine and mass discourse moves beyond an alternation between fascination and disgust into more rigorous forms of analysis. The essays and short fiction examined in this chapter clearly suggest that it does. To the extent that Woolf's aesthetic is defined by subscription to the 'Time-mind', popular relativism, and the close-up on the moment, this entails neither an eclipse of the object world nor the evasion of money and politics. The turn to relativism liberates a critical, anti-authoritarian perspective, not a disintegration into private realities and percepts. Contrary to Lewis's argument, the writing that ensues from it does not create a time outside history, installing pseudo-objects in the place of the real, and a fashioned 'personality' in place of the historical subject.

Woolf uses fashion, 'the ruler of any age', though not in the way Lewis had in mind when in 1919 he called upon 'a few men' to do so. Within Lewis's cultural critique, fashion as mass discourse signifies the end of mind and its common-sense grasp of the object world; for Woolf fashion is a phenomenon of the mass – linked to the culture of advertisement and the operations of the market, but never a monolithic discourse. In Lewis's 'externalist' aesthetic, clothes can function only as satire; ironically, with Woolf's 'internalist' approach, clothes emerge as commodities within an economy and signs within a socio-semiotic system. Placed within this complex perspective, clothes as well as fashion become instrumental in subtle analyses of the relations between the individual and the structures of experience defined by the culture of the commodity, giving the cue for perceptive explorations of the relationship between subject and object that so deeply worried Wyndham Lewis, rather than signifying its imminent collapse.

Notes

1. Lewis 1987: 103, 132. According to Lewis's biographer Jeffrey Meyers, Clive and Vanessa Bell appear in this satire as the Jonathan Bells, Vanessa portrayed as 'a picturesque plein-air drudge . . . an indistinct Chelsea gypsy',

a 'West End bohemian after the manner of Augustus John'. See Lewis 1965: 88, 131–2, 562–3. The character Horace Zagreus was apparently a composite of George Borrow and Horace de Vere Cole, Adrian Stephen's friend who took part in the *Dreadnought* hoax (Meyers 1980: 160, 165).

2. It is interesting to observe in this connection that MacCarthy places the Omega work in the context of the more frivolous of Bloomsbury activities – the playfulness of fancy-dress parties and the *Dreadnought* hoax.

3. Woolf's complex and contradictory relations with the market have been noted by a number of scholars commenting on the ambivalences involved in Woolf's obvious fascination with consumption and commodity culture, compounded by a class- and gender-based critique of patriarchal capitalism; equally the potential contradictions of a promotional policy which aligns itself with *Vogue* on the one hand while evading literary commodification through a privately owned press on the other. For discussion of these and related matters, see, for instance, Wicke 1994 and 1996; Abbott 1992; Mao 1998; Simpson 2005; Mahood 2002; Garrity 1999 and 2000; Hankins 2000; Marcus, L. 1996.

4. Douglas Mao, with reference to Michael Tratner and others, points out that 'the economic theories that modernists found most intriguing (those of Maynard Keynes and C. H. Douglas, for example) advocated an increase in consumption as the remedy for economic ills, imperialism and war'. Mao also supports Tratner's view that 'modernism's declared liberation from Victorian constraints owed much both to political economy and to sexology, which lent new respectability to what Lawrence Birken names . . . "consuming desire"' (Mao 1998: 18–19).

5. In his chapter on Woolf in *Men Without Art* Lewis writes with ironic circumspection: 'while I am ready to agree that the intrinsic importance of Mrs. Woolf may be exaggerated by her friends, I cannot agree that as a symbolic landmark – a sort of party-lighthouse – she has not a very real significance' (Lewis 1987: 132).

6. Lewis was writing in reply to Stephen Spender's review of *Men Without Art* in *The Spectator* of 19 October 1934, which described Lewis's attack on Woolf as unnecessary and 'malicious'.

7. I am not suggesting that Woolf wrote this story somehow 'in response' to Einsteinian relativity-physics, or that she was indeed familiar with the theory of relativity at the time of writing. Though, according to Michael Whitworth, Leonard Woolf was noting the revolutionary impact of Freud, Rutherford and Einstein as early as 1911, as Whitworth also observes, non-specialist accounts of the theories began to appear in Britain only in 1918, in large numbers from late 1919, when the experimental proof of Einstein's General theory was made public (Whitworth 2001). Scholarly work by Gillian Beer, Michael Whitworth, Holly Henry, Anne Banfield and others, has revealed the extent of Woolf's borrowing from scientific disciplines and vocabularies, including physics, but the eclectic and allusive nature of this borrowing suggests that it serves largely as confirmation of ideas, metaphors and intuitions already in circulation, furthering ideological as well as epistemological speculations. The 'relativity' of Woolf's story is philosophical rather than physical, indirectly anticipating Lewis's critique of the popular conflation of philosophy and physics and its alignment with ideology, though not in the

manner Lewis predicted. Where, for Lewis, the outcome of 'relativity' is a threatening fragmentation, for Woolf it is a liberating condition of particularity and difference.

8. This short fiction was published in *Forum* (New York) in January 1928. Woolf refers to it in letters as 'a nice little story about Sapphism' and 'my little Sapphist story of which the Editor has not seen the point' (*L*: 3, 397, 431; *CSF*: Notes and Appendices, p. 306). Recent critical response has divided on the question of whether the story is of lesbian initiation or of misrecognition. For instance, Janet Winston ('Reading Influences: Homoeroticism and Mentoring') places it in a tradition of Sapphist mentoring narratives, while to Susan Clements ('The Point of "Slater's Pins": Misrecognition and the Narrative Closet') the story is a study of the cultural and narrative forces through which lesbians come to misrecognise their sexual identity. Kathryn Simpson ('Economies and Desire: Gifts and the Market in "Moments of Being: 'Slater's Pins Have No Points'"') offers a highly perceptive reading of the homoerotic implications of this story in light of textual interconnections between monetary, libidinal, and gift economies, arguing persuasively that a feminine gift economy operates alongside market economies in Woolf's text to generate homoerotic desire as well as a sense of resistance to sexual and economic conventions.

9. See, for example, Man Ray's photograph for Tristan Tzara's essay 'On a Certain Automatism of Taste' (1933), both of which examine the similarity in appearance of the female genitalia and certain shapes of women's hats. See also Lehmann's *Tigersprung* (2000: 354–8).

Chapter 5

Civilised Minds, Fashioned Bodies and the Nude Future

In her study of twentieth-century performance cultures, *Theatre, Sacrifice, Ritual* (2005), Erika Fischer-Lichte traces a transition, defining European arts and academia between the turn of the twentieth century and the First World War, from what she understands as predominantly 'textual' to prevailingly 'performative' modes of cultural and artistic articulation. Performatives are understood in this context as acts that bring something into being; they are not representational or referential; what they bring forth 'comes into being only by way of the performative act'; further, 'they mean what they bring forth – and, in this way, constitute reality' (Fischer-Lichte 2005: 27). Rather than speech-acts, Fischer-Lichte's focus is on bodily acts: specifically the potential of bodily acts to bring forth a community, and 'the potential of a collective to execute performative acts that . . . bring forth culture' (ibid.: 27, 32).

Among the premises for this analysis is the observation that, at the end of the nineteenth century, modern European culture conceptualised and represented itself as a 'text' culture, defined in contradistinction to 'primitive', 'performative' cultures based in spectacle and ritual performance. The shift Fischer-Lichte accounts for involves a re-evaluation of the relations between 'primitive' and 'modern' cultures, but also, as she expertly shows, of 'the relationship between individual and community in modern society, and the role and function of the human body with regard to culture' (Fischer-Lichte 2005: 13). Such re-evaluations were taking place across the humanities, in theatre studies, religious studies, anthropology and the classics, converging and connecting with certain pressing concerns about modern society expressed by contemporary social commentators: the increasing alienation and fragmentation of perspective following from the specialisation and division of labour; the potentially explosive conflict between the cult of individualism, on the one hand, and the growth of anonymous masses, on the other. The question, as posed for instance by Emile Durkheim in 1898, was of how individual and community were interconnected in a society on the verge of disintegration, and what forms of communal integration might be entrusted to reverse and hopefully heal the disintegrating process.

Fischer-Lichte's study demonstrates how the European elite responded to such urgent issues by rethinking classical culture as a model of performative community, and by turning to the performative mode of festival and mass spectacle, as with Max Reinhardt's Theatre of the Five Thousand and the reopening of the Olympic Games in 1896. My interest here, however, is not in the elaboration of new rituals but in the redefinitions to which two relationships were subjected, the relationships between mind/body and individual/community, and particularly the terms in which such redefinitions occurred. If we take it as a given that a centre of modern concerns, in the period Fischer-Lichte defines, is the relationship between individual and society – with questions being asked about what regulates this relationship in modern, democratic societies, and what cultural articulations and performances might ensure a state of equilibrium – it is a striking fact that these various (re)definitions were often made and contested in terms of body and fashion as competing 'paradigms' of modernity. Along the lines of analysis pursued by Simmel, fashion is thought of both as a model of social organisation and as the dominant mode of negotiation between individual and society, subjective and objective culture, in the modern metropolis. Fashion is the paradigmatic embodied practice that permits and indeed enables individuation without threatening integration; in fact it is precisely this illusion of individual performative space provided by fashion that keeps modern society from disintegrating. On the other hand – against the conformity of fashion and what is thought of as its constrictive, deforming and degenerating uniformisation – the liberated body, nude or clad in communal, timeless garments, is idealised as the basis of a performative culture capable of establishing community.

Even as the disastrous aftermath of the modern romance with ritual and spectacle begins to enter the public consciousness with the performative interpellation and deployment of (dressed) bodies by the new totalitarian regimes in the build-up to the Second World War, the body continues to be idealised in progressive circles which define the agents of democracy and peaceful community as embodied, ego-driven minds. As we shall see, these questions – the relation between individual and collective; the difference between 'primitive' and modern in this respect; the performative turn with its validations of ceremonies, rituals, and symbols – are all of urgent concern to Leonard and Virginia Woolf as political agents and cultural analysts at this time, given most extensive treatment in two related texts: *Quack, Quack* (1935) and *Three Guineas* (1938).

Significantly, both texts are particularly aware of the communicative and performative charge inherent in dressed bodies and vestimentary signs, and both present sophisticated analyses of such modes of signification, though with strikingly different conclusions. Where Leonard trusts in the capacity of the rational mind and a civilised discourse based in the constative to heal wounds of division and counteract the irrationality of performative culture, Virginia attends to gender as a fundamental line of cultural division, imposing its own limits on the notion of a civilised community and on the idea of a conclusive differentiation between rational and irrational, constative and performative.

Theorists of fashion have often emphasised its equalising, levelling effect – a principle of democracy that aligns it with the modern. Wyndham Lewis, as shown in Chapter 4, pointed to the alignment between fashion and mass democracy. Less contentiously, and decades earlier, Herbert Spencer's *Principles of Sociology* (1902) identifies ceremonial and fashion as the distinguishing marks of pre-industrial monarchic regimes and modern democracies respectively (Spencer 2004). Spencer's distinction is made to explain the different types of conformity that regulate 'primitive' monarchical as opposed to modern democratic societies. Drawing on contemporary anthropology, Spencer concludes that the enforcement of ancient rituals is very different from the mass conformity of modern industrial society. In the ceremonial institutions of monarchical regimes, writes Spencer, in 'the Mutilations, the Presents, the Visits, the Obeisances, the Forms of Address, the Titles, the Badges and Costumes . . . we see enforced, not likeness between the acts of higher and lower, but unlikeness: that which the ruler does the ruled must not do; and that which the ruled is commanded to do is that which is avoided by the ruler' (Spencer 2004: 329). The enforcement of ritual, moreover, occurs with impunity as a compulsory form of cooperation. By contrast, the conformity that rules modern democratic societies operates as an entirely different mode of social control:

> As now existing, fashion is a form of social regulation analogous to constitutional government as a form of political regulation: displaying, as it does, a compromise between governmental coercion and individual freedom. Just as, along with the transition from compulsory co-operation to voluntary co-operation in public action, there has been a growth of the representative agency serving to express the average volition; so has there been a growth of this indefinite aggregate of wealthy and cultured people, whose consensus of habits rules the private life of society at large. And it is observable in the one case as in the other, that this ever-changing compromise between restraint and freedom, tends towards increase of freedom. For while, on the average, governmental control of individual action decreases, there is a decrease in the rigidity of Fashion; as is shown by the greater latitude of private judgment

exercised within certain vaguely marked limits. . . . Fashion has ever tended towards equalization. Serving to obscure, and eventually to obliterate, the marks of class distinction, it has favored the growth of individuality; and by so doing has aided in weakening Ceremonial, which implies subordination of the individual. (Spencer 2004: 332)

The regulatory mode and the social glue of modern society, then, is the voluntary compromise between individual restraint and freedom, whereby the growth of individuality is held in check by the consensus of disembodied opinion. The name for this modern regulation is Fashion.

In keeping with Spencer's lines of demarcation, yet sceptical of the alleged homogenising effects of fashion, the sociologist Ferdinand Tönnies formulates a distinction between *Gemeinschaft* and *Gesellschaft* which applies to the different modes of life of traditional rural community and modern urban society and which maps on to the different sartorial logics of the traditional, 'timeless' *Tracht* and cosmopolitan, ephemeral fashion (Tönnies 2004: 333). Working from this map he presents an analysis of the forms of disintegration at work in modern societies but also points to a potential for integration between what appeared at the turn of the twentieth century as two opposing principles: society and community. His analysis retains Spencer's differentiation between ceremonial, or in Tönnies' term, custom, as characteristic of traditional, pre-modern communities, and fashion as distinctive of modern society, though he goes beyond Spencer in conceding the complexity of volition, agency, and 'legislative will', that is involved in either (ibid.: 336). Ultimately, however, Tönnies thinks of customs as establishing themselves with a kind of necessity that is absent from fashion; customs have the endurance of religious practices, while fashion 'is always a factor and symptom of the dissolution of custom' (ibid.: 337). Moreover,

as the subject and bearer of fashion, *society* stands in a certain necessary opposition to customs. Society is modern, educated, cosmopolitan. It represents completely different principles, it seeks progress, not inactivity. Trade, the production of goods, manufacture, and the factory are the elements with which it spreads its nets out over the entire inhabited earth. Society wants movement, and indeed accelerated movement. It must dissolve custom in order to develop a sense and taste for the new, for imported goods. It relies on individual incentive, particularly on youth's curiosity and the love of finery, and on the desire to exchange and procure what pleases. Here all attachment or loyalty to what is passed down, what is one's own, what is inherited, must yield. Commerce has a dissolving and destructive effect everywhere. Trade and commerce, urban life, the growth of cities, the power of money, capitalism, the division of classes, general bourgeois life, and the striving for education – all of these, aspects of the same development of *civilization*, favor fashion and impair custom. (Tönnies 2004: 339)

Nonetheless, and perhaps paradoxically, the possibility for overcoming this process of dissolution and disintegration lies precisely in the spirit of modernity itself, in its civilising, forward movement. The hope, expressed by Tönnies, is that the civilising process will eventually bring forth a society 'capable of producing a rational will', liberating it equally from 'the whims of fashion' and from ceremonial 'superstition, ghosts, and magic' (Tönnies 2004: 340). What is envisaged at a more evolved stage of modernity, in other words, is the *Gesellschaft als Gemeinschaft* – released both from fashion as the principle of irrationality, and from those aspects of custom that are at odds with modern rationality.

As we shall see, the totalitarian regimes both in Italy and Germany made active use of Tönnies' differentiation in their cultural politics, investing heavily in regional costume as the proper dress for the social body, expressing communal and national values and identities. For the moment, however, we shall stay with Tönnies' optimistic vision, the dream of modern integration based in the principles of an embodied rationality, which we find variously expressed in progressive circles in several parts of Europe. The aesthetic and ultimately moral community envisaged by the proponents of the *Gesamtkunstwerk* may be illustrated by the thoughts of Henry van de Velde, presenting himself as one of the main activists in the modern renaissance of the applied arts launched by Morris and Ruskin. Lecturing and writing around 1900, van de Velde's concern is 'that the diverging demands of individuality and community come together today in our efforts to establish a readjustment of social conditions' (Stern 2004: 132). In the area of dress, he argues, these two demands are not mutually exclusive. While 'there are circumstances in human life in which everyone's dress should be different – indoors, for example', 'there are others, mainly in the street, in which dress should be alike. A third circumstance, celebrations and great events, requires uniform dress' (ibid.: 132). The ugliness of a crowd or a social gathering dressed in a heterogeneous way creates aesthetic and social disorder. The stylisation imposed by fashion merely 'follows its own fantasies' and thus is incapable of harmonious integration. The artistic anti-fashion clothing proposed by van de Velde, by contrast, was 'based on the organic principles of logical construction' established through the evolutionary theory of dress elaborated by George H. Darwin, and in accordance with modern modes of life and rationality (ibid.: 133). Where Morris had promoted Pre-Raphaelite iconography as the ideal of classical organicism, van de Velde proposed a 'timeless' assimilation of classical Greek, Gothic and modern.

While the rationale behind the *Gesamtkunstwerk* movement was a belief in the moral redemption and communal integration effected by

a total aesthetic approach to all daily objects, the physical culture movement of the interwar years and its affiliated ventures in dress reform gave
more emphasis to the body as reality principle, substituting progressive ideas of modern subjects as embodied, rational, democratic agents
for the vague 'moral redemption' of the arts and crafts movements.
As Fischer-Lichte points out, the trans-European, though German-
dominated, *Nacktkultur* and *Lebensreform* movements may be understood as one of many parallel instances of the performative turn; more or
less coincident proclamations in many fields of the idea of the body, or
the embodied mind, as the basis of culture. The British nudist and physical culture movements after the First World War may to some extent
have been looking back to the 'neo-pagan' lifestyles, the rural romance
and the modest sexual freedoms enjoyed by the Pre-Raphaelites in the
previous century and the 'Neo-Pagans' in the years before the war.[1] The
body culture of the interwar years, however, was much more explicitly
directed towards the connections between progressive, embodied minds
and the creation of democracy and international peace. Founded on evolutionary ideas of civilisation, a belief in the connection between modern
vitalism and rationality, as well as the logical evolution towards nudity
and the reality priciple of the body, this culture was given discursive
and organisational support by writers like Havelock Ellis, J. C. Flügel,
Gerald Heard and John Langdon Davies, and associations like The FPSI,
The Federation of Progressive Societies and Individuals.

Writing his *Anatomy of Clothes* in 1924, Gerald Heard elaborates a
radical evolutionary history of dress, founded not on social processes
but on the vitalist principle of a 'Life Force'. By projected evolution,
passing from the body to its environs in ever-widening circles, a line
of development may be envisaged which takes the form of 'a constant
reciprocation' between the dressed body and its material environment:
'a lighter, stronger architecture imposing cleaner, closer, more convenient clothing. Colour will come back onto building surfaces, and men's
dress will begin to flush in reflection' (Heard 1924: 142). Though the
expected reciprocation between technology and clothing can be seen
in its beginnings in the youth who lives beside his car – 'as advanced
in his fashion as the limousine in whose panels he is reflected' (ibid.:
153) – there is no doubt in Heard's mind that the remoter future is
nude. When the reasons for wearing clothing – modesty, protection,
display – have been eliminated by evolution (in morality, architecture,
technology and engineering), hygiene and the care for our bodies will
'no doubt strip us naked', he predicts (ibid.: 146). On the same note,
John Langdon-Davies declares in *The Future of Nakedness* (1929)
that science (health and hygiene) 'has undertaken the rehabilitation of

nakedness' by documenting the healthy effects of sun and fresh air, and that 'nothing could better illustrate our distance from the Victorian Age, even from its rebels', than the body-denying 'haberdashery' of Carlyle's clothes philosopher in *Sartor Resartus* (Langdon-Davies 1929: 43). The turn to the reality principle of the body, for these commentators, is the distinguishing mark of the twentieth century. The point to be made here, obviously, is not that the views of Heard and Langdon-Davies are representative either of intellectual or popular opinion in the interwar years, but that they are voiced in the context of a progressive community, to some extent a counter-culture, which quite consistently identifies modernity, democracy and pacifism with the liberated (nude) body and with the embodied mind. Significantly, and relevant to an understanding of Leonard's as well as Virginia's projects in *Quack, Quack* and *Three Guineas*, this is a culture with which both Woolfs, directly or by indirection, were affiliated.

Leonard Woolf, along with other radical intellectuals like Bertrand Russell, H. G. Wells and Rebecca West, was one of twenty-two Vice-Presidents of the Federation of Progressive Societies and Individuals, formed in 1933 to provide, as announced in the Federation's Manifesto, 'a common platform and objective' for groups with a shared commitment to 'an all-round progressive programme' for social and economic reform. What is at stake is to organise a wealth of scattered and ineffectual initiatives directed towards 'rational progress', against the compact forces of reaction: 'The chaos of international relations, the failure to balance production and consumption, the nationalist policies pursued by governments with their appeals to fear, greed and self-interest under the guise of patriotism', and, ultimately, 'the breakdown of civilization' (Joad 1933: 22). With such collaboration in view, the Federation 'seeks to show the common philosophical background of all progressive thought, and to give concrete expression to this background by common effort in practical work' (ibid.: 22). The Manifesto outlines Federation policies in the areas of economy and politics, education, social life, including 'the release of personal conduct from all taboos and restrictions', as well as civil and religious liberties, such as 'the securing for the individual of the most complete freedom of conduct and self-expression that is consistent with the common welfare', an objective which lists among other practical policies the 'abolition of restrictions relating to dress' (ibid.: 24–5).

What is particularly interesting here, is what this attempt to organise such scattered efforts suggests: in effect a performative understanding of individuals as cultural and political agents; of subjects as embodied minds acting within specific spaces and environments; of culture and politics as pervading even the most trivial aspects of human life. This impression is strengthened by the variety of societies giving their support to the Federation's objectives. The FPSI consisted of a number of groups, including The Peace Group, The Political and Economics Group, The Education Group, The Sex Reform Group, The Law Reform and Civil Liberties Group, The Town and Country Planning Group, and The Pictorial Propaganda Group. Among the affiliated societies were The World League for Sexual Reform and The Gymnic Association of Great Britain. The range of membership suggests a 'total' modernising project, directed towards virtually every area of culture – public and private, mental and physical. An impression of the collaborative relations existing between the various associations, the sense of a movement with a shared purpose, may be had by a look at some of their publications. The Federation published *PLAN for World Order and Progress. A Constructive Monthly Review* which contains advertisements for *Gymnos, The Official Organ of the Gymnic Association of Great Britain*, which in turn advertises *PLAN*, the Men's Dress Reform Party, as well as reform garments designed and approved by the MDRP such as 'The New M.D.R.P. Tennis Shorts', 'Bathing Slip', and 'Golf Ensemble' (Vols I–II, 1933–4). Introducing itself in *Gymnos*, the Gymnic Association claims to represent a modern vitalist principle, 'the new and vital impulse which is stirring mankind throughout the world' (I.1, 3). The cultural and political benefits of Gymnosophy as 'all-round regeneration' (I.2, 13) are brought forth: practising nudity is to realise a 'living force which brings calm and contentment to the mind, and healing to the body' (I.1, 3). While the *Freikörperkultur* is still in its infancy in Britain, it is predicted a great future, in parallel with the movement's success in Germany and other countries. The Gymnic Association is affiliated with the European Union for *Freikörperkultur*, and reports with great enthusiasm on the movement's European success, especially as seen in the highly organised activities in Germany.

The chapters making up the Manifesto – contributed by H. G. Wells, C. E. M. Joad, W. Arnold Forster, Francis Meynel, Janet Chance and J. C. Flügel, among others – stress the logical connection between civil liberties; liberated bodies; liberal, pacifist minds; national and ultimately international democracy; and world peace. J. C. Flügel's contribution is a chapter entitled: 'A Psychology for Progressives – How Can They Become Effective?', defining the 'psychology' that unites the variety of societies and individuals comprised by the Federation, as well as setting down the strategy by which such a psychology may be rendered useful, which is to say: translated into politically efficient performance. Flügel finds this common psychological foundation in the word 'progressive'

– a mental attitude described as predominantly scientific and psychological, in contradistinction to the 'moral' attitude of other regimes, the 'blind reliance on outworn loyalties, conventions, and taboos' necessary to societies run on 'rigidly conservative, communist, or fascist lines' (Flügel 1933: 302–3). Originating in the super-ego and the primitive instincts of the id, the 'moral' attitude is by definition a 'rigid and archaic one, which adapts itself only with the utmost difficulty to the changing conditions of modern life' (ibid.: 296). The aim of the progressive, like the aim of psychoanalysis, is to modernise the mind by strengthening the control of the ego over the super-ego and the id, making conscious and sublimating the primitive and archaic elements which stand in the way of progress. Creating modern subjects is to achieve a freer, less oppressive society run on principles of reason and science, and ultimately to prevent war. Such subjects perceive themselves as performing bodies, but of a new kind: free, rational agents, different both from the primitive ceremonial culture resurfacing in the new totalitarian regimes, and from the rigid conformity of modern bourgeois societies regulated by the principles of fashion.

Flügel's civilised modernity represented by conscious reason was asserted in other progressive publications in the contemporary debate, notably *The Intelligent Man's Way to Prevent War* (1933), edited and introduced by Leonard Woolf. Pointing to 'human psychology, the beliefs and desires of human beings,' as the ultimate reason for war, the book's contributors propose to consider 'these psychological factors and the part which education must play in creating the psychology of peace' (Woolf 1933: 16). Flügel's particular contribution in the FPSI Manifesto as well as in his two books, *The Psychology of Clothes* (1930) and *The Psycho-Analytic Study of the Family* (1921), both published by the Woolfs at The Hogarth Press, was to theorise the connection between the progressive, pacifist mind and society's regulation of dressed bodies. Like Simmel and Spencer, Flügel regards fashion as the regulatory mode of modern society, but in addition to social factors he accounts for psychological ones and also considers modes of regulation as dividing along lines of gender. While certain archaic remnants of primitive, ceremonial culture are to be found in the sartorial practices of modern society, the main lines of division in Flügel's historiography are drawn between female sartorial emancipation, on the one hand, and a development which coincides with modernity and which he names 'The Great Masculine Renunciation,' on the other (Flügel 1930: 110).

Flügel's concern is the idea that modernising the mind effectively depends on modernising the body. Hence the project of the clothes psychology, of describing how bodies and minds are fashioned by clothing, as well as how dressed bodies signify and perform within a culturo-symbolic order. Integrating clothing into a general theory of human development, Flügel understands dress as a gendered discourse invested with narcissistic/exhibitionistic and phallic symbolic value. On the journey from naked infant to clothed and civilised adult, clothing emerges as an important component in drawing the infant out of the primary, id-dominated condition. Simplified, clothing mediates paternal law, the prohibition placed upon the narcissistic and auto-erotic pleasures the infant gains from his or her naked body. Clothing also signifies the individual's position with respect to the phallus. Turning to Herbert Spencer and writings in anthropology, Flügel finds that many of the decorative features of our clothing were originally connected with the wearing of trophies, in which phallic symbolism plays an important part: trophies are generally used as signs of (phallic) power, whereas the removal of trophies from dead enemies serves as symbolic castration. The case among primitive people for men to be more decorated than women, and the remnants of this in some European customs, suggests that men are inherently more inclined to decoration and women more inclined to modesty in dress. Traces of the primitive state are seen in ceremonial dress, in military and ecclesiastical hierarchies, and in academic robes, also in the forms of social convention which require men to remove a garment as a sign of respect, e.g. the hat on entering a church. Thus 'in men, castration itself is symbolised by the removal of garments, while the possession or display of the corresponding garments serves, in virtue of their phallic symbolism, as a reassurance against the fears of castration' (Flügel 1930: 104–5).

In modern times, according to Flügel, sexual difference divides along different lines. Apart from the anachronistic remnants of primitive phallic display seen in ceremonial dress, modern males are ruled by clothes regimes which abound 'in features which symbolise [man's] devotion to the principles of duty, renunciation, self-control' – in other words, the law of the father and the excessive moralism of the super-ego (Flügel 1930: 113). The adoption of such clothes regimes Flügel links to the emergence of modern bourgeois society. Effectively preventing sublimation of infantile narcissism onto clothing, male bourgeois dress is the result of 'The Great Masculine Renunciation': a willing subordination (on the part of bourgeois males) of individual distinction and satisfaction to the demands of society (ibid.: 110). In contrast, the so-called 'sartorial emancipation of women' has introduced modes of dress that combine a principle of decorative clothing with exposure of the naked body (as with the *décolleté*) (ibid.: 105). This is to say that women's fashion allows for sublimated narcissism as well as the auto-erotic pleasures, the skin-and-muscle eroticism of actual exposure. Sublimated narcissism is understood to be of benefit to the individual and culture, carrying a certain ego-liberating, hence progressive, potential. The auto-erotic element, argues Flügel, brings women's fashion into line with the rationale of the nude culture movement and its emphasis on the auto-erotic constituents of the pleasures connected with the naked body – a modern attitude to the relations between clothes and body 'that appears to be quite foreign to the primitive mind' (ibid.: 225).

The route to modern bodies and progressive psychology as Flügel maps it, goes via modes of dress which permit sublimation while removing undue elements of corporeal discipline and primitive phallic display.[2] Modern clothing should exhibit the progressiveness and adaptability of fashion, 'while eliminating the pernicious element of change for change's sake' (Flügel 1930: 220). The Men's Dress Reform Party has 'issued a preliminary call to freedom', but the forces behind the Great Masculine Renunciation – the moral symbolism and phallic value attaching to conventional male clothing – are still at work, associating dress reform with guilt and castration fears (ibid.: 220). The final step, however, depends on realising the reality principle of 'the natural, corporeal body,' persisting under our artificial sartorial one, as the 'essential, permanent, and inescapable element of our being' – a reality principle, moreover, to which 'the new science of eugenics, emphasising the importance of sexual selection for future human welfare, adds its own argument' (ibid.: 222–3).

Grounded in the ego and the reality principle of the body, Flügel's modern subject is a rational, independent and democratic agent, capable of resisting the excessive conformity of bourgeois fashion as well as the archaic remnants of a primitive culture built on unthinking obedience to rituals and symbols. Both his prediction of a nude future and his ideas regarding the connection between nudity and civilised, pacifist subjects, were supported by other progressive commentators in the 1920s and 1930s. By May 1933, however, the FPSI was expressing concern that Hitler's suppression of *Freikörperkultur* and *Nacktkultur* in Germany represented a revival of 'war-fervour' (*Gymnos* I.4, 12); by June the latest news from Germany was that the remaining FKK groups were to be turned into specifically militaristic channels (I.5, 14). When Leonard and Virginia wrote *Quack, Quack* and *Three Guineas* in 1935 and 1938 they were responding to this reactionary (Fascist/National Socialist) context, though equally to a progressive one. Both texts are concerned with the symbolic modalities that bring the collective, the mass, into being; with Fischer-Lichte one might call this the performative modality. Moreover, both address the possibility of preventing war by creating resisting subjects: subjects capable of resisting cultural and ideological interpellation by ceremonies, rituals and symbols of various kinds, for instance the symbols of nationalism, patriotism or fascism. It is a reflection on their analytic powers that these texts serve to reveal and effectively anticipate the degree to which the performative turn was expropriated and deployed in Nazi and Fascist cultural politics, specifically by the conscription of dressed bodies into German and Italian propaganda machines.

I have briefly noted the suppression of the *Freikörperkultur* by the Nazi regime and its reinvention in useful bodies. Much has been written about the idealisation and eroticisation of the male uniform in the Third Reich as part of the visual politics of National Socialism.[3] As Irene Guenther documents in her book *Nazi Chic? Fashioning Women in the Third Reich* (2004), the Nazi propaganda machine also invested heavily in sartorial regimes that would subsume German women into the *Einheitlichkeit* and *Gleichheit* of the *Volksgemeinschaft* (Guenther 2004: 13, 121). Organisational uniforms and the revival of traditional folk costume – the *Tracht* – were promoted as the visual embodiments of ideal German femininity (the woman as the mother of the *Volk*), defined in contradistinction to the artificiality, distortion, and degeneration of 'jewified', French-dominated, international fashion (ibid.: 98–9, 145). *Tracht* figured prominently in the carefully choreographed spectacles staged by the National Socialist Party and in a broad range of Party-sponsored occasions, historical German celebrations and folk festivals (ibid.: 112). Organisational uniforms, such as the *Führer*-approved uniform of the *Bund deutscher Mädel* (League of German Girls) expressed the Party's demand for unity and commonality, while offering possibilities for distinction through an elaborate system of cords, braids and badges (ibid.: 120–1). Such awareness of the seemingly innocent performative force of fashion was matched by the Italian fascist regime during the 1930s. Eugenia Paulicelli's *Fashion under Fascism* (2004) documents the massive investments by the regime both in the nationalisation of the clothing industry and at the level of display and spectacle. Widespread use of uniforms created and displayed a disciplined social body, while dress based on rural tradition was enlisted to project an invigorated national identity – the 'new Italians' of a 'new Italy' – against the degenerate cosmopolitanism and international capitalism represented by (French-dominated) fashion (Paulicelli 2004: 51).

If Fascist and National Socialist cultural politics is defined by its sophisticated understanding of iconography and performance in the interpellation and creation of a community, Leonard Woolf, in writing *Quack, Quack*, is concerned precisely with the 'political magic' (Woolf

1935: 37) of the grand spectacle and the mass suggestion brought about by, and on, phenomenal bodies. *Quack, Quack* is a tract against what Leonard names 'quackery', the return in Western culture of the 'superstitions of the savage', of primitive, ceremonial cultures based on custom, rituals and taboos, and on the inspired claim to absolute truth of the priest or king. Beginning in the early nineteenth century this cultural regression to primitive instincts and morality, as Leonard depicts it, has taken on increasing intensity since the 1880s, coinciding in that respect with Fischer-Lichte's historiography of the performative turn. Leonard traces it through the Hegelians, Carlyle, Nietzsche and Bergson, to its culmination in fascist ideology: 'the supreme example in modern times of the reversion to savagery and the belief in political magic' (ibid.: 37).

Juxtaposing photographs of Hitler and Mussolini with effigies of Polynesian war-gods, Leonard Woolf's point is to show that the corporeal manifestation of inspiration (and its performative effect) is virtually identical in all cases, the significant point being 'the psychological effect which the facial appearance is clearly meant to produce . . . the superhuman sternness of the god and the terror which he instils' (Woolf 1935: 47). Hence, writes Leonard, 'the description by travellers of the behaviour and state of mind of the inspired leaders and their followers are almost exactly applicable to that of a fascist meeting addressed by a Mussolini, Hitler, Göring, or Göbbels'. In support of his claims, he quotes at length from Frazer's *The Golden Bough* (1890):

> As soon as the god had entered the king or priest, 'the latter became violently agitated, and worked himself up to the highest pitch of apparent frenzy, the muscles of the limbs seemed convulsed, the body swelled, the countenance became terrific, the features distorted, and the eyes wild and strained'. . . When the Polynesian had reached this state, 'he often rolled on the earth, foaming at the mouth, as if labouring under the influence of the divinity by whom he was possessed, and, in shrill cries, and violent and often indistinct sounds, revealed the will of the god' . . . The Polynesian Führer sometimes 'continued for two or three days possessed by the spirit or deity; a piece of native cloth, of a peculiar kind, worn round one arm, was an indication of inspiration, or of the indwelling of the god with the individual who wore it' . . . In Germany and Italy the inspiration of Hitler and Mussolini is permanent. Hence the wearing of a piece of cloth of a peculiar kind (e.g., inscribed with the swastika) has also become permanent and has extended from the God-inspired leader to the leader-inspired followers, for it indicates that the wearer has accepted the inspiration either directly or indirectly. (Woolf 1935: 45–7; internal quotations from Frazer's *The Golden Bough*)

The performative force of the inspired Führer depends on the audience's belief in, and ratification of, the performance as emanating from a transcendent authority. Leonard's juxtaposition of photographs is intended to demonstrate that Hitler and Mussolini establish the credibility, and thus authority, of their performance by invoking, or citing, what is in effect conventions of prophetic speech: the bodily marks and sartorial symbol of inspiration. Moreover, this juxtaposition serves to reveal how the vestimentary object takes on the function of a sign: able to circulate freely without the body of which it is the metonym, always capable of invoking its referent – the source of prophetic inspiration and its authority.

Frazer, as shown by Fischer-Lichte, is one of the agents in the transition from textual to performative conceptualisations of culture. *The Golden Bough* contributes to overturning the nineteenth-century distinctions between primitive and civilised, performative and textual in demonstrating that European culture had evolved from a culture based on sacrificial ritual, a performative modality, moreover, which still existed among the segments or layers that constituted modern culture. Another key figure in the performative (re)turn is Nietzsche, whose *Birth of Tragedy* (1872) was instrumental to the late nineteenth-century reconceptualisation of theatre and ritual through the scandalous claim that the ancient Greek theatre originated in a Dionysian ritual which transformed performers as well as audience into an ecstatic community. Nietzsche's description of the transformative effects brought about by bodies in a state of ecstasy (Fischer-Lichte 2005: 39), is clearly reminiscent of Leonard's inspired bodies in *Quack, Quack*.

Nietzsche's as well as Frazer's thoughts on the ritual origins of culture were picked up and developed by the Classics scholar (and friend of Virginia Woolf) Jane Ellen Harrison and the so-called Cambridge Ritualists (Gilbert Murray and Francis MacDonald Cornford). What is particularly interesting in their theory of ritual as physical, performative acts, is the idea of the originary rite as a communal presencing or bringing forth of the (Bergsonian) *durée* (Fischer-Lichte 2005: 41). Once more, this is what worries Leonard Woolf in *Quack, Quack*. For Leonard (who based much of his critique on Karen Stephen's *The Misuse of Mind: A Study of Bergson's Attack on Intellectualism*), what a 'civilised' man such as Bergson has in common with the fascists and the primitive 'quacks' is a claim to inspiration combined with symbolic opacity: the fiction of synthetic intuitions communicable only by bodily performance or as visual and verbal symbols which work by their materiality and demand instinctive, emotional response. In conveying such intuitions,

> the oracle itself has lost all perception of what is imagery and metaphor and simile and what is the truth which it is seeking to express through imagery, metaphor, or simile . . . the quack himself can no longer distinguish between the symbol and the thing symbolized. (Woolf 1935: 133)

There goes a line, as Leonard perceives it – a 'wave of unreason' – from the performative culture of the savage to the embodied mode of knowing idealised by Bergson and the performative aesthetic of modernism (the opaque symbols which mean what they are); finally to the 'political magic' of fascist mass spectacles, ceremonies, and opaquely suggestive symbols (Woolf 1935: 193). What is desperately called for at a moment which seems to be the crest of the wave, is the reinstatement of mind and the reinforcement of the lines of demarcation suspended in the performative turn: the boundaries between mind and body; textual and performative; rational and irrational; civilised and primitive; and ultimately, between democracy and totalitarianism.

J. C. Flügel and Leonard Woolf both direct their analysis towards the relations between individual and society, attempting to find viable answers to the question of how democratic subjects are constituted. Their modernising projects spring from the conviction that the performative symbols of ceremonial culture uphold their authority by the combined forces of id and super-ego, hence their recommendations consist in liberating the conscious mind from the remnants of primitive, archaic instincts and the moral response of the super-ego. While Leonard emphasises the education of the rational mind as a counter-measure to the Nazi's primary object of education, 'the rearing of strong bodies' (Woolf 1935: 81), Flügel is particularly concerned with the idea that modernising the mind effectively depends on modernising the body. As such he continues the emphasis given to the body as the basis of culture which Fischer-Lichte defines as the performative turn, though with the important difference that Flügel's priority is the conscious embodied mind rather than unconscious bodily processes, and that, like Leonard, he insists on the careful differentiation of civilised from primitive.

This, then, is the argumentative context into which Virginia throws her 'revolutionary bomb of a book', in the words of a contemporary commentator (Bosanquet 1938). *Three Guineas* has many points of contact with *The Psychology of Clothes* as well as *Quack, Quack*. It is a tract against war which addresses the temptations and dangers of culturo-symbolic interpellation and which conducts much of its analysis through the operations of sartorial regimes. Like Flügel's book it presents a gendered analysis of the relations between dressed bodies and the social order, but with different conclusions, refusing Flügel's historiography of The Great Male Renunciation and Female Sartorial Emancipation by rethinking narcissism as male vanity, and by introducing a parallel history of female chastity. Like *Quack, Quack*, it despairs at fascism's collective bodies, but disagrees with Leonard's diagnosis of symbolic processes and with the prescribed cure of education.

The questions Woolf puts forward for discussion in *Three Guineas* are 'Why war?' and 'What can be done to prevent it?' The answers she provides depend on an analogy between patriarchy and fascism; an understanding of the inextricable connectedness between the private and the public. Appropriately, her rhetorical strategy could be described as one of montage or patchwork – a patchwork which brings together, in her own words, the 'outsides' of things with the 'insides'; the seemingly trivial with the ostensibly serious. This involves the use of a series of photographs which, though they are never referred to in the text, serve to illustrate a sartorial analysis which is central to Woolf's argument. One might say that Woolf here takes the look of civilisation, its sartorial regimes, as symptom of its pathology, subjecting it first to a semiotic, then to a psychoanalytic analysis which, in its complexity and sheer audacity, is sophisticated, ironic and sometimes amusing. From a defamiliarising perspective she defines as 'through the shadow of the veil that St Paul still lays upon our eyes' (*TG*: 22), Woolf shows that garments and vestimentary objects speak a number of languages – among them the language of commodities, of exchange value, of advertisement, but also of mystification and veiling, as when the *langue* pretends not to be a system; the sign pretends to be simply an object. She examines dress as it signifies and regulates the performance of culture, of gender and power within a patriarchal order. Ironically, though, in an economy of exchange value, the modes of display which advertise women's value on the marriage market turn out to be essentially no different from the way educated men wear their robes and regalia: like 'the tickets in a grocer's shop', to exhibit their value to the gross national product (ibid.: 24). Dress as women use it,

> is comparatively simple. Besides the prime function of covering the body, it has two other offices – that it creates beauty for the eye, and that it attracts the admiration of [the male] sex. Since marriage until the year 1919 . . . was the only profession open to us, the enormous importance of dress to a woman can hardly be exaggerated. (*TG*: 24)

Male dress has a similar 'advertisement function' as the essay shows by juxtaposing the stars and ribbons that advertise men's intellect to powder and paint, a woman's chief method of advertising her professional asset, and by setting the sum paid for a knighthood next to the sum paid for a yearly dress allowance.

Significantly, Woolf's analysis does not make the Spencerian distinction between ceremonial and fashion, revealing instead that the distinction is inoperative in modern democracy because both are cases of 'voluntary' conformity. Examining forms of seemingly voluntary

Figure 9   'A University Procession', from *Three Guineas*

cooperation, Woolf shows how individuals are systematically interpellated by ceremonies and symbols even of an 'innocent' kind, revealing that the presence of ceremonial and its performative force in the midst of civilisation – as in the academic and ecclesiastical processions of educated men – amounts to more than the anachronisms or 'archaic remnants' which Flügel suggests. To the gaze from behind the veil, the look of civilisation attains a queer visibility – 'Your clothes in the first place make us gape with astonishment':

> How many, how splendid, how extremely ornate they are – the clothes worn by the educated man in his public capacity! Now you dress in violet; a jewelled crucifix swings on your breast; now your shoulders are covered with lace; now furred with ermine; now slung with many linked chains set with precious stones. Now you wear wigs on your heads; rows of graduated curls descend to your necks. Now your hats are boat-shaped, or cocked; now they mount in cones of black fur; now they are made of brass and scuttle shaped; now plumes of red, now of blue hair surmount them. Sometimes gowns cover your legs; sometimes gaiters. Tabards embroidered with lions and unicorns swing from your shoulders; metal objects cut in star shapes or in circles glitter and twinkle upon your breasts. Ribbons of all colours – blue, purple, crimson – cross from shoulder to shoulder. After the comparative simplicity of your dress at home, the splendour of your public attire is dazzling. (*TG*: 23)

On the one hand, ceremonial dress appears to be a highly regulated system in which the symbolical meaning of every 'button, rosette and stripe' is unequivocal; signifier corresponding to signified in a hierarchy of power. Thus,

> some have the right to wear plain buttons only; others rosettes; some may wear a single stripe; others three, four, five, or six. And each curl or stripe is sewn on at precisely the right distance apart; it may be one inch for one man, one inch and a quarter for another. Rules again regulate the gold wire on the shoulders, the braid on the trousers, the cockades on the hats. (*TG*: 23–4)

At the same time, however, the ritual character of ceremonial has the effect of transposing the sign into the mystifying incarnation of the symbol, with the effect that what is enacted is not so much the relations and hierarchies of power as its blinding mystery and absolute logic. Ritual and its sartorial properties interpellate and discipline individual bodies, bringing forth a collective with performative, perlocutionary force:

> Here you kneel; there you bow; here you advance in procession behind a man carrying a silver poker; here you mount a carved chair; here you appear to do homage to a piece of painted wood; here you abase yourselves before tables covered with richly worked tapestry. And whatever these ceremonies may mean you perform them always together, always in step, always in the uniform proper to the man and the occasion. (*TG*: 24)

There is a different performative dimension to ceremonial dress than the ritual which is no less blinding in its effect. This Woolf's analysis also serves to bring out. In the case of the judge pronouncing judgement in the court of law, the garments he is wearing are signs of investment; they invest him with the power of office, thus supplying the Austinian 'appropriate circumstances' to make the speech act operative in the judicial sense. Woolf shows us this, but also makes us aware of the theatrical and comical elements of such investiture and its (self-)blinding effects:

> Thus the late Mr Justice MacCardie, in summing up the case of Mrs Frankau, remarked: 'Women cannot be expected to renounce an essential feature of femininity or to abandon one of nature's solaces for a constant and insuperable physical handicap . . . Dress, after all, is one of the chief methods of women's self-expression . . . In matters of dress women often remain children to the end. The psychology of the matter must not be overlooked. But whilst bearing the above matters in mind the law has rightly laid it down that the rule of prudence and proportion must be observed.' The Judge who thus dictated was wearing a scarlet robe, an ermine cape, and a vast wig of artificial curls. Whether he was enjoying 'one of nature's solaces for a constant and insuperable physical handicap', whether again he was himself observing 'the rule of prudence and proportion' must be doubtful. But 'the psychology of the matter must not be overlooked'; and the fact that the singularity of

his own appearance together with that of Admirals, Generals, Heralds, Life Guards, Peers, Beefeaters, etc., was completely invisible to him so that he was able to lecture the lady without any consciousness of sharing her weakness, raises two questions: how often must an act be performed before it becomes tradition, and therefore venerable; and what degree of social prestige causes blindness to the remarkable nature of one's own clothes? Singularity of dress, when not associated with office, seldom escapes ridicule. (*TG*: 170)

It is probably not coincidental that a reader of Carlyle's *Sartor Resartus* might detect a certain echo in Woolf's observations on this point, of the clothes philosopher's example of how a red coat may get a blue coat hanged:

You see two individuals, [the clothes philosopher] writes, one dressed in fine Red, the other in coarse threadbare Blue: red says to Blue, 'Be hanged and anatomised;' Blue hears with a shudder, and (O wonder of wonders!) marches sorrowfully to the gallows; is there noosed-up, vibrates his hour, and the surgeons dissect him, and fit his bones into a skeleton for medical purposes. How is this . . .? Red has no physical hold of Blue, no *clutch* of him, is nowise in *contact* with him: neither are those ministering Sheriffs and Lord-Liutentants and Hangmen and Tipstaves so related to commanding Red, that he can tug them hither and thither; but each stands distinct within his own skin. Nevertheless, as it is spoken, so is it done; the articulated Word sets all hands in Action; and Rope and Improved-drop perform their work. (Carlyle 1869: 40)

As both Woolf and Carlyle have noticed, what authorises the power of the word and extends its field of operation beyond the limits of language in this case, is the fact that the word is clothed:

Has not your Red hanging-individual a horsehair wig, squirrel skins, and a plush-gown; whereby all mortals know that he is a JUDGE? – Society, which the more I think of it astonishes me the more, is founded upon Cloth. (Carlyle 1869: 41)

Significantly, however, such points of coincidence between Woolf's and Carlyle's sartorial analysis are limited to observations of the communicative charge inherent in clothing, and do not extend to their various critiques of the system. It is hardly surprising that Carlyle's concern is to preserve the sacred nature of the emblem from appropriation by unworthy individuals. His strategy is that of imaginatively and comically undressing falsely expropriated power – letting 'the Clothes fly off the whole dramatic corps [of] Dukes, Grandees, Bishops, Generals, Anointed Presence itself,' to see 'the whole fabric of Government, Legislation, Property, Police, and Civilised Society . . . *dissolved*, in wails and howls' (Carlyle 1869: 41–2). Woolf's politics, though it shares Carlyle's dissolving laughter, is much more radical. In her analysis there is no sacred emblem, and a strategy of undressing the clothes of culture would hardly be sufficient to reveal the operations through which cultural signification is practiced and performed.

Woolf's analysis, consequently, does not limit itself to clothing's performative effects; by recourse to psychoanalysis, or rather by ironic appropriation of some current psychoanalytic terms, it goes in search of motivations and origins. The connection that occurs to Woolf between 'the sartorial splendours of the educated man' and the consequences of war documented daily in newspaper images of ruined houses and dead bodies, is vanity – a condition, she observes, whose trivial associations serve to mask its true implications: 'Your finest clothes are those you wear as soldiers'; the 'red and the gold, the brass and the feathers' are invented 'partly in order to impress the beholder with the majesty of the military office, partly in order through their vanity to induce young men to be soldiers' (*TG*: 25). Similarly,

> for educated men to emphasize their superiority over other people, either in birth or intellect, by dressing differently, or by adding titles before, or letters after their names are acts that rouse competition and jealousy – emotions which, as we need scarcely draw upon biography to prove, nor ask psychology to show, have their share in encouraging a disposition towards war. (ibid.: 25–6)

To persuade the reader of the full range of implications behind that trivial 'vanity', Woolf imports an explanatory model from contemporary psychoanalysis. She cites a professor of theology who refers 'the general acceptance of male dominance [and] feminine inferiority, resting upon subconscious ideas of woman as "man manqué"', to 'infantile fixation' and the 'castration complex' (*TG*: 144). Treating the evidence and the rhetoric with customary irony, Woolf nonetheless appropriates them for her own purposes, proceeding to trace the manifestations of infantile fixation – culturally sanctioned and supported – in a range of areas and discourses. In making the point that clothing – like trophies in primitive culture – has phallic value, signifying possession of the phallus as well as the fear of losing it, Woolf concurs with Flügel's clothes philosophy. Woolf's particular contribution, however, consists in demonstrating the consequences of phallic law, as an order depending on the woman cast in the role of envious admirer, and as an order of competition and jealousy among men. Thus, the uniform of the fascist dictator, with its medals and mystic symbols, is essentially no different in its performative modality from the gold, the brass and the feathers which adorn educated men. In both cases a single pathology is at work: phallic fixation and castration fears.

In her search for origins, Woolf posits two foundational performative moments in Western culture, both speech acts which lay down a law: Creon's law in the *Antigone* and St Paul's law in his letter to the Corinthians – the foundational text for the ruling Western assessment of chastity, in Woolf's conception. Springing from the same source – phallic fixation – between them these moments establish two traditions: the traditions, respectively, of subjection and resistance; the enunciation of a decree and the speech act which refuses its authority. Woolf's essayist reflects at length on the subconscious motivations behind St Paul's 'famous pronouncement upon the matter of veils', recognising its subconscious motivations in the castration fears 'of the virile or dominant type, so familiar at present in Germany':

> Chastity then as defined by St Paul is seen to be a complex conception, based upon the love of long hair; the love of subjection; the love of an audience; the love of laying down the law, and, subconsciously, upon a very strong and natural desire that the woman's mind and body shall be reserved for the use of one man and one only. (*TG*: 186–7)

As the woman is of and for the man, according to St Paul, 'for this cause ought the woman to have a sign of authority on her head' (*TG*: 187). Reflecting on the Pauline precept as a phallic scene of law allows Woolf to trace the history of the veil as a vestimentary sign of subjection, thus substituting a history of chastity for Flügel's narrative of female historical emancipation. Her concern, undoubtedly, is to show that the performative force of the Pauline argument, underscored by the ideological and material interests of patriarchy, still persists.

Once more, then, clothes regimes that Flügel describes as remnants of a primitivism destined to be dispelled by modernity's liberating force, are shown by Woolf to have continued actuality. Women's so-called sartorial emancipation is revealed as the modern obverse of chastity, involved in the same economy of demand and exchange. In the nineteenth century to be veiled was to be 'accompanied by a male or a maid' (*TG*: 188). To the maid acting as veil in public, the knowledge that 'she was putting into practice the commands laid down by St Paul [and] doing her utmost to deliver her mistress's body intact to her master' may have offered some solace but even so, 'in the darkness of the beetle-haunted basement she must sometimes have bitterly reproached St Paul on the one hand for his chastity, and the gentlemen of Piccadilly on the other for their lust' (ibid.: 186). Nowadays, concedes Woolf, 'chastity has undergone considerable revision', though not to the point of a real emancipation. In fact, as she notes ironically, 'there is said to be a reaction in favour of some degree of chastity for both sexes. This is partly due to economic causes; the protection of chastity by maids is an expensive item in the bourgeois budget' (ibid.: 189). The threads and filaments of desire, phallic power, and the economic as well as psychological advantages of marking women's bodies as the property of one man and hence prohibited to others, still persist.

Three Guineas' second letter, asking for the second guinea, comes as a request for cast-off garments for 'women whose professions require that they should have presentable day and evening dresses which they can ill afford to buy' (*TG*: 179). Debating with herself whether to contribute her guinea to dressing women for the professions, with the prospect of one day being allowed to wear a judge's wig, an ermine cape, a military uniform, the essayist reflects that opening the professions to women is in effect to substitute one system of exchange value (work) for another (sex). Moreover, this new exchange system comes with a set of ties – dog collars, ribbons and badges inscribed with the duties of God and Empire – which chastity did not have. With a choice between the veil and the dog collar, and the recognition of a degree of freedom behind the veil – the freedom of 'derision' as well as freedom from 'unreal loyalties' – chastity is a real option (ibid.: 90). In the end, the essayist's guinea comes with the condition that bodily chastity is translated, not into Flügel's narcissism and nudity, but into mental chastity: the state of dressing for the professions without marrying them, of remaining sceptical of patriarchy's symbolic systems and their enunciative force, retaining the defamiliarising gaze from behind the veil.

The veil thus is a metaphor – of a position and a mode of seeing within the symbolic order – that serves to deconstruct the boundaries between primitive and civilised. Flügel places the veil safely with the primitive others: in connection with his discussion of modesty he refers to 'Moslem theory' according to which woman is the property of man, with the consequence that outdoor dress for women is designed to avoid the arousal of sexual desire in men (Flügel 1930: 61). It is interesting to compare this observation not only with Woolf's argument in *Three Guineas* but also with her reflections on the topic as early as 1906 during a trip to Constantinople. Exhilarated by the sartorial culture of the 'Gorgeous East' – 'a various torrent of red fezes, turbans, yashmaks, & European respectability' – she notes in her journal that

> the facts contradict the preconception that the Turks belong to a different stage of civilisation & so require women to be veiled: in fact the veil is a very frail symbol; worn casually, & cast aside if the wearer happens to be curious. (*PA*: 351–2)

If it is a frail symbol in the East, however, Woolf's alternative historiography shows it to be a strong symbol in Western, Christian culture, even in 'modern' Victorian and post-Victorian society.

A similar inversion of terms and suspension of boundaries informs Woolf's other foundational moment in Western culture: the performative force of Creon's edict in the *Antigone*. As critics have pointed out, Sophocles' Antigone is perhaps 'the principal character in our culture . . . who is defined, and who defines herself, in a speech act of refusal'; whose defiance of Creon's law, that is, consists not primarily in a physical act (of honouring her dead brother), but rather in the public proclamation of her action: 'I say I did it; I do not disavow it!' (Gould 1995: 34; Sophocles 1991: 487).[4] The significance of Woolf's invocation of this primary scene resides in the act of civil disobedience performed and proclaimed by a woman marginally placed with respect to the Polis. The significance is also that the force of Creon's command is caught up with the question of gender: the force with which he reaffirms and maintains his decree through the play originates in the horror of yielding to advice that coincides with that of a woman. Thus the play demonstrates the consequences of male vanity, with Creon being made to experience the destructive force not only of his own law, but of forcefully refusing the persuasive speech of others.

It is instructive to compare Virginia's invocation of this scene of law to Leonard's appeal to Greek culture as the origin of civilisation in *Quack, Quack*. As we have seen, Leonard's argument with its distinctions between civilised and primitive, textual and performative, depends on resisting and effectively reversing the reconceptualisations of Greek culture that empowered the performative turn: the re-evaluation of ritual carried out by Nietzsche, Harrison and the Cambridge Ritualists. The Greeks were the first to understand the obligations and standards of intellectual morality, insists Leonard; theirs is the moment when superstition was overcome. The young Virginia Stephen can be seen to participate in the idealisation of Greek culture and the idea of its ritual basis. On her visit to Greece in 1906, she writes in her journal of the supreme beauty of classical sculpture and of Eleusis, the place of secret fertility rites associated with the goddess Demeter and the 'Cult of the Mysteries': 'On such days, we know, the people of Athens formed together, garlanded in fine draperies, & marched in procession to their mystic rites which none might know' (*PA*: 324). Imagining the pre-historic Greeks, she writes: 'the king wore purple robes, & his limbs shone with beaten gold . . . they marched . . . in ceremonial procession, glittering in dyed clothing & ornament & gold' (ibid.: 332). Such imaginative investment in Greek culture and its dressed bodies remains as a source of metaphor throughout her work. In the context of *Three Guineas*, however, the rhetorical purpose is a different one. Where Leonard makes his appeal to classical Greek reason and civilisation, the point of Virginia's gendered analysis is to show the presence of unreason and division – the irrationality of vanity, phallic law and its consequence of subjection – at the origin of culture, an origin, moreover, which makes the idea of a community (whether as *Gemeinschaft* or democratic *Gesellschaft*) an impossibility. Gender, then, is the fundamental question to be resolved.

It is the question of force that interests Woolf in her two foundational moments and in the performative in general: the history of force, its investments, its modus operandi, and its inextricable connectedness with subjection, and signs of subjection, such as the veil. Leonard's concern was with the Nazi armband as the signifier of a performative mode of signification which created loyal subjects and automatised response. His recommended strategy for the resisting subject seemed to rest on a rhetoric of the constative and of subjecting assertions to the test of verification. In Leonard's thinking, transparent reasoning and the tactic of setting sceptical reason against the perlocutionary force of symbols provide the only hope of redeeming civilisation from the inspired bodies of metaphysical and ideological quackery (and with them the useful bodies of the fascist machinery of war). It is hardly surprising that Virginia has a different conception of the traffics and complexities of signification than Leonard. Her analysis of how culture is founded and performed, brought forth and practised, allows her to see that the performative force of symbols will not be dispelled by decree of reason, civilisation or the ego, but also that the 'reason' and 'civilisation' of educated man exist on a continuum without safe boundaries. Thus the cultural critique of *Three Guineas* engages not only the enforced performance of totalitarian regimes, but also various integrative projects of democratic societies, including progressive attempts to enlist the dressed body as signifier and performer of modern rationality. Where Leonard juxtaposes two kinds of savagery, two primitive performative cultures, Virginia, as we have seen, reveals the presence of ceremonial, performative culture in the midst of civilisation. The field of agency she defines for the resisting (female) subject is circumscribed by 'mental chastity' – suggesting a need to remain chaste under the force of the law and the sign of subjection; to counter it, like Antigone, with speech acts of refusal – but also with jokes, parody, ridicule, irony; etiolations of the speech act's performative force. Women she says, should pronounce an opinion upon outsides, because the outside is usually connected with the inside – which, presumably, amounts to saying that the fragment may provide access to the totality, the trivial to the serious, and the most naturalised everyday act to the system of cultural performance.

Finally, what Woolf proposes is a reconceptualised education – not the civilising process of the educated man, but an education in what one might call signifying practice:

> the arts of human intercourse; the art of understanding other people's lives and minds, and the little arts of talk, of dress, of cookery, that are allied with them. The aim of the new college, the cheap college, should be not to segregate and specialize, but to combine. It should explore the ways in which mind and body can be made to cooperate; discover what new combinations make good wholes in human life. (*TG*: 40)

What seems to be envisaged here is a redefined humanism and a signifying practice based on combinations rather than boundaries, on human intercourse rather than dominance and subjection. This, it seems, would be to found a true community, to reopen the space of counsel closed by Creon, and to finally divest the performative of its phallic force.

Notes

1. Woolf, along with other members of Bloomsbury, had a brief fling with neo-pagan 'gypsy' fashion, outdoor life and cult of nudity. See for instance Paul Delany (1987).
2. One of Flügel's proposals, consequently, concerns the establishment of a 'Clothing Board' to deal with clothing according to principles of modernity such as 'practical suitability', 'economic reasonableness', and 'the advances of modern science' (Flügel 1930: 219).
3. See e.g. Susan Sontag 1980 and Elizabeth Wilson 1990.
4. I am indebted to Timothy Gould's reading of *The Antigone* in 'The Unhappy Performative' (1995) for this understanding of the play.

Chapter 6

Hats and Veils: *Texere* in the Age of Rupture

The words Leonard Woolf chose for his wife's epitaph in 1941 Woolf herself set down on paper ten years earlier as Bernard's last words in *The Waves*: 'Against you I will fling myself, unvanquished and unyielding, O Death!' To many readers this is a phrase of considerable beauty; it is also one which focuses a critical disagreement, or rather a discomfort with Woolf's novel: the embarrassment which seems to ensue from the high style of apostrophe and soliloquy, and the uncertainty surrounding two familiar Woolfian voices: the elegiac and the satiric; or the 'impassioned' and the ironic.[1] Similar alternations inform *Jacob's Room* and *To the Lighthouse*, though within a stylistic range which seems to curtail both the doubts and the embarrassment. Following from Jane Marcus's groundbreaking postcolonial reading of the novel, however, the consensus tends towards some variant of the satiric reading, by which *The Waves* gives us 'the swan song of the white Western male author with his Romantic notions of individual genius', with Bernard as 'Byronic man, the Romantic artist-hero, sing[ing] his last aria against death' (Marcus 1993: 235). Marcus deals with the embarrassment ensuing from the high style of apostrophe and soliloquy by reading it as a strategy of ironic undercutting: the impassioned invocations like Bernard's above constitute 'a postmodern pastiche of quotation from the master texts of English literature', while the form of the soliloquy 'enacts a discursive infantilization' which 'mocks the Western valorization of individual selfhood' (ibid.: 231, 236, 235). Woolf's uncomfortable mysticism is dealt with within a framework of postcolonial critique in which the novel as a whole is a narrative about imperialist culture making and the interludes readable as homage to Indian religious philosophy as mediated (among others) by Woolf's cousin Dorothea Stephen in her *Studies in Early Indian Thought*.

The influence of Marcus's essay is shown in the number of critics who have followed suit in reading the high style as part of a parodic/

satiric project, choosing to deal with the novel's mysticism by locating it within particular contemporary discourses or discursive formations, whether the 'new physics' of the 1920s and 1930s or the interest in non-Christian, non-deistic spirituality which was another prominent phenomenon of these years. Emily Dalgarno reads *The Waves* as Woolf's response in fiction to a precise cultural moment: the introduction (via new visual technologies and the new physics) of a 'new sense of the visible and a new discursive formation', a turn towards representation summed up in Martin Heidegger's 1938 lecture 'The Age of the World Picture': 'The fundamental event of the modern age is the conquest of the world as picture' (Dalgarno 2001: 101). In Dalgarno's reading the novel represents Woolf's most consistent attempt to step outside an anthropocentric model of the gaze caught up with Imperialist notions of race and gender, a critical project in light of which Bernard's final apostrophe (along with the novel's Romantic allusions) reads as satire; the self-dramatisation of the Romantic artist-hero asserting his centrality within the humanist visual paradigm.

Several commentators address Woolf's 'mysticism' by making the connection between mysticism as a cultural phenomenon between the wars and the change in scientific thinking occasioned by the new theories in physics. Gillian Beer, Holly Henry and Julie Kane point out that James Jeans and Arthur Eddington, along with other prominent physicists of their day, were led by the new findings toward a mystical world view. The titles of their works point us in this direction. Kane quotes Eddington's *Science and the Unseen World* (1929), where he writes that

> Perhaps the most essential change [in scientific thinking] is that we are no longer tempted to condemn the spiritual aspects of our nature as illusory because of their lack of concreteness . . . matter and all else that is in the physical world have been reduced to a shadowy symbolism. (Eddington 1929: 21–2; Kane 1995: 344)

Henry refers to the public interest surrounding Jeans's *The Mysterious Universe* (1930) with its 'quasi-theological claims that structure in the universe implied the universe was formed by a creator-mathematician' (Henry 2003: 93). The openness to mysticism comes from the physicist's world of 'inaudible tones, invisible light, imperceptible heat', from which any conception of substance is 'wholly lacking' (Beer 1996: 117, 112). Woolf scholars have tended to 'redeem' Woolf's mysticism in this perspective, by seeing the 'mystical, eyeless vision' as decentred; anthropofugal rather than anthropocentric, a dispersal which resists aggressive imposition of human-centred paradigms, and so on. In Henry's reading the hybrid generic form and dispersed aesthetic vision demonstrated by *The Waves* accounts for the decentring of humans produced by contemporary scientific and technological developments (Henry 2003: 107), a reading which aligns itself with Pamela Caughie's assertion that 'Woolf relinquishes in *The Waves* the belief that art has a center of vision, that it can reveal some truth or effect some "ultimate synthesis"' (Henry 2003: 105; Caughie 1991: 50).

What is at issue here – the question raised by Bernard's final words (and Woolf's epitaph) – is how to read the 'poetry' (the 'impassioned prose' and the mysticism) of *The Waves*, and, connected with that, how to understand Woolf's response to the symbolic world of physics, to a universe which, as Jeans put it in 1930, 'begins to look more like a great thought than like a great machine' (Kane 1995: 345). Popularised science, at the time when Woolf was composing her novel, was describing a universe of waves and particles, entropy and dissipation, and a discipline whose representations and symbolisations were in all likelihood little more than convenient human projections: a position in which there can be no great difference between scientist and nature, representation and reality (Beer 1996; Whitworth 2001). *The Waves* may well be read as Woolf's response to this changed world of matter and the limitations of human modes of cognition, but that does not mean that the world it presents is without essence or that its literary project is primarily deconstructive and satiric. From my perspective, the 'look through clothes', one of the striking aspects of *The Waves* is the recurrence of sartorial items and tropes throughout the text – a recurrence, I wish to suggest, which points towards alternative readings of both of the questions above. What I want to argue is that the sartorial performs much of the novel's work, and that this work, as the title of this chapter indicates, may be described as attempting an allegorical *texere* in an age of rupture, a textual weaving which establishes connections between literary acts of investiture and divestiture, and which asserts the mysteries of material presence through a series of unfoldings and envelopments. In short, reading 'through clothes' enables us to see that Woolf's response to the changed appearance of matter and the move to a symbolic world was not to relinquish the belief that art can reveal truth, but rather to posit it as an alternative mode of cognition and knowledge, a modelling or projecting which is not so much based on science as parallel to it.

With such a perspective, what takes place in the interludes emerges as a kind of *poiesis*, a process in which the natural order produces itself as continuance and difference; an unconcealment of which the sun is constituted as the primary agent. Garments and textiles are closely involved in figuring nature's creative work and in investing the sun with animating, creative powers. Before sunrise the sea is a creased cloth that sweeps a veil of white water across the sand (*TW*: 3). Sartorial accessories personify Dawn, adorning her with water-coloured jewels and a fan that makes a finger-print of shadow upon a white blind (ibid.: 3–4). The sun's poiesis 'stitches white tablecloths with fine gold wires', touches a red-edged curtain to bring out circles and lines, gathers 'flocks of shadow . . . in many-pleated folds' (ibid.: 20, 55, 82). Waves and landscapes are animated and endlessly transformed under the sun's gaze, metamorphosing into horses, birds, 'a regiment of plumed and turbaned soldiers' (ibid.: 81–2). Shadows are 'blown like grey cloths over the sea', curtains and blinds are animated, enlisted in the sun's work of transforming appearances into apparitions (ibid.: 139–40). With the evening sun the sky's cloth becomes a 'fleecy canopy' under which, lined with shadows, chairs and tables are made to seem 'more ponderous'; knives, forks and glasses 'portentous'; an iron black boot transformed into 'a pool of deep blue' (ibid.: 159–60). In the end sky and sea are indistinguishable, the room 'hung with vast curtains of shaking darkness' which, endlessly metamorphosing, performs its work, enveloping, covering everything (ibid.: 181–2).

Traditionally, the sun is a figure of knowledge as well as of nature. As Michael Ferber writes, the sun is the most striking thing to be seen, also a condition of sight itself (Ferber 1999). For the Greeks, to be alive was to see the sun, but equally, as suggested in the Homeric invocation of the sun as the ever-present witness, to be seen by it. Giving face and dress to the sun and its agents is to invest the universe with sentient and potentially responsive forces, an auratic veiling which Benjamin also finds in the recurring prosopopoeias of Baudelaire's poetry. Against the background of interludes, the soliloquies give us voices speaking to themselves or overheard, possibly witnessed by and even addressed to the sun. The soliloquies are vocative; they draw attention to voice, to the modality of address – in this, as we have said, resides much of their embarrassment; the embarrassment of the high style. Strangely, they assert the temporality of the pure present against the 'said' of the recording instance and the past tense of the interludes; they soliloquise on writing, they speak in quotations, they invoke the muse. Jonathan Culler writes of the apostrophe that it could be taken as the figure 'of all that is most radical, embarrassing, pretentious, and mystificatory in the lyric' (Culler 1981: 137). If that is indeed the case, this is an embarrassment that the apostrophe would seem to share with the soliloquy in that both are spoken to be overheard rather than heard, the speaker normally pretending to be addressing someone other than his listeners. In both cases, too, what seems to be involved is what Culler describes for the apostrophe as a 'deflection of message', a 'troping on the circuit or situation of communication' which asserts that the feeling involved is for the act of addressing itself, for the vocative, optative, and imperative functions, rather than simply signifying the depth of the speaker's emotions (ibid.: 135).

We shall have cause to return to the question of address and its functions at a later stage in this discussion, specifically in connection with the reading of Bernard's final apostrophe. For the moment, however, I want to turn to another source of difficulty, and potential embarrassment, in this text: its disparity of rhetorical levels and thematic concerns – disparities which the sartorial signifiers both seem to open up and connect. As many readers have observed, much of the content of the soliloquies is taken up with what seems to be a characteristically modern experience of becoming a subject, a process which, in the subject/object relations which define the modern visual field, entails becoming a picture: being represented by one's appearance, learning to make an impression rather than a spectacle of oneself. Superficially, these are trivial concerns, though, as every modern subject knows, with existential as well as socio-economic ramifications. The cultural moment in which these soliloquies are uttered is one where, in the area of psychology, J. C. Flügel finds himself called upon to write at length on the role of clothing in psycho-sexual and socio-cultural inscriptions, while, in ethnology, Marcel Mauss elaborates his ideas on the social nature of the habitus and bodily techniques – both concerned with culture as mediated through the body. Woolf, it seems, is absorbed by related ideas: the 'civilising process' as working through dressed bodies; the 'concourse of the body and moral and intellectual symbols' which Mauss was thinking about at the same time; and the importance of tradition in this process: the authority of example (Mauss 2005: 76). 'There is no technique and no transmission in the absence of tradition', writes Mauss: 'In all these elements of the art of using the human body, the facts of education [are] dominant' (ibid.: 75). No doubt, Woolf would have concurred. In *The Waves*, however, the text goes beyond the psycho-somatic and socio-cultural concerns of Flügel and Mauss. With an approach to clothes that has many points of contact with that of Carlyle in *Sartor Resartus*, Woolf draws on the sartorial to connect pathos and bathos, the trivial and the elevated, satire and mysticism.

Recently, historians and theorists of dress have claimed *Sartor Resartus* as a foundational text for contemporary dress studies as a field of cultural enquiry, on the grounds that this strange piece of writing prefigures and so is particularly apposite for the preoccupations that define the 'society of the sign': the valorisation of the symbolic, the attention to material and visual cultures, the concern with questions of identity, representation and lifestyles (Keenan 2001: 1–15; Carter 2003: 1–17). Keenan and Carter both give emphasis to *Sartor*'s project of social and cultural critique, based on its understanding of clothes as resonant social symbols, emblematic of social relations, and instrumental to the 'sacralization of individual and corporate bodies' (Keenan 2001: 15). What is equally interesting about this text however (as both Keenan and Carter point out) is its particular type of materialism and the hermeneutics it proposes for the material world. In Carlyle's theory of the Symbol the quotidian has a meaning that transcends itself. All visible things are emblems; metaphors and symbols: 'Matter exists only spiritually, and to represent some Idea, and body it forth. Hence Clothes, as despicable as we think them, are so unspeakably significant' (Carlyle 1869: 49). The clothes philosopher's gaze through 'the Clothes-Screen' purports to see daily life 'girt with Wonder, and based on Wonder': 'Rightly viewed no meanest object is insignificant; all objects are as windows, through which the philosophic eye looks into Infinitude itself' (ibid.: 187, 49). As Carter glosses it, *Sartor*'s hermeneutics arises from the idea of the world as a conjoining of spirit and matter that can only be grasped by the labour of interpretation (Carter 2003: 14). What results is a hermeneutic of the layered worlds of meaning within the material, and a mode of interpretation which gives attention at once to the literal and the allegorical, the prosaic and the sublime. In its association with German Idealist philosophy Carlyle's materialism may be difficult to countenance, as Keenan observes in pointing to the distance between the contemporary position and Carlyle's 'reverential . . . regard for the "ordinarily sacred" in the midst of our everyday lives'; the Romantic, innocent vision 'that matter matters in the ultimate scheme of things' (Keenan 2001: 19). Nonetheless, as the renewed interest in *Sartor Resartus* indicates, Carlyle's metaphysical materialism resonates in the context of various modern approaches to the material world, from that of the Surrealists to contemporary 'Thing theory' and enquiries in 'material culture'.

In the context of *The Waves*, what is particularly suggestive about *Sartor Resartus* is that Carlyle is writing within a cultural moment which to him is dominated by instrumental reason, when 'Science' and the utilitarian spirit have destroyed 'Wonder' (Carlyle 1869: 46), and that he fastens on clothes as the vehicle for his cultural critique as well as for the attempt to restore a lost hermeneutic capacity. In a text which combines 'Descendentalism' and 'Transcendentalism' (ibid.: 44), satire and mysticism; which veers hazardously between levels and styles, clothes as material things invested with a rich allegorical potential are enlisted to perform the turns and establish the connections between discourses and worlds. The philosophy of clothes, in other words, allows Carlyle to say something about the nature of culture as a system of symbolic relations, and about the nature and meaning of human life. Turning to the sartorial preoccupations of *The Waves*, a number of similarities between the two texts suggest themselves. While proposing *Sartor* as an intertext for Woolf's novel – with the implication that Woolf is now somehow taking seriously the allegorical approach to things that she parodies in *Freshwater* and *Orlando* – may be perceived as stretching the evidence too far, at the very least it should be recognised that Carlyle's understanding and deployment of clothing have something to offer in reading the significance and function of the sartorial in Woolf's text, and in negotiating the stylistic and thematic disparities critics have found so troublesome.

Quite consistently, the characters in *The Waves* are known by their relation to clothing, specifically by certain recurring tags or epithets which seem to represent them to themselves and the world. Clearly this is a mode of signification that differs from the impressionist sketch of a character's appearance, functioning more as a textual insistence, a refrain which gestures towards something beyond the subject/object relation. From the beginning, garments and textiles are part of the world that comes into being, making up the prosaic ordinariness as well as the strangeness of the everyday world, signalling one of the central preoccupations of the soliloquies. The first thing Jinny sees is a 'crimson tassel twisted with gold threads', next the house 'with all its windows white with blinds' (*TW*: 6). Susan observes how 'Mrs Constable pulls up her thick black stockings,' while Rhoda's gaze at 'the table-cloth, flying white along the table' invests it with secret meaning, of a flag signalling, or a shroud (ibid.: 6). Louis is known to himself and the others as 'a boy in grey flannels with a belt fastened by a brass snake' (ibid.: 7, 13). This, he points out, is his appearance 'up here', though the mystery of the snake signals a connection to what he is 'down there', in the world of stone figures and 'men in turbans'; to his 'roots . . . threaded like fibres' (ibid.: 13). Susan's refrain is the pocket-handkerchief which contains her childhood agony, referred to five times within a brief soliloquy and remaining with her, screwed tight into a ball or nervously twisted, as a signature property (ibid.: 8–10). Another early memory, of illicit desire, is signified by washing blown out hard on the clothesline (ibid.: 17, 93). Later in life a range of sartorial epithets define her mode of being, alternating between the organic and the maternal: clothes like skins and furs; aprons, stockings and slippers; meshes, covers, cocoons in which she wraps plants and children. She despises the futility of fashion; 'would wear a plain straw hat on a summer's day', is the pre-modern mother/muse who inspires calm and reverence; forever 'stitching . . . under a quiet lamp in a house' (ibid.: 79, 72–3). Bernard's summing up at the end picks up on the refrain for each: the grey flannel with a snake belt, the pocket handkerchief, clothes blown out hard on the line (ibid.: 184–8). His own defining memory of being 'covered with warm flesh,' he thinks of as an experience that is generally human, describing it in Carlylean terms, of the body as garment: 'We become clothed in this changing, this feeling garment of flesh' (ibid.: 18, 93). Individuation occurs as the 'wax that coats the spine' melts in different patches for each: 'Thus . . . in great streaks my waxen waistcoat melted' (ibid.: 185, 190).

The *habitus*, as Mauss would say, is 'instilled from above' (Mauss 2005: 75), massively so through the uniformisation and sartorial hierarchies of school, to which they go 'with the regulation number of socks and drawers' (*TW*: 93), to be acculturated and gendered through embodiment: 'the concourse of the body and moral and intellectual symbols' (Maus 2005: 76). Education occurs as imitation: the boys imitate Percival's normative gestures, just as the teachers attempt to imitate the headmaster – though, 'wearing grey trousers, they will only succeed in making themselves ridiculous' (*TW*: 25–6). The characters are differentiated by their relation to cultural symbols and the regime of corporeal inscription. Where Louis finds all his doubts laid by the sign of the headmaster's authority, his crucifix, to Neville the gilt cross heaving on his waistcoat is like Carlyle's hollow garments: the sign of a 'sad religion', 'words of authority . . . corrupted by those who speak them' (ibid.: 24–5, 22). Repeatedly, the text looks back to the process of dressing, weaving and plaiting that hollowed out the character of Jacob Flanders, while also anticipating the sartorial semiotics of *Three Guineas* and *Between the Acts*. Bernard, in another Carlylean echo, undercuts authority by inventing a story in which he imagines Dr Crane undressing '(let us be trivial, let us be intimate)': unfastening his sock suspenders, taking the coppers from his trouser pockets, swinging his braces (ibid.: 36–7). It is Bernard, too, who meditates on ceremonial symbols in parodic terms in the Hampton Court episode: 'Our English past – one inch of light. Then people put teapots on their heads and say, "I am a king."' 'Soon one recovers belief in figures but not at once in what they put on their heads' (ibid.: 174). As in the carnivalesque pageant of *Between the Acts*, history and anthropology reduce to costume, with picture-book juxtapositions carrying much of the satire: the imperialist's 'sun-helmet' next to men in 'loin-cloths' (ibid.: 102); Percival's billycock hat against the 'Oriental' turban.

Rhoda's existential pain, the agony of being exposed to the 'arrows' of another's gaze, is consistently expressed in terms of dress or nudity, face or facelessness. At school the regimentalisation of brown serge deindividuates her (*TW*: 23–4). Being a subject is to be in possession of the requisite bodily techniques; having no face, no identity or sense of connection with a world of substance comes from not being able to pull up one's stockings with certainty or resoluteness (the way Jinny and Susan do), not knowing how to tie a bow (ibid.: 31, 98). At the party she stands 'trapped in silk', thinking of 'mothers from whose wide knees skirts descend': 'Hide me . . . the most naked of you all' (ibid.: 79). Rhoda anticipates Percival's death in a vision that places him at the centre of an ancient ritual of investiture, draped in garlands and laurel leaves – but 'death is woven in with the violets' (ibid.: 105–6). Her extreme alienation at his death is figured by the serialisation of the crowd of shoppers: 'faces and faces, served out like soup-plates by scullions; coarse, greedy, casual; looking in at shop-windows with pendant parcels' (ibid.: 120). Fashion is also renewal, however: the procession of life as habit and phantasmagoria moves on with the decision to go to Oxford Street to buy stockings for a party. In the shop, beauty returns among laces and coloured ribbons: 'Pain is suspended as a girl silently slides open a drawer' (ibid.: 120–1). Yet alienation remains Rhoda's mode of being. As she looks back on her life towards its end, 'all were dressed in indeterminate shades of grey and brown, never even a blue feather pinned to a hat' (ibid.: 156). Climbing the Spanish hill and dreaming of dying, she feels 'there is only a thin sheet between me now and the infinite depths . . . The sheets spotted with yellow holes let me fall through' (ibid.: 157–8).

From childhood Jinny's fantasies of the future revolve around dress, of fabric 'veined', 'shot with red threads', winding and billowing round her, of leaving school and wearing long skirts; necklaces and sleeveless dresses at night (*TW*: 24, 40). At home in 'the great society of bodies' (ibid.: 46), her embodiment is mediated by dress as a natural extension of the body, animated by its movements, sending out signals on its behalf. To her the sexual exchange economy has the appearance of ritual, stylised and formal, enacted by dress (ibid.: 76). In middle age she knows 'I shall soon raise my arm in vain and my scarf will fall to my side without having signalled' (ibid.: 148). Once more, however, clothes represent routine and renewal, life's triumph over the 'abysses' of time and space 'with rouge, with powder, with flimsy pocket-handkerchiefs' (ibid.: 175). Far from Rhoda's alienated vision, fashion signifies variety and differentiation, movement and progress, traffics and journeys: the 'infinite variety of women's dresses' delight her, as do uniforms, wigs and gowns, bowler hats and 'tennis shirts beautifully open at the neck' (ibid.: 169). In the 'triumphant procession' of shoppers the symbols of

fashion have taken over for the ceremonial 'banners and brass eagles
and heads crowned with laurel-leaves won in battle'. This is the modern
'army of victory', the peak of civilisation, at the other end of which are
'savages in loin-cloths, and women whose . . . long breasts sag': 'I too,
with my little patent-leather shoes, my handkerchief that is but a film
of gauze, my reddened lips and my finely pencilled eyebrows, march to
victory with the band' (ibid.: 149).

Like Rhoda, Louis's sense of unreality stems from his conception that
there is a norm for being a body in the world; 'the mean', 'the average',
which is beyond him, outside his possession: 'I look at the little men at
the next table to be sure that I do what they do' (*TW*: 69). His life is spent
in 'antics', smoothing his hair lest someone should laugh at him (ibid.:
95). Like Rhoda, too, he has access to two realities: 'some far horizon'
and the flux of the metropolis, where clothes have supplanted character
and individuals are metonymically represented by their headgear: 'hats
bobbing up and down in perpetual disorder' (ibid.: 70). As poet and
observer he imagines himself addressed by the procession of fashion
– the 'aimless passing of billycock hats and Homburg hats and all the
plumed and variegated head-dresses of women' – his ambition 'to make
a steel ring of clear poetry that shall connect . . . the church spire and
the bobbing billycock hats' (ibid.: 70, 96). His destiny, as he perceives
it, is the poet's plaiting and weaving (ibid.: 154). Ironically, however,
his days are spent 'lac[ing] the world together' with ships, spinning the
webs of commerce, extending the fabric of capitalism (ibid.: 127, 153).
In the evenings, he divests himself of the signs of his authority – hat and
stick, white waistcoat, 'gold and purple vestments' – to resume 'that
curious attempt', invoking the spirit of poetry in an apostrophe which
transmutes ironically into prose: 'O western wind . . . O western wind
you are at enmity with my mahogany table and spats', with my mistress
who tumbles the floor 'with dirty under-linen' (ibid.: 168–9, 153–4).

The Waves gives us clothing's material shaping of individuals through
habit or *habitus*; the ideological and ideational effects of the material world, but also the human attempt at shaping the material world
through types of figuration, interpretation and investment. Fashion
figures modern metropolitan experience (as aimless serialisation or consuming desire), while webs, nets and filaments signify depths of being
and transindividual, transhistorical connections; yielding veils, sheets
and curtains separating one world from another, draperies enveloping
in ambiguity. Neville at Hampton Court figures his body as 'unprotected
fibre', also 'a net whose fibres pass imperceptibly beneath the world'
(*TW*: 164). Between Bernard and Neville a line extends: 'the line that
is spun from us lengthening its fine filaments across the misty spaces of

the intervening world' (ibid.: 66). At a moment of connection in the restaurant, Rhoda observes: 'our eyes . . . seem to push through curtains of colour . . . which yield like veils and close behind them'. 'Yes, said Jinny, our senses have widened. Membranes, webs of nerve . . . have filled and spread themselves and float round us like filaments' (ibid.: 101). From childhood Rhoda figures consciousness as a 'thin sheet', and sleep as falling through it into waves of 'black plumes' and 'wings' (ibid.: 19). Like Louis she is conscious of 'a world immune from change', though her vision is figured in different terms, as 'people without faces, leaning like statues against the sky'; 'faces rid of features, robed in beauty' (ibid.: 79–80). Watching their friends return, the 'conspirators' Rhoda and Louis see them as androgynous, numinous figures: 'Are they men or are they women? They still wear the ambiguous draperies of the flowing tide . . . Wonder and awe change as they put off the draperies of the flowing tide' (ibid.: 177–8).

The presence of sartorial items consistently invites a hermeneutic approach. Through repetition and the high style, clothes and textiles are in many cases imbued with a mystery that places them outside the order of objects and objectivist discourses. The effect is similar but not identical to the modern materialism practised by the surrealist avant-garde, which strove to grant things – including clothes – their potency, cognizant of the work matter performs in moving, shaping, impinging on people (Lehmann 2000; Brown 2001). As Ulrich Lehmann writes, dadaists and surrealists imbued clothes and sartorial items with a magic that arose from their perception of everyday objects in a manner alien to their proper purpose: things approach the realm of the mythic and the surreal when liberated from their cultural framework (Lehmann 2000). Benjamin, in his reflections on surrealism in 1929, refers to this as an anthropological (as opposed to metaphysical or romantic) materialism, but modern materialisms like Woolf's are not necessarily caught up with a Benjaminean dialectical optics (Benjamin 2007: 192). Presenting things in their surreal, mythical or mystical aspect, is, as exponents of 'thing theory' have shown, to deny modernity's artificial distinctions between inanimate objects and human subjects, to assert that the world's subjects and objects are involved in complex patterns of interrelation and circulation, perhaps also to suspend clear distinctions between the material and the immaterial, between appearances and apparitions. The sartorial as it operates in *The Waves* evokes the mysteries of material presence partly because it operates on a boundary between the animate and the inanimate, representing a material shaping of the subject while establishing connections to different worlds through organic surfaces, webs and fabric. Animated by the wind or made transparent by the sun, clothes and textiles turn into the signals or apparitions of alternative topographies, temporalities and rationalities. *The Waves* is, among other things, a modern metropolitan novel that makes use of a sartorial tropology to depict the metropolis as both an existential and a numinous space. The sartorial, one might say, serves to bring out two metropolitan topographies: the phantasmagoria and the alienation of the big city, and, as a submerged territory or *unground*,[2] a world of apparitions and mysteries.

The novel's meditations on different kinds of writing are figured through cloth and clothing. Where Louis's high modernist poem aims to create order in the procession of hats, to connect – in a steel ring – the church spire and the billycock hat, the plumed head-dresses of Oxford Street and the women bearing pitchers of water by the Nile, Bernard's compulsive phrase-making, his prose, takes the form of 'a wandering thread, lightly joining one thing to another': 'My mind hums hither and thither with its veil of words for everything' (*TW*: 36, 88). 'I am wrapped round with phrases, like damp straw'; 'I keep my phrases hung like clothes in a cupboard, waiting for someone to wear them' (ibid.: 166–7). The progression towards the percipient, androgynous prose of Bernard's final summing up goes through a renunciation of self which also takes the form of an unclothing. 'I am no hoarder', reflects the middle-aged Bernard, 'I shall leave only a cupboard of old clothes when I die – and am almost indifferent to the minor vanities of life which cause Louis so much torture' (ibid.: 100). From the Byronic posturing of youth, where his friends see him throwing off his cloak, flinging down his hat and stick with practised bravado, he arrives at a place and a mood from which his usual self 'looks like a heap of old clothes', its 'warm coverings' and 'familiar veils' fallen, new stages of life approaching, 'wearing robes of solemnity' (ibid.: 56, 143–4). The end of writing comes with the loss of self, the absence of regard: 'I saw but was not seen. From me had dropped the old cloak, the old response': 'let me cast and throw away this veil of being . . . Unregarded I need no words' (ibid.: 220, 227).

The novel's final moments bring 'the eternal renewal' of nature's poiesis, the sun's eye returns, Pegasus rises, and Bernard rides in the face of his enemy: 'Against you I will fling myself, unvanquished and unyielding, O Death!' (*TW*: 228). Jonathan Culler reads invocation as a figure of vocation:

> Voice calls in order to be calling, to dramatize its calling, to summon images of its power so as to establish its identity as poetical and prophetic voice . . . The poet makes himself a poetic presence through an image of voice, and nothing figures voice better than the pure O of undifferentiated voicing. (Culler 1981: 142)

Here we return to the question that opened these reflections: of whether Bernard's 'pure O' is uttered with the stageyness of the Byronic hero and ironically undercut by Woolf's quotational, allusive style. The 'retailoring of the tailor' that makes up *Sartor*'s central narrative, occurs through a renunciation which is suggestively reminiscent of that described for Bernard above. On his wild wanderings through the 'Wilderness' of 'the World in an Atheistic Century', Carlyle's tailor-poet reaches the 'Centre of Indifference' by his first 'moral Act: Annihilation of Self'. Way-weary and life-weary he asks merely to rest: 'to live or to die is alike to me' (Carlyle 1869: 128–30). Strikingly (or ironically), *Sartor*'s concept of Renunciation (Goethe's *Entsagen*) entails the hero's renunciation of his Byronic yearning for infinite happiness ('Foolish soul! What act of legislature was there that thou shouldst be Happy?' 'Close thy Byron; open thy Goethe' (ibid.: 132)), and the beginning of a sincere engagement with the world. The act of renunciation unseals his 'mind's eyes', allowing him to see that the universe is not 'dead and demoniacal', and to look upon his 'fellow man' with love and pity (ibid.: 128–30). Through affliction, concludes Carlyle's text, life 'triumphs over Death. On the roaring billows of Time, thou art not engulfed, but borne aloft into the azure of Eternity'. 'This is the Everlasting Yea' (ibid.: 133).

Needless to say, accepting *Sartor Resartus* among Woolf's intertexts in *The Waves* hardly serves by itself to dispel the argument for a satiric reading. When I still want to take seriously Bernard's affirmation of the vocation of writing as a vocative which makes the objects of the universe potentially responsive forces, solicits regard, and so creates the fabric of allegory, I do so against the background of the larger intertextual web into which *The Waves* enters, and which, I suggest, has something significant to say about Woolf's response to the insubstantial, symbolic world of science. In Volume 4 of his autobiography, covering the years 1919 to 1939, Leonard Woolf writes with the discomfort of the rationalist about his wife's beliefs in the afterlife of the writer: 'I suspect that Virginia, though she did not believe in life after death, did believe in her life after death in *The Waves*, and not merely in the life of *The Waves* after her death' (Woolf, L. 1967: 206). As Woolf's readers after three-quarters of a century we may not be better placed to say what she (or he) meant by this, though perhaps to dispel some of the discomfort. Several of Woolf's essays express the (post-Romantic) idea that writers live on as voice in their writing; a voice that can be reconstructed by means of careful listening to the text in its rhythm, its breath. Texts are also *tupoi*; imprints and integuments that take the imprint of the author's body and mind. Both are conceptualisations, as Woolf herself says, that give rise to a critical activity of exhumation and reanimation rather than the autopsy or dissection.[3] Woolf's thoughts on the posthumous are not always caught up with the voice and vocation of the author, however. Throughout her fictional and autobiographical writing, as is well known, Woolf expresses her intuitions of the existence of other temporal and spatial domains: depths of experience and existence to which one has only fleeting access; a temporality beyond individual and generational memory. It seems to be an intuition of this order, and its connection to nature, she expresses in this much cited passage from her diary:

> [I] got then to a consciousness of what I call 'reality': a thing I see before me, something abstract; but residing in the downs or sky; beside which nothing matters; in which I shall rest & continue to exist. Reality I call it. And I fancy sometimes this is the most necessary thing to me: that which I seek . . . Now perhaps this is my gift, this perhaps is what distinguishes me from other people. (*D* 3: 196)

The 'gift' she speaks of here seems to be the gift of the reality of an afterlife, one that is connected with nature; an affinity with a particular landscape, perhaps a sense of nature as emblematic; meaningful. As with so many nineteenth-century themes in Woolf's writing, such conceptions are subjected to ironic as well as serious treatment. Most famously the topos of living on, in nature and/or the monument of one's works, is ironically deployed in the characterisation of Mr Ramsay in *To the Lighthouse*, where such ideas, along with Victorian anthropomorphism and sentimentalised beliefs in immortality, are spoofed as part of the rhetoric of valediction and the tributary modes Woolf is parodying. At the same time, as the alternations in tone between the ironic and the elegiac suggest, Woolf's parodic working-through of this rhetoric does not leave it without continued effect, does not root it out of Woolf's imagination or the 'whispering-gallery' of voices and quotations that recur and resound in the writer's mind.

There can be no doubt that Woolf is interested in what Esther Schor calls 'the vitality and legacy of the dead' in many senses, also in the reality of an afterlife (Schor 1994). As the narrating voice says in *Melymbrosia*, 'Nothing is stranger than the position of the dead among the living' (*MEL*: 18). What is equally clear is the prominence of a sartorial tropology both in Woolf's critique of a conventionalised rhetoric of mourning as well as in her figurations of the afterlife. Veils, draperies and garments signify excess, concealment and conventionality in a Victorian culture of mourning (the shrouded, curtained rooms muffling and covering up any sense of reality at her mother's death; the 'passionate lamentations that . . . hung about the genuine tragedy with folds of Eastern drapery' (*MOB*: 92–3, 40)), but also index death as state and 'de-temporalised space' in a private allegory of life: the continued life of the dead as ghosts or spirits, the possibility of crossing and re-crossing thresholds of life and afterlife.[4]

Nature and its agents appear clothed throughout Woolf's writing. The sea is like a cloth, the water a veil, the air gauze and mesh, sea and sky are all one fabric. Cliffs and ships signal secret messages as if part of a meaningful web. There is writing on the landscape: a scroll of smoke droops in valediction; the topography is a writing that signifies 'the nature of things' (*TTL*: 204). These tropes are all from *The Waves* and *To the Lighthouse*, but there is also nature's 'secret signalling' in *Mrs Dalloway*, by which

> every moment Nature signified by some laughing hint . . . her determination to show by brandishing her plumes, shaking her tresses, flinging her mantle this way and that, beautifully, always beautifully, and standing close up to breathe through her hollowed hands Shakespeare's words, her meaning. (*MD*: 124)

Shakespeare, Woolf's primary embodiment of the powers of literary language, is thus included in a textual weave of draped apparitions and natural agents, a *texere*, moreover, which entails the chiasmic, in the sense of a crossing or crossover of the boundaries of life and death. 'Shakespeare's words, [Nature's] meaning' is the dirge from *Cymbeline*, 'Fear no more' – speaking, as Jeremy Tambling points out in a reading of the play, of a 'knowledge . . . accrued from beyond death', from the 'detemporalised unground' of the 'post-humus' (Tambling 2001: 38).[5] With such resonances the draped figure becomes a composite of emblematic nature and writing itself: the vocation of writing as well as its ability to suspend conditions of life and death.

Woolf's persistent clothing of nature and its agents represents a relation to nature which is openly anthropomorphic, which not only invests the inanimate world with the possibility to look at us in return, as Benjamin writes of Baudelaire's auratic veiling, but which clothes it in garments that are surely allusive in more than one sense. Clearly Woolf's dressing of nature alludes to an iconographical and topological tradition in which veils, robes and draperies suggest revelation and concealment (or rather revelation *as* concealment) of ideal celestial or mythological truths; a traditional usage by which vestmentiary epithets qualify Dawn, the Seasons, the Muses, the Nereids, and other representatives of nature and myth; and where fabrics and textiles symbolise the union of opposites, the resolution of conflict, the healing of rifts.[6] At the same time, as we have seen, Woolf's writing establishes its own intertextual framework within which to read the clothed apparitions, a framework that has more in common with Carlyle's emblematic world than with a Romantic materialism whose aim is the symbolic union of subject and object. The insistent anthropomorphism of 'Time Passes' may be taken as illustrative of this point, divided between an ironic and a serious dressing of nature, indicating different conceptions of the symbol and the relations between the human and the material world. 'Divine goodness' – 'twitching the cord' and 'drawing the curtain' of mystery – clearly falls under Woolf's ironic anthropomorphism, as does the mystic walking the beach, 'stirring a puddle, looking at a stone' and asking the naive questions of an anthropocentric metaphysics: 'What am I? What is this?' (*TTL*: 139, 143). Invested with a different seriousness, the body of Time appears in a series of prosopopoeias, as airs which 'fold their garments'; clothed allegorical figures which invest the world with meaning by clothing, veiling, enveloping. Silence is a 'veil' enveloping the house and a 'swaying mantle' that weaves into itself cries of birds, ships hooting, the hum of the fields. These passages have the tone of the revelation, an unveiling: we are on the scene of what is concealed from us, a landscape of anteriority and posteriority, not as naked nature but as 'Loveliness itself', 'Stillness' itself (ibid.: 137–42).

The clothes left behind in the house figure in a symbolism that hesitates between the human and the non-human. Of course something similar applies to the house itself; the human *étui* overtaken by nature's plots, but the clothes left behind are even more poignant, invested with a stronger mnemonic force than other human possessions: 'What people had shed and left – a pair of shoes, a shooting cap, some faded skirts and coats in wardrobes – those alone kept the human shape and in the emptiness indicated how once they were filled and animated'. 'For there were clothes in the cupboards; they had left clothes in all the bedrooms'; 'boots and shoes', 'handkerchiefs, bits of ribbon' (*TTL*: 141, 148). These sartorial images seem to be on a level with Mrs Ramsay's grey cloak as it occupies Mrs McNab's memory: what some would call 'souvenirs', and others 'material hauntings'; reminders of human presence. Mrs Ramsay's shawl, however, is one sartorial item that begins to speak a different language. To begin with the shawl serves as an *Andenken* of Mrs Ramsay's apotropaic veiling of death; through its recurrence, however, it becomes involved in nature's signalling, like the autumn trees 'tak[ing] on the flash of tattered flags' (ibid.: 139); a symbolism that is by turns uncanny, gentle, aimless; beyond anthropocentrist decoding: 'as . . . a rock rends itself from the mountain . . . one fold of the shawl loosened and swung to and fro'; 'the rock was rent asunder; another fold of the shawl loosened; there it hung, and swayed'; 'idly, aimlessly, the swaying shawl swung to and fro' (ibid.: 142, 145, 150). By contiguity and suggestion the shawl becomes enveloped in a symbolic order suggested by nature's curtains of darkness, folds of blackness, night's wrapping, dawn's weaving, the sun's lifting of curtains and breaking of veils: the order of 'what is there when we are not there' and what, did we deserve it, 'should be ours always' (ibid.: 155, 139).

Woolf's 'mystical' and 'eyeless' writing in 'Time Passes', like the interludes of *The Waves*, is often read in light of contemporary epistemology and philosophy of science. Gillian Beer's reading of *To the Lighthouse* alongside some central concerns in post-empiricist enquiry has been influential in this direction: Mr Ramsay's 'subject and object and the nature of reality', the survival of the object without a perceiver, the possibility of unoccupied perspectives (*TTL*: 28). Anne Banfield's *The Phantom Table* (2000) develops Beer's arguments by reading Woolf's fiction together with Post-Impressionist formalism and Russellian theory of knowledge as parallel projects. In Banfield's reading, Woolf's 'acquaintance-based aesthetic' (Banfield 2000: 130) corresponds to the Impressionist analysis of sense experience, while Woolf's larger aim, like those of Russell and Fry, is projection of knowledge into unknown worlds. Here Banfield gives emphasis to the I/eye-less vision of unoccupied perspectives (in *The Waves* and 'Time Passes') and Woolf's experiments with sense-data caught on the periphery of perspectives, 'as if the sense-organs don't always require a mind' (ibid.: 130). My point here is not by any means to suggest that such readings are misdirected or wrong; on the other hand, nor should they be allowed to occlude those aspects of Woolf's thinking on literary language and the relations between the material and the symbolic that the sartorial tropes and the link to Carlyle bring to attention. The question I am putting for consideration is whether Woolf's consistent foregrounding of garments as objects, things and symbols points towards a rhetorical awareness of mediacy and the cognitive competence of literary language, and further, that dimension of metaphor that Goethe referred to as *unerforschlich* as well as *unaussprechlich* – or, in Carlyle's terms, where silence and speech act together.[7]

As shown in the discussion of *Freshwater* in Chapter 2, Carlyle's argument 'that all Symbols are properly Clothes' (Carlyle 1869: 187), involves an understanding of the proper function of linguistic mediacy and the relation of individual symbols to a universal allegory of the divine. 'Language is the Flesh-Garment . . . of Thought', writes Carlyle:

> I said that Imagination wove this Flesh-Garment; and does not she? Metaphors are her stuff: examine Language; what, if you except some few primitive elements (of natural sound), what is it all but Metaphors, recognised as such, or no longer recognised . . . If those same primitive elements are the osseus fixtures in the Flesh-Garment, Language, – then are Metaphors its muscles and tissues and living integuments. (Carlyle 1869: 49)

The point made here is that language is woven, and that it is (excepting a few primitive sounds) metaphorical in origin – a theory of language one might describe as Nietzschean. Unlike Aristotle's theory of tropes which assumes the ability to know the essence of things through the senses, and unlike the traditional empiricist account of the image as the causal result of a process that starts with objects in the world, Carlyle (like Nietzsche) understands metaphor as involving some kind of turn or leap from one sphere to another, an 'overleaping' or '*Überspringen*', in Nietzsche's term. Metaphorical transference creates relations between phenomena and linguistic expressions which were previously unrelated. For Carlyle, as G. B. Tennyson writes, metaphor illuminates relationships, reveals connections between things not at first evident, thus suggesting some meaningful scheme in the universe (Tennyson 1965). This scheme, however – the 'Living Garment' of which all nature and life are part – is not vouchsafed by means of Romantic translucence, by the spirit shining through nature. If 'all visible things are emblems', then, on the other hand, 'all Emblematic things are properly Clothes, thought-woven or hand-woven' (Carlyle 1869: 141; 49). By 'the wondrous agency of Symbols', revelation comes as concealment: 'In a Symbol there is concealment and yet revelation: here therefore, by Silence and by Speech acting together, comes a double significance' (ibid.: 151). In sum, this amounts to a non-perceptual theory of metaphor and symbol as cognitive and transcendent; a theory whose concern is not to join subject and object; which locates truth in mediacy, concealment and silence; and which takes as its metaphor the garment rather than the body.

Beer reads 'Time Passes' as a post-empiricist revision of Hume (and Leslie Stephen) in the question of subject/object, a revision in which language, or rather its inherent anthropomorphism, deconstructively intervenes. The idea is that where 'Time Passes' moves beyond the limits of empiricism to posit the empty or unoccupied perspectives of logical realism, the insistent anthropomorphism of the passage inevitably reintroduces human perspective (Beer 1996). In my reading, the anthropomorphism of this section is a poetic dressing by which meaning is simultaneously, and undecidably, created and uncovered; which may be thought of in terms both of investiture and divestiture. Distinct from *aletheia*, by which a metaphysical truth unveils itself, I think of this dressing as literary acts which are connected in Woolf's mind with a larger textual fabric and which serve to bring to mind not the object, but what Mrs Ramsay calls 'the nature of things'.

Reflecting on what she calls 'Darwin's Romantic materialism', Gillian Beer observes that Darwin shares with other Victorian writers . . . the feeling for the thisness [*haeccitas*] of things which signals both their full presence and their impenetrability . . . their resistance to interpretation in terms of man's perceptions and needs, and yet man's profound need to join himself to them which may be expressed linguistically through metaphor. (Beer 1986: 221)

or, we might add, the Romantic symbol. Such questions, as we have seen, had become different and more complex by the time Woolf was writing *The Waves*, with the advent of the symbolic, insubstantial and endlessly relativised world of the new physics. Between Carlyle's (and the Cameron circle's) emblematic matter, on the one hand, and the 'shadowy symbolism' of Eddington and Jeans, on the other, Woolf's tropology of the garment suggests an approach that is ultimately distinct from either. Perhaps it makes sense to describe it as a modern take on Carlyle's 'Natural Supernaturalism': a hermeneutics of the material world that takes clothes as particularly illustrative examples of the mysteries residing in the profane.

In 1938 Benjamin writes about Kafka in terms which have some relevance to *The Waves*:

Kafka's work is an ellipse; its widely spaced focal points are defined, on the one hand, by mystical experience (which is, above all, the experience of tradition) and, on the other hand, by the experience of the modern city-dweller . . . the contemporary of modern physicists. . . . If one states . . . that an enormous tension exists between such experiences in Kafka . . . one has stated only a half-truth. What is actually . . . crazy about Kafka is that this absolutely new world of experience comes to him by way of the mystical tradition . . . Kafka listened attentively to tradition . . . This listening requires great effort because only indistinct messages reach the listener. There is no doctrine to be learned, no knowledge to be preserved. What are caught flitting by are snatches of things not meant for any ear. (Benjamin 2007: 325–6)

One may well say that Woolf's work around 1930 occupies a similar ellipse. What she falls back on confronted with conceptions of reality increasingly prone to subjectivism, mentalism and even solipsism, is not the mysticism of Jewish tradition but the 'whispering-gallery' and 'continuing presences' of writing. The 'magical experiments with words' of the continental avant-garde aimed to create new plastic and synthetic realities as complex as those referred to by new collectives such as 'the crowd', 'the nation', 'the universe'. In these experiments, 'image and language take precedence' – before meaning and before the self, producing realities based on chance, analogies, montage (Benjamin 2007: 184, 179). These principles also inform the surrealist's approach to the material world, the 'profane illumination': an 'anthropological' as opposed to 'metaphysical' materialism which brings out 'the immense forces of "atmosphere"' concealed in things, a materialism in which 'ghostly signals flash from the traffic and inconceivable analogies and connections . . . are the order of the day', an optic that perceives 'the everyday as impenetrable, the impenetrable as everyday' (ibid.: 182–3, 190). Such comparisons may help us some way towards understanding how language and things perform in *The Waves*. However, there are important differences between the anthropological materialism Benjamin finds in French surrealism and Woolf, as there are differences between the materialism of *The Waves* and that of *Between the Acts*. Woolf's illumination of things in *The Waves* is not dialectical in the way Benjamin thinks of the surrealist profane illumination whose canon of things reveal their revolutionary energies in the object that has begun to be extinct, substituting a political for a historical view of the past. (This is closer to Woolf's practice in *Between the Acts*.) Nor does Woolf's use of rhythm and allusion, the juxtaposition of high and low, and so on, map on to the transformational linguistic games of the surrealists. Clearly, certain distinctions need to be made.

Benjamin points to the connections between the modern encounter with the atmospheric object and the attempt to discover or map a cosmological order under Baroque emblematics (Mao 1998: 6). With *Sartor Resartus* Carlyle writes himself into this series of attempts to 'gain insight into some underlying order by means of discrete objects' (ibid.: 6). The difference in Carlyle's venture is brought about by his choice of garments as objects. Through clothes he explores the sociology and semiotics of matter. Expanding and elaborating upon the clothes metaphor allows him to develop a theory of language (specifically metaphor and symbol) that emphasises its cognitive and performative force. Like Carlyle, Woolf foregrounds clothes in her explorations of the modes in which matter is present in our lives as objects and things, and how one may read through such fragments to the totality of an order of production or signification. The clothes that fill the pages of *The Waves* represent one way of understanding modern culture through its material aspect. For Woolf, too, as for Carlyle, the garment becomes the thing that figures the capacity of language to impact upon the world by writing it. Most obviously, of course, language has the capacity to create 'Wonder', in Carlyle's phrasing, to alter the familiarity and triviality of the material world that so often make us leave it unquestioned. Beyond that, as Carlyle, Woolf and the Surrealists knew in different ways, language represents a knowledge beyond the subject and as such possesses the potential to disclose as much as create structures of reality, signification and truth. Woolf discovered this potential in linguistic rhythm and recurring phrases, the culture's rags and tags. In her writing it is also signified in the literary topos of draperies, robes, mantles and veils, with its suggestion of thresholds and de-temporalised spaces, suspensions of time as well as the limits of life and death.

Bernard's final apostrophe is prefigured in Louis's invocation of the Western Wind as a spirit of inspiration. However, unlike Louis with his vanities – his spats and white waistcoat, his I, I, I – Bernard succeeds in making himself a writer, a weaver of disparate threads, in the final summing up. His 'pure O' voices his engagement with death, but also with the vocation of writing. To the extent that his words continue to figure Woolf after her death, as Leonard seemed to intend they should, they align her with a similar engagement. Woolf's response to the insubstantial world of modern physics was the texting of *The Waves*: a weaving of the mundane with the sublime, revealing the fabrics that contain and connect modern subjects to social and historical texts as well as to nature's *poiesis*.

Notes

1. 'Impassioned Prose' is the title of Woolf's 1926 essay on the prose of Thomas de Quincey, written, as Andrew McNeillie points out in his Introduction to Volume 4 of Woolf's essays, at a key stage, while drafting the 'Time Passes' section of *To The Lighthouse*. McNeillie considers Quincey's 'impassioned prose' a 'cousin' to the type of fiction Woolf envisaged for *The Waves* in 'The Narrow Bridge of Art' (1927): a work 'written in prose, but in a prose which has many of the characteristics of poetry' (*E* 4: xviii–xix; Woolf's essay is also known as 'Poetry, Fiction and the Future').
2. I am indebted to J. Hillis Miller's *Topographies* (1995) for the idea of an atemporal 'unground'.
3. See for instance Woolf's essay 'Donne After Three Centuries' (CR 2), as well as essays on Wordsworth, Coleridge and de Quincey.
4. For a fuller exploration of these ideas, see R. Koppen, 'Sartorial Adventures: Woolf and the (Other-)Worldliness of Dress', in H. Southworth and E. K. Sparks (eds), *Woolf and the Art of Exploration: Selected Papers from the Fifteenth International Conference on Virginia Woolf*, Clemson, SC: Clemson University Digital Press, 2006, pp. 212–20.
5. I am indebted to Jeremy Tambling's valuable reading of *Cymbeline* in *Becoming Posthumous* (2001) for this understanding of the posthumous as a trope and as the dominant figure of *Cymbeline*.
6. See, for instance, John Scheid and Jesper Svenbro, *The Craft of Zeus: Myths of Weaving and Fabric* (1996).
7. For more on Goethe's terms, see Bengt A. Sørensen, *Allegorie und Symbol: Texte zur Theorie des dichterischen Bildes im 18. und frühen 19. Jahrhundert*, Frankfurt am Main: Athenaum, 1972, pp. 133–4.

Bibliography

Abbs, Carolyn (2006), 'Writing the Subject: Virginia Woolf and Clothes', *COLLOQUY: Text, Theory, Critique*, 11: 209–25.

Abbott, Reginald (1992), 'What Miss Kilman's Petticoat Means: Virginia Woolf, Shopping, and Spectacle', *Modern Fiction Studies*, 38, 1: 193–216.

Anderson, Mark M. (1992), *Kafka's Clothes: Ornament and Aestheticism in the Habsburg Fin de Siècle*, Oxford: Clarendon Press.

Anscombe, Isabelle (1981), *Omega and After: Bloomsbury and the Decorative Arts*, London: Thames and Hudson.

Anthony, Katharine (2004), 'Some Realizations in Dress Reform', in Purdy 2004, pp. 117–25.

Ashelford, J. (1996), *The Art of Dress*, London: National Trust.

Banfield, Anne (2000), *The Phantom Table: Woolf, Fry, Russell and the Epistemology of Modernism*, Cambridge: Cambridge University Press.

Barthes, Roland (1990), *The Fashion System*, Berkeley: University of California Press.

Baudelaire, Charles ([1859] 1964), 'The Painter of Modern Life', in J. Mayne (ed.), *The Painter of Modern Life and Other Essays*, London: Phaidon Press, pp. 1–40.

Beer, Gillian (1986), '"The Face of Nature": Anthropomorphic Elements in the Language of the Origin of Species', in Ludmilla Jordanova (ed.), *Languages of Nature: Critical Essays on Science and Literature*, London: Free Association Books, pp. 207–43.

— (1996), *Virginia Woolf: The Common Ground*, Edinburgh: Edinburgh University Press.

Beerbohm, Max (2004), 'The Pervasion of Rouge', in Purdy 2004, pp. 226–31.

Bell, Quentin (1968), *Bloomsbury*, London: Weidenfeld and Nicolson.

— (1972), *Virginia Woolf: A Biography*, 2 vols, London: Hogarth Press.

— (1976), *On Human Finery*, London: Hogarth Press.

Benjamin, Walter (1998), *Illuminations: Essays and Reflections,* ed. H. Arendt, New York: Schocken Books.

— (1999), *The Arcades Project*, Cambridge, MA: The Belknap Press.

— (2006), *The Writer of Modern Life: Essays on Charles Baudelaire*, ed. M. W. Jennings, Cambridge, MA: The Belknap Press.

— (2007), *Reflections: Essays, Aphorisms, Autobiographical Writings*, ed. P. Demetz, New York: Schocken Books.

Berg, M., ed. (1999), *Consumers and Luxury*, Manchester: Manchester University Press.

Berman, J. and J. Goldman, eds (2007), *Virginia Woolf Out of Bounds: Selected Papers from the Tenth Annual Conference on Virginia Woolf*, New York: Pace University Press.

Birken, Lawrence (1988), *Consuming Desire: Sexual Science and the Emergence of a Culture of Abundance, 1871–1914*, Ithaca, NY: Cornell University Press.

Blair, Kirstie (2004), 'Gypsies and Lesbian Desire: Vita Sackville-West, Violet Trefusius, and Virginia Woolf, *Twentieth Century Literature*, 50, 2: 141–66.

Blair, Sara (2004), 'Local Modernity, Global Modernism: Bloomsbury and the Places of the Literary', *ELH* 71: 813–38.

Bosanquet, Theodora (1938), *Time and Tide*, 4 June: 788–90, in *Virginia Woolf: The Critical Heritage*, ed. Robin Majumdar and Allen McLaurin, London: Routledge and Kegan Paul, 1975, p. 402. Quoted in Hermione Lee's introduction to *Three Guineas*, London: Hogarth Press, 1991, p. vii.

Bowlby, Rachel (2001), *Carried Away: The Invention of Modern Shopping*, New York: Columbia University Press.

Boxwell, D. A. (1998), '(Dis)orienting Spectacle: The Politics of *Orlando*'s Sapphic Camp', *Twentieth Century Literature*, 44, 3: 306–27.

Breward, Christopher (1999), *The Hidden Consumer*, Manchester: Manchester University Press.

Breward, Christopher, Becky Conekin and Caroline Cox (2002), *The Englishness of English Dress*, Oxford and New York: Berg.

Brown, Bill (2001), 'Thing Theory', *Critical Inquiry*, 28, 1: 1–22.

Buci-Glucksmann, Christine (1986), 'Catastrophic Utopia: The Feminine as Allegory of the Modern', *Representations*, No. 14, *The Making of the Modern Body: Sexuality and Society in the Nineteenth Century*, pp. 220–9.

Butler, Judith (1990), *Gender Trouble: Feminism and the Subversion of Identity*. New York: Routledge.

Calefato, Patrizia (2004), *The Clothed Body*, Oxford and New York: Berg.

Cameron, Julia Margaret (1973), *Victorian Photographs of Famous Men and Fair Women*, London: Hogarth Press.

— (1986), *Whisper of the Muse: The Overstone Album and Other Photographs*, Malibu, CA: The J. Paul Getty Museum.

Carlyle, Thomas (1869), *Sartor Resartus: The Life and Opinions of Herr Teufeldrockh in Three Books*, London: Chapman and Hall.

Carter, Michael (2003), *Fashion Classics from Carlyle to Barthes*, Oxford and New York: Berg.

Caughie, Pamela (1991), *Virginia Woolf and Postmodernism: Literature in Quest and Question of Itself*, Urbana: University of Illinois Press.

Cervetti, Nancy (1996), 'In the Breeches, Petticoats, and Pleasures of *Orlando*', *Journal of Modern Literature*, 20, 2: 165–75.

Clements, Susan (1994), 'The Point of "Slater's Pins": Misrecognition and the Narrative Closet', *Tulsa Studies in Women's Literature*, 13, 1: 15–26.

Cohen, Lisa (1999), '"Frock Consciousness": Virginia Woolf, the Open Secret, and the Language of Fashion', *Fashion Theory*, 3, 2: 149–74.

Collins, Judith (1983), *The Omega Workshops*, London: Secker and Warburg.

Cohen, Margaret (1993), *Profane Illumination: Walter Benjamin and the Paris of Surrealist Revolution*, Berkeley: University of California Press.

Culler, Jonathan (1981), *The Pursuit of Signs: Semiotics, Literature, Deconstruction*, London and Henley: Routledge and Kegan Paul.

Dalgarno, Emily (2001), *Virginia Woolf and the Visible World*, Cambridge: Cambridge University Press.

de Gay, Jane (2001), "". . . though the fashion of the time did something to disguise it": Staging Gender in Woolf's *Orlando*', in Berman and Goldman 2001, pp. 31–8.

Delany, Paul (1987), *The Neo-pagans: Friendship and Love in the Rupert Brooke Circle*, London: Macmillan.

Derrida, Jacques (1987), *The Truth in Painting*, Chicago: Chicago University Press.

Doherty, Brigid (1995), 'Fashionable Ladies, Dada Dandies', *Art Journal*, 54, 1: 46–50.

Eddington, Arthur S. ([1929] 1930), *Science and the Unseen World*, London: Allen and Unwin.

Edson, Laura Gwynn (1997), 'Kicking off her Knickers: Virginia Woolf's Rejection of Clothing as Realistic Detail', in Gillespie and Hankins 1997, pp. 119–24.

Ellis, Havelock (1928), *Studies in the Psychology of Sex: Eonism and Other Supplementary Studies*, Vol. VII, Philadelphia, PA: F. A. Davis.

Entwistle, Joanne (2000), *The Fashioned Body: Fashion, Dress and Modern Social Theory*, Cambridge: Polity Press.

Esty, Jed (2004), *A Shrinking Island: Modernism and National Culture in England*, Princeton, NJ: Princeton University Press.

Farfan, Penny (2004), *Women, Modernism, and Performance*, Cambridge: Cambridge University Press.

Felshin, Nina (1995), 'Clothing as Subject', *Art Journal*, 54, 1: 20–9.

Felski, Rita (1995), *The Gender of Modernity*, Cambridge, MA and London: Harvard University Press.

Ferber, Michael (1999), *Dictionary of Literary Symbols*, West Nyack, NY: Cambridge University Press.

Fillin-Yeh, Susan (1995), 'Dandies, Marginality and Modernism: Georgia O'Keeffe, Marcel Duchamp and Other Cross-Dressers', *Oxford Art Journal*, 18, 2: 33–44.

Fischer-Lichte, Erika (2005), *Theatre, Sacrifice, Ritual: Exploring Forms of Political Theatre*, London and New York: Routledge.

Flügel, J. C. (1921), *The Psycho-analytic Study of the Family*. The International Psycho-Analytical Library No. 3, London: Hogarth Press.

— (1930), *The Psychology of Clothes*, The International Psycho-Analytical Library No. 18, London: Hogarth Press.

— (1933), 'A Psychology for Progressives: How Can They Become Effective?' in Joad 1933, pp. 292–313.

Flynn, Deirdre (1999), 'Virginia Woolf's Women and the Fashionable Elite: On Not Fitting In', in J. McVicker and L. Davis (eds), *Virginia Woolf and Communities: Selected Papers from the Eighth Annual Conference on Virginia Woolf*, New York: Pace University Press, pp. 167–73.

Fry, Roger (1973), 'Mrs Cameron's Photographs', in Cameron 1973, pp. 23–8.

Fuchs, Eduard (2004), 'Bourgeois Dress', in Purdy 2004, pp. 317–27.

Garber, Marjorie (1992), *Vested Interests: Cross-Dressing and Cultural Anxiety*, New York and London: Routledge.

Garrity, Jane (1999), 'Selling Culture to the "Civilized": Bloomsbury, British *Vogue* and the Marketing of National Identity', *Modernism/Modernity*, 6, 2: 29–58.

— (2000), 'Virginia Woolf, Intellectual Harlotry, and 1920s British *Vogue*', in P. L. Caughie, ed., *Virginia Woolf in the Age of Mechanical Reproduction*, New York and London: Garland Publishing, pp. 185–218.

Gilbert, Sandra M. (1980), 'Costumes of the Mind: Transvestism as Metaphor in Modern Literature', *Critical Inquiry*, 7, 2: 391–417.

— (1993), 'A Note on the Illustrations', in Virginia Woolf, *Orlando*, xlvii–xlviv.

Gillespie, D. F. and L. K. Hankins, eds (1997), *Virginia Woolf and the Arts: Selected Papers from the Sixth Annual Conference on Virginia Woolf*, New York: Pace University Press.

Glendinning, Victoria (1983), *Vita: The Life of V. Sackville-West*, New York: Alfred A. Knopf.

Goody, Alex (2000), 'Ladies of Fashion/Modern(ist) Women: Mina Loy and Djuna Barnes', *Women: A Cultural Review*, 10, 3: 266–82.

Gould, Timothy (1995), 'The Unhappy Performative', in A. Parker and E. K. Sedgwick (eds), *Performativity and Performance*, New York and London: Routledge.

Green, Barbara (1996), 'Advertising Feminism: Ornamental Bodies/Docile Bodies and the Discourse of Suffrage', in K. J. H. Dettmar and S. Watts (eds), *Marketing Modernisms: Self-Promotion, Canonization, Rereading*, Ann Arbor: University of Michigan Press.

Guenther, Irene (2004), *Nazi Chic? Fashioning Women in the Third Reich*, Oxford and New York: Berg.

Gutzov, Karl (2004), 'Fashion and the Modern', in Purdy 2004, pp. 196–205.

Gymnos: The Official Organ of the Gymnic Association of Great Britain, Vol. 1, No. 4, London: May, 1933.

Hamnett, Nina (1932), *Laughing Torso*, London: Constable.

Hankins, Leslie K. (2000), 'Virginia Woolf and Walter Benjamin Selling Out(siders)', in P. L. Caughie, ed., *Virginia Woolf in The Age of Mechanical Reproduction*, pp. 3–35.

Haralson, E. (2003), *Henry James and Queer Modernity*, Cambridge: Cambridge University Press.

Harvey, J. (1995), *Men in Black*, London: Reaktion.

Heard, Gerald (1924), *Narcissus: An Anatomy of Clothes*, London: Kegan Paul, Trench Trubner & Co.

Henry, Holly (2003), *Virginia Woolf and the Discourse of Science: The Aesthetics of Astronomy*, Cambridge: Cambridge University Press.

Hollander, Anne (1988), *Seeing Through Clothes*, New York: Penguin Books.

— (2000), *Feeding the Eye*, Berkeley: University of California Press.

— (2002), *Fabric of Vision: Dress and Drapery in Painting*, London: National Gallery Company.

Hovey, Jaime (1997), '"Kissing a Negress in the Dark": Englishness as a Masquerade in Woolf's *Orlando*', *PMLA*, 112, 3: 393–404.

Hughes, Clair (2001), *Henry James and the Art of Dress*, London: Palgrave Macmillan.
— (2006), *Dressed in Fiction*, Oxford and New York: Berg.
Humm, Maggie (2002), *Modernist Women and Visual Cultures: Virginia Woolf, Vanessa Bell, Photography and Cinema*, Edinburgh: Edinburgh University Press.
— (2006), *Snapshots of Bloomsbury: The Private Lives of Virginia Woolf and Vanessa Bell*, New Brunswick, NJ: Rutgers University Press.
Huyssen, Andreas (1986), *After the Great Divide: Modernism, Mass Culture, Postmodernism*, Bloomington: Indiana University Press.
Jeans, James (1930), *The Mysterious Universe*, New York: Macmillan.
Joad, C. E. M. (1933), *Manifesto: Being the Book of the Federation of Progressive Societies and Individuals*, London: Allen and Unwin.
Jones, Amelia (1995), '"Clothes Make the Man": The Male Artist as a Performative Function', *Oxford Art Journal*, 18, 2: 18–32.
Kane, Julie (1995), 'Varieties of Mystical Experience in the Writings of Virginia Woolf', *Twentieth Century Literature* 41, 4: 328–49.
Keenan, William J. F., ed. (2001), *Dressed to Impress*, Oxford and New York: Berg.
Kennard, Jean E. (1996), 'Power and Sexual Ambiguity: The *Dreadnought* Hoax, *The Voyage Out*, *Mrs Dalloway*, and *Orlando*', *Journal of Modern Literature*, 20, 2: 149–64.
Knopp, Sherron E. (1988), '"If I Saw You Would You Kiss Me?": Sapphism and the Subversiveness of Virginia Woolf's *Orlando*', *PMLA*, 103, 1: 24–34.
Kraus, Karl (2004), 'The Eroticism of Clothes', in Purdy 2004, pp. 239–44.
Kuryluk, Ewa (1999), *Veronica and Her Cloth: History, Symbolism, and Structure of a 'True' Image*, London: Basil Blackwell.
Laing, Katherine S. (1997), 'Addressing Femininity in the Twenties: Virginia Woolf and Rebecca West on Money, Mirrors, and Masquerade', in Gillespie and Hankins 1997, pp. 66–74.
Langdon-Davies, John (1929), *The Future of Nakedness*, London: Noel Douglas.
Lee, Hermione (1997), *Virginia Woolf*, London: Vintage.
Lehmann, Ulrich (2000), *Tigersprung: Fashion in Modernity*, Cambridge, MA: MIT Press.
Lewis, Wyndham, ed. (1914), *BLAST* No. 1, London: John Lane.
— (ed.) (1915), *BLAST* No. 2, London: John Lane.
— (1927), *Time and Western Man*, London: Chatto & Windus.
— ([1936] 1973), *The Roaring Queen*, ed. Walter Allen, London: Secker and Warburg.
— (1963), *The Letters of Wyndham Lewis*, ed. W. K. Rose, London: Methuen & Co.
— (1965), *The Apes of God*, Harmondsworth: Penguin Books.
— (1986), *The Caliph's Design*, ed. Paul Edwards, Santa Barbara, CA: Black Sparrow Press.
— (1987), *Men Without Art*, ed. Seamus Cooney, Santa Rosa, CA: Black Sparrow Press.
Loos, Adolf (2004), 'Men's Fashion' and 'Men's Hats', in Purdy 2004, pp. 93–101.

Luckhurst, Nicola (1997), 'Vogue . . . is going to take up Mrs Woolf, to boom her', in Gillespie and Hankins 1997, pp. 75–84.

— (1998), *Bloomsbury in Vogue*, London: Cecil Woolf.

MacCarthy, Fiona (1984), 'Roger Fry and the Omega Idea', in *The Omega Workshops 1913–19: Decorative Arts of Bloomsbury*, London: Crafts Council Gallery.

Mackrell, Alice (2005), *Art and Fashion*, London: B. T. Batsford.

Mahood, Aurelea (2002), 'Fashioning Readers: The *Avant garde* and British *Vogue*, 1920–9', *Women: A Cultural Review*, 13, 1: 37–47.

Man, Paul de (1971), *Blindness and Insight: Essays in the Rhetoric of Contemporary Criticism*, New York: Oxford University Press.

Mankoff, Debra N. (2000), *Jane Morris: The Pre-Raphaelite Model of Beauty*, San Francisco: Pomegranate.

Mao, Douglas (1998), *Solid Objects: Modernism and the Test of Production*, Ewing, NJ: Princeton University Press.

Marcus, Jane (1989), 'The Asylums of Antaenus: Women, War, and Madness – Is There a Feminist Fetishism?' in H. Aram Veeser (ed.), *The New Historicism*, London and New York: Routledge, pp. 132–51.

— [1992] (1993), 'Britannia Rules The Waves', in Margaret Homans (ed.),*Virginia Woolf: A Collection of Critical Essays*, Englewood Cliffs, NJ: Prentice Hall, pp. 227–47.

Marcus, Laura (1996), 'Virginia Woolf and the Hogarth Press', in Willison 1996, pp. 124–50.

Mauss, Marcel (2005), 'Techniques of the Body', in M. Fraser and M. Greco (eds), *The Body: A Reader*, London and New York: Routledge, pp. 73–7.

Mendes, Valerie (1992), *The Victoria and Albert Museum's Textile Collection: British Textiles from 1900 to 1937*, London: V&A Publications.

Mendes, Valerie and Amy de la Haye (1999), *Twentieth Century Fashion*, London: Thames and Hudson.

Meyers, Jeffrey (1980), *The Enemy: A Biography of Wyndham Lewis*, London: Routledge.

Miller, J. Hillis (1995), *Topographies*, Stanford, CA: Stanford University Press.

Morrison, Kathryn (2003), *English Shops and Shopping: An Architectural History*, New Haven, CT: Yale University Press.

Mouton, Janice (2001), 'From Feminine Masquerade to Flâneuse: Agnès Varda's Cléo in the City', *Cinema Journal*, 40, 2: 3–16.

Neverow, Vara (2001), 'Freudian Seduction and the Fallacies of Dictatorship', in M. Pawlowski (ed.), *Virginia Woolf and Fascism*, pp. 56–72.

Newton, Esther (1984), 'The Mythic Mannish Lesbian: Radclyffe Hall and the New Woman', *Signs: Journal of Women in Culture and Society*, 9, 4: 557–75.

Noble, Joan R. (ed.) (1972), *Recollections of Virginia Woolf by Her Contemporaries*, London: Peter Owen; New York: William Morrow & Co.

Nord, Deborah E. (1998), '"Marks of Race": Gypsy Figures and Eccentric Femininity in Nineteenth-Century Women's Writing', *Victorian Studies*, 41, 2: 189–210.

Outka, Elizabeth (2001), '"The shop windows were full of sparkling chains": Consumer Desire and Woolf's *Night and Day*', in Berman and Goldman 2001, pp. 229–35.

Park, Sowon S. (2005), 'Suffrage and Virginia Woolf: "The Mass Behind the Single Voice"', *The Review of English Studies*, 56, 223: 119–34.

Paulicelli, Eugenia (2004), *Fashion under Fascism: Beyond the Black Shirt*, Oxford and New York: Berg.

Pawlowski, Merry M., ed. (2001), *Virginia Woolf and Fascism: Resisting the Dictator's Seduction*, London: Palgrave.

Phillips, Kathy J. (1994), *Virginia Woolf Against Empire*, Knoxville: University of Tennessee Press.

Purdy, Daniel L., ed. (2004), *The Rise of Fashion: A Reader*, Minneapolis: The University of Minnesota Press.

Rappaport, Erika D. (2000), *Shopping for Pleasure: Women in the Making of London's West End*, Princeton, NJ: Princeton University Press.

Reed, Christopher (1996), *A Roger Fry Reader*, Chicago: University of Chicago Press.

— (2004), *Bloomsbury Rooms: Modernism, Subculture, and Domesticity*, New Haven, CT and London: Yale University Press.

Ribeiro, Aileen (1995), *The Art of Dress*, New Haven, CT: Yale University Press.

— (2005), *Fashion and Fiction: Dress in Art and Literature in Stuart England*, New Haven, CT and London: Yale University Press.

Rosenfeld, Natania (2001), 'Monstrous Conjugations: Images of Dictatorship in the Anti-Fascist Writings of Virginia and Leonard Woolf', in Pawlowski 2001, pp. 122–36.

Rosner, Victoria (2005), *Modernism and the Architecture of Private Life*, New York: Columbia University Press.

Scheid, John and Jesper Svenbro (1996), *The Craft of Zeus: Myths of Weaving and Fabric*, Cambridge, MA: Harvard University Press.

Schlack, Beverly Ann (1979), *Continuing Presences: Virginia Woolf's Use of Literary Allusion*, University Park and London: Pennsylvania State University Press.

Schor, Esther (1994), *Bearing the Dead: The British Culture of Mourning from the Enlightenment to Victoria*, Princeton, NJ: Princeton University Press.

Shaw, Mary Lewis (1992), 'The Discourse of Fashion: Mallarmé, Barthes and Literary Criticism,' *SubStance*, 21, 2: 46–60.

Shone, Richard (1999), *The Art of Bloomsbury: Roger Fry, Vanessa Bell and Duncan Grant*, London: Tate Gallery Publishing.

Simmel, Georg (1971), *On Individuality and Social Forms: Selected Writings*, ed. Donald N. Levine, Chicago and London: University of Chicago Press.

Simpson, Kathryn (2005), 'Economies and Desire: Gifts and the Market in "Moments of Being: 'Slater's Pins Have No Points'"', *Journal of Modern Literature*, 28, 2: 18–37.

Snaith, Anna (2000), *Virginia Woolf: Public and Private Negotiations*, London: Palgrave Macmillan.

Sontag, Susan (1980), 'Fascinating Fascism', in Susan Sontag, *Under the Sign of Saturn*, New York: Farrar Straus Giroux.

Sophocles (1991), *The Antigone, in Sophocles I*, trans. David Grene, Chicago: University of Chicago Press.

Spalding, Frances (2006), *Vanessa Bell*, Stroud, Gloucestershire: Tempus.

Spencer, Herbert [1902] (2004), 'Fashion' (From *The Principles of Sociology*), in Purdy 2004, pp. 328–32.

Stallybrass, Peter and Ann R. Jones (2001), 'Fetishizing the Glove in Renaissance Europe', *Critical Inquiry*, 28, 1: 114–32.

Steele, Valerie (1985), *Fashion and Eroticism: Ideals of Feminine Beauty from the Victorian Era to the Jazz Age*, New York and Oxford: Oxford University Press.

Stern, Radu (2004), *Against Fashion: Clothing as Art, 1850–1930*, Cambridge, MA: MIT Press.

Strachey, Lytton (1922), 'Lady Hester Stanhope', *Books and Characters*, London: Chatto and Windus.

Tambling, Jeremy (2001), *Becoming Posthumous: Life and Death in Literary and Cultural Studies*, Edinburgh: Edinburgh University Press.

Tennyson, G. B. (1965), *Sartor Called Resartus: The Genesis, Structure, and Style of Thomas Carlyle's First Major Work*, Princeton, NJ: Princeton University Press.

Theweleit, Klaus (1987), *Male Fantasies*, Cambridge: Polity Press.

Tickner, Lisa (1987), *The Spectacle of Women: Imagery of the Suffrage Campaign 1907–14*, London: Chatto & Windus.

Tratner, Michael (1995), *Modernism and Mass Politics: Joyce, Woolf, Eliot, Yeats*, Stanford, CA: Stanford University Press.

Tönnies, Ferdinand ([1909] 2004), 'Customs', in Purdy 2004, pp. 333–40.

Veblen, Thorsten (1994), *The Theory of the Leisure Class*, Harmondsworth: Penguin.

— (2004), 'Conspicuous Consumption' and 'Dress as an Expression of the Pecuniary Culture', in Purdy 2004, pp. 261–88.

Vischer, Friedrich (1867), *Vernünftige Gedanken über die jetzige Mode: Kritische Gärge*, new series, book 3, Stuttgart.

— (2004), 'Fashion and Cynicism', in Purdy 2004, pp. 153–62.

Weaver, Mike (1986), Introduction, in Cameron 1986.

Whitlock, Gillian (1987), '"Everything Is Out of Place": Radclyffe Hall and the Lesbian Literary Tradition', *Feminist Studies*, 13, 3: 554–82.

Whitworth, Michael H. (2001), *Einstein's Wake: Relativity, Metaphor, and Modernist Literature*, Oxford: Oxford University Press.

Wicke, Jennifer (1994), '*Mrs Dalloway* Goes to Market: Woolf, Keynes, and Modern Markets', *Novel* (Fall): 5–23.

— (1996), 'Coterie Consumption: Bloomsbury, Keynes, and Modernism as Marketing', in K. J. H. Dettmar and S. Watt (eds), *Marketing Modernisms: Self Promotion, Canonization and Rereading*, Ann Arbor: University of Michigan Press.

— (2001), 'Frock Consciousnes: Virginia Woolf's Dialectical Materialism', in Berman and Goldman 2007, pp. 221–9.

Wilde, Oscar (2004), 'The Suitability of Dress', in Purdy 2004, pp. 232–8.

Willison, Ian, Warwick Gould and Warren Chernaik, eds (1996), *Modernist Writers and the Marketplace*, Basingstoke: Macmillan.

Wilson, Elizabeth (1990), 'All the Rage', in Jane Gaines and Charlotte Herzog (eds), *Fabrication: Costume and the Female Body*, New York: Routledge.

— (2003), *Adorned in Dreams*, London: Tauris.

Wilton, Andrew and Robert Upstone (1997), *The Age of Rossetti, Burne-Jones and Watts: Symbolism in Britain,* London: Tate Gallery Publishing.

Winston, Janet (1997), 'Reading Influences: Homoeroticism and Mentoring in Katherine Mansfield's "Carnation" and Virginia Woolf's "Moments of Being: 'Slater's Pins Have No Points'"', in E. Barrett and P. Cramer (eds), *Virginia Woolf: Lesbian Readings,* New York and London: New York University Press, pp. 57–77.

Woolf, Leonard, ed. (1933), *The Intelligent Man's Way to Prevent War,* London: Victor Gollancz.

— (1935), *Quack, Quack,* London: Hogarth Press.

— (1963–9). *Autobiography,* 5 vols., New York and London: Harcourt Brace Jovanovich.

Woolf, Virginia (1942), *The Death of the Moth and Other Essays,* London: Hogarth Press.

— (1952), *The Moment and Other Essays,* London: Hogarth Press.

— (1973), 'Julia Margaret Cameron', in V. Woolf and R. Fry (eds), *Victorian Photographs of Famous Men and Fair Women by Julia Margaret Cameron,* London: Hogarth Press; Boston: David R. Godine (first published in 1926).

— (1975–80), *The Letters of Virginia Woolf,* ed. N. Nicolson, 4 vols, London: Hogarth Press.

— (1977), *A Room of One's Own,* London: Granada.

— (1977), *The Years,* London: Granada.

— (1979), '"Anon" and "The Reader": Virginia Woolf's Last Essays', ed. B. R. Silver, *Twentieth Century Literature,* 25, 3–4: 356–441.

— (1982), *The Diary of Virginia Woolf,* London: Penguin Books.

— (1984), *The Common Reader: First Series,* ed. Andrew McNeillie, London: Hogarth Press.

— (1985), *Freshwater: A Comedy,* Orlando, FL: Harcourt Brace Jovanovich.

— (1985), *Moments of Being: A Collection of Autobiographical Writing,* ed. Jeanne Schulkind, San Diego: Harcourt Inc.

— (1986), *The Second Common Reader,* ed. Andrew McNeillie, London: Hogarth Press.

— (1986–2009), *The Essays of Virginia Woolf,* ed. Andrew McNeillie, vols. 1–4, ed. Stuart N. Clarke, vol. 5, London: Hogarth Press.

— (1989), *The Complete Shorter Fiction,* ed. Susan Dick, San Diego: Harcourt Brace & Company.

— (1991), *Three Guineas,* London: Hogarth Press.

— (1992), *Between the Acts,* Oxford: Oxford University Press (World's Classics).

— (1992), *Jacob's Room,* London: Penguin Books.

— (1992), *Mrs Dalloway,* London: Penguin Books.

— (1992), *Night and Day,* London: Penguin Books.

— (1992), *To the Lighthouse,* London: Penguin Books.

— (1992), *The Voyage Out,* London: Penguin Books.

— (1992), *The Waves,* London: Penguin Books.

— (1993), *The Crowded Dance of Modern Life,* ed. Rachel Bowlby, London: Penguin.

— (1993), *Orlando,* London: Penguin Books.

— (2002), *Melymbrosia*, ed. Louise DeSalvo, San Francisco: Cleis Press.
— (2003) *Roger Fry: A Biography*, London: Vintage.
— (2003), *Carlyle's House and Other Sketches*, ed. David Bradshaw, London: Hesperus Press.
— (2004), *A Passionate Apprentice: The Early Journals 1897–1909*, ed. M. A. Leaska, London: Pimlico.

Index

Note: *page numbers in italics denote illustrations*